Ius Gentium: Comparative Perspectives on Law and Justice

Volume 122

Ius Gentium is a book series which discusses the central questions of law and justice from a comparative perspective. The books in this series collect the contrasting and overlapping perspectives of lawyers, judges, philosophers and scholars of law from the world's many different jurisdictions for the purposes of comparison, harmonisation, and the progressive development of law and legal institutions. Each volume makes a new comparative study of an important area of law. This book series continues the work of the well-known journal of the same name and provides the basis for a better understanding of all areas of legal science.

The *Ius Gentium* series provides a valuable resource for lawyers, judges, legislators, scholars, and both graduate students and researchers in globalisation, comparative law, legal theory and legal practice. The series has a special focus on the development of international legal standards and transnational legal cooperation.

Ines Kajiru • John Cantius Mubangizi
Elia Mwanga • Leonard Chimanda Joseph
Editors

Economic Development and Human Rights in Contemporary Sub-Saharan Africa

Springer

Editors
Ines Kajiru
School of Law
University of Dodoma
Dodoma, Tanzania

John Cantius Mubangizi
University of the Free State
Bloemfontein, South Africa

Elia Mwanga
School of Law
University of Dodoma
Dodoma, Tanzania

Leonard Chimanda Joseph
School of Law
University of Dodoma
Dodoma, Tanzania

ISSN 1534-6781 ISSN 2214-9902 (electronic)
Ius Gentium: Comparative Perspectives on Law and Justice
ISBN 978-3-031-81402-0 ISBN 978-3-031-81400-6 (eBook)
https://doi.org/10.1007/978-3-031-81400-6

This Springer imprint is published by the registered company Springer Nature Switzerland AG
The registered company address is: Gewerbestrasse 11, 6330 Cham, Switzerland

Foreword

The thematic focus on human rights law and economic development in Africa is distinct. Despite the voluminous materials on the subject of human rights and economic development, this has long been a neglected topic in and regarding Africa.

African scholarship and academia have largely been silent in this area of research, writing and teaching. In this proposed book, the essays focus on the historical, contemporary and future aspects of human rights law and economic development in Africa. The editors and contributors are Africans based in sub-Saharan Africa. The situation in the three main geopolitical blocks in Africa (West, Eastern, and Southern Africa), including national case studies, is given much attention. While regional contributions are provided, making this edited volume a comprehensive collection of African voices on the topic will be taken into account. It blends the use of case studies and doctrinal legal research approaches that espouse transformations in and of human rights law and economic development in Africa and its future orientation from the perspectives of Indigenous African scholars, experts and practitioners.

The book combines contributions from senior and emerging African and internationally recognised scholars in the field of human rights law, economic development and African studies. It makes a comprehensive and rigorous overview of the salient content and major developments in human rights law and economic development in sub-Saharan Africa. It explores the core concepts and principles, theories and practices, accountability mechanisms and key challenges to human rights law in Africa in the era of global economic development. The book offers a unique insight into the development, domestication and implementation of challenges relating to human rights law, economic development and governance in Africa. Readers will gain a discerning insight into the nuances of human rights law and economic development regulation in Africa from this extensive review. This necessary exploration of human rights law and economic development from an African perspective will be an indispensable reference point for academics and advanced students of international human rights and business law, in particular, and international law, in general.

Essentially, the book contributes to the development of sub-Saharan African scholarship and the reinforcement of the international discourse on the future of human rights law and economic and African development. The key contributions of the book are its perspectives and enunciation of the specificities of the African context and its appraisal and (re-)theorisation of the conceptual legal links between human rights, climate change, and the environment to appreciate these differences and peculiarities.

University of Dodoma
Dodoma, Tanzania

Razack Lokina

Preface

This book contains contributions from senior and emerging scholars in sub-Saharan Africa. The book appraises the nexus between sub-Saharan Africa's economic development and human rights. The chapters in the book have been peer-reviewed and reworked by the authors. The main objective of the book is to add to the sub-Saharan African scholarship and to strengthen the African dialogue on economic development and human rights in a time of digital change. The analysis of this book is based on the crucial contributions provided to its specificities of the sub-Saharan African context and its assessment and jurisprudence of economic development and human rights to escalate these variances and idiosyncrasies.

Moreover, various challenges that encumber the promotion, protection and realisation of the rights of economic development in sub-Saharan Africa were analysed. The evidence indicates that experience has varied from one country to another.

It is important to note that legislators have an opportunity to bring changes, and it is commendable that they pursue the trails that advance and offer sustainable and complete protection for economic development and human rights in sub-Saharan Africa. A strong will and agenda and multi-stakeholder teamwork are sources for effective protection in this respect.

This book emphasises that policy resolutions made today will determine whether the legal protective system of the future is capable of providing through its four key obligations of human rights: protection, promotion, respect and fulfilment.

The existing system is embedded with so many challenges due to path enslavements from the historical over- (or under-)prioritising of one of these four key universal human rights law obligations. Decisions that optimise the protection of human rights while focusing on economic growth without leaving any one behind. Looking forward to balancing the four objectives will ultimately deliver a national human rights system that is sustainable, vigorous, reliable and comprehensive.

The book therefore calls for the building of strong institutions as well as the involvement of both state and non-state actors in advancing and safeguarding human rights and sustainable economic development in sub-Saharan Africa through legal reforms and robust institutional mechanisms for the enforcement of relevant laws and policies.

The book should be of great interest to practitioners, scholars, government officials' students and those dedicated to economic development and human rights in sub-Saharan Africa and beyond. As editors of this book, we are proud to find excellent authors (contributors) from different countries in sub-Saharan Africa who are experts in their respective fields.

Dodoma, Tanzania — Ines Kajiru
Bloemfontein, South Africa — John Cantius Mubangizi
Dodoma, Tanzania — Elia Mwanga
Dodoma, Tanzania — Leonard Chimanda Joseph

Acknowledgement

The preparation and final publication of this book is a manifestation of the efforts of many individuals. While it is impossible to mention all of them, the editors wish to acknowledge the significant efforts made by chapter contributors. Indeed, without their contribution, this book would not have been published.

In a special way, the editors wish to thank the management of the University of Dodoma and the School of Law for supporting the initiative to have this book published.

Last but not least, the editors wish to thank the publisher for accepting our idea and being ready to publish this book.

Contents

About the Editors and Contributors

About the Editors

Ines Kajiru PhD in Law from Kwazulu-Natal, South Africa and LL.B and LL.M from Mzumbe University, Tanzania; Dean at the University of Dodoma School of Law.

John Cantius Mubangizi LL.B (Makerere University), LL.M (University of Cape Town), LL.D (University of KwaZulu-Natal), Professor, Free State Centre for Human Rights, Faculty of Law, University of the Free State, Bloemfontein, South Africa. E-mail: MubangiziJC@ufs.ac.za.

Elia Mwanga LL.B (Hons); LL.M; PhD (Law) from the University of Dar es Salaam; Senior Lecturer of Law at the University of Dodoma; Advocate; Coordinator—Postgraduate Studies and Research—School of Law, University of Dodoma. E-mail: elia.mwanga@udom.ac.tz.

Leonard Chimanda Joseph LL.B, LL.M (University of Dar es Salaam), Advocate, Contributor to the Local Engagement Refugee Research Network, Member to the University of Dar es Salaam Research Chair on Forced Displacement, PhD in Law Candidate at University of Sussex (United Kingdom).

Contributors

Ayoola Abuloye Faculty of Law, Obafemi Awolowo University, Ile Ife, Nigeria

Vimbai Chibango Durban University of Technology, Durban, South Africa

Leonard Chimanda Joseph School of Law, University of Dodoma, Dodoma, Tanzania

Julius Cosmas Private Law Department, Faculty of Law, Mzumbe University, Morogoro, Tanzania

Justina M. Danda School of Law, University of Dodoma, Dodoma, Tanzania

Stanley Osezua Ehiane Department of Political Science and Administrative Studies, University of Botswana, Gaborone, Botswana
Department of Development Studies, School of Social Sciences, University of South Africa (UNISA), Pretoria, South Africa

Ines Kajiru School of Law, University of Dodoma, Dodoma, Tanzania

Scholastica Mality School of Law, University of Dodoma, Dodoma, Tanzania

Bontle Masilo Department of Political Science and Administrative Studies, University of Botswana, Gaborone, Botswana

Baraka Mkami School of Law, University of Dodoma, Dodoma, Tanzania

Sekela Kalangson Mlungu School of Law, University of Dodoma, Dodoma, Tanzania

Vicent Bartholomew Mtavangu Mzumbe University Mbeya Campus College-Department of Legal Studies (DLS), Mbeya, Tanzania

John C. Mubangizi University of the Free State, Bloemfontein, South Africa

Saudin Jacob Mwakaje University of Dar es Salaam, School of Law, Dar es Salaam, Tanzania

Elia Mwanga School of Law, University of Dodoma, Dodoma, Tanzania

John S. Ombella Economic Law Department, Faculty of Law, Mzumbe University, Mzumbe, Morogoro, Tanzania
Private Law Department, Faculty of Law, Mzumbe University, Morogoro, Tanzania

Amiri Sharifu Dar es Salaam CPA Review Center, Dar es Salaam, Tanzania
Anjarwalla & Khanna Tanzania, Dar es Salaam, Tanzania

Towards a Human-Rights-Based Approach to Economic Development in Africa

John C. Mubangizi

1 Introduction

One of the first instruments to formally acknowledge the relationship between human rights and economic development was the 1984 Lomé III Convention,[1] which mentioned human rights in its preamble and in the joint declarations attached to it. Two years later, the United Nations Declaration on the Right to Development[2] also recognised the close relationship between human rights and development. This recognition was strongly endorsed by the 1993 World Conference on Human Rights. The Vienna Declaration and Programme of Action,[3] which emanated from that conference, clearly recognised the interdependence and mutually reinforcing relationship between "democracy, development and respect for human rights and fundamental freedoms".[4] In 1998, a United Nations Development Programme (UNDP) Policy Document on Integrating Human Rights with Sustainable Development emphasised the link between human rights and development and concluded that "human rights and sustainable development are inextricably linked,

This chapter is a significantly revised and updated version of an earlier publication in the *Journal of Social Sciences* 39(1): 67–76 (2014). The permission of the publishers, Kamla-Raj Enterprises, to revise and update the publication is hereby acknowledged.

[1] Signed at Lomé on 8 December 1984 between the European Community and its partner states in Africa, the Caribbean and the Pacific.

[2] Resolution A/RES/41/128, adopted by the UN General Assembly on 4 December 1986.

[3] Resolution A/CONF.157/23, adopted by the UN General Assembly on 12 July 1993.

[4] Article 8.

J. C. Mubangizi (✉)
University of the Free State, Bloemfontein, South Africa
e-mail: mubangiziJC@ufs.ac.za

I. Kajiru et al. (eds.), *Economic Development and Human Rights in Contemporary Sub-Saharan Africa*, Ius Gentium: Comparative Perspectives on Law and Justice 122, https://doi.org/10.1007/978-3-031-81400-6_1

complementary and multidimensional".[5] Furthermore, a 2013 study also showed that "human rights and development are considered 'parallel streams' which address similar problems and share similar views".[6]

As will be seen later, the *2030 Agenda for Sustainable Development*[7] also recognises the important relationship between human rights and development. It states that "the Agenda is grounded in the Universal Declaration of Human Rights, and international human rights treaties, among other things and is informed by other instruments such as the Declaration on the Right to Development".[8]

There are a number of reasons why the relationship between development and human rights is critical and, therefore, why a human-rights-based approach to economic development is essential—particularly in Africa. Such an approach, according to former UN Secretary General Kofi Annan, "empowers people to demand justice as a right, not as a charity, and gives communities a moral basis from which to claim international assistance where needed".[9] It may well be argued that for African communities to claim or demand such international assistance, they ought to meet internationally accepted norms of human rights and democratic values, which will ensure that such assistance is properly utilised to the benefit of the communities concerned. Furthermore, human rights form an important component of good governance and democratisation. Since good governance and democracy are integral prerequisites for sustainable development, human rights protection inevitably becomes part of the equation. The UNDP has captured this relationship in the following terms:

> Development is unsustainable where the rule of law and equity do not exist; where ethnic, religious or sexual discrimination are rampant; where there are restrictions on free speech, free association and the media; or where large numbers of people live in abject and degrading poverty.[10]

Paragraph 20 of the 2030 Agenda for Sustainable Development, referred to earlier, states, for instance, that "the achievement of full human potential and of sustainable development is not possible if one half of humanity continues to be denied its full human rights and opportunities".[11]

Indeed, poverty is one of the main challenges facing Africa today—although there are many more. Because of such challenges, it is argued that adopting a human-rights-based approach to economic development in Africa is imperative and critical. In so arguing, this chapter explores and acknowledges the level and extent of the current practices of integrating human rights and economic development in Africa—paying specific attention to the roles and dimensions of civil and political rights, on

[5] UNDP (1998).

[6] D'Hollander et al. (2013).

[7] UN General Assembly (2015).

[8] Ibid.

[9] Quoted in Danish Mission Council Development Department (DMCDD), Position Paper.

[10] UNDP (1998).

[11] UN General Assembly (2015).

one hand, and socio-economic rights, on the other, and how they impact economic development in different but important ways. Paying particular attention to the strategies of the United Nations Sustainable Development Goals in the context of adopting a human-rights-based approach to economic development, opportunities and prospects are explored—before highlighting the challenges and conditions prevailing in Africa that may, and do have, significant implications for the said approach.

2 Understanding the Concepts and Their Relationship

In order to understand the opportunities and challenges of adopting a human-rights-based approach to economic development in Africa, it is necessary to first unpack the important concepts and how they relate to each other. The starting point is a general understanding of "a human rights-based approach"—before seeing it in the context of development. In that regard, the Scottish Human Rights Commission (SHRC) has described a human-right-based approach as one that "empowers people to know and claim their rights and [increases] the ability and accountability of individuals and institutions who are responsible for respecting, protecting and fulfilling human rights".[12] Accordingly, such an approach should give people "greater opportunities to participate in shaping the decisions that impact on their human rights [and should increase] the ability of those with responsibility for fulfilling rights to recognize and know how to respect those rights…"[13] More importantly, the SHRC believes that a human-rights-based approach "is about ensuring that both the standards and principles of human rights are integrated into policy making as well as the day to day running of organizations".[14] What this means is that human rights should provide the guiding framework for policymaking, development planning and organisational behaviour. It also means that "development policies and programs must contribute explicitly to human rights … and … must be organized in a way that will strengthen the capacities of individuals (rights holders) to exercise and demand respect for their rights, and of states (duty bearers) to fulfil their human rights obligations".[15]

The most succinct definition of "a human rights-based approach" is provided by the United Nations, which sees such an approach as "a conceptual framework for the process of human development that is normatively based on international human rights standards and operationally directed to promoting and protecting human rights".[16] This definition is indeed consistent with the key principles of a human

[12] SHRC (n.d.).

[13] SHRC (n.d.).

[14] SHRC (n.d.).

[15] CIFEDHOP (2012).

[16] OHCHR (2006). Frequently Asked Questions on a Human-Rights-Based Approach to Development Cooperation, https://www.ohchr.org/documents/publications/faqen.pdf.

rights-based approach outlined by the European Union. These include a linkage between development challenges and rights, the empowerment of rights holders to claim their rights, their participation in all processes that affect them, the non-discrimination and inclusion of vulnerable groups and the accountability of duty bearers towards rights holders.[17]

Defining "economic development" is a bit more difficult as it has to be seen in the context of the concept of "development" whose definitions are diverse and sometimes contentious. This is because development is often seen and defined in relation to various contexts—resulting in terminology such as "human development", "sustainable development" and, of course, "economic development". Sometimes a combination of these terms is used, resulting in terminology such as "sustainable human development". Indeed, today, development is increasingly seen as such. In that regard, human development has been described as "the process of enlarging the range of peoples' choices from a sound physical environment to economic and political freedoms".[18] It is in this same context that Amartya Sen has seen development as freedom and argues that it is a process of expanding the real freedoms that people enjoy.[19] He contrasts development as human freedom with what he calls "narrower views of development, such as identifying development with the growth of gross national product, or with the rise in personal incomes, or with industrialisation, or with technological advance, or with social modernization".[20]

Whereas the definitions of development may be diverse, the basic consensus on the concept is achieved through the definition provided by the 1986 United Nations Declaration on the Right to Development—which defines development as

> a comprehensive economic, social, cultural and political process, which aims at the constant improvement of the well-being of the entire population and of all individuals on the basis of their active, free and meaningful participation in development and in the fair distribution of benefits resulting there from.[21]

However, it is the concept of "economic development" that this discussion focuses on. Unfortunately, like the definition of "development" itself, "economic development" might mean different things to different people. In that regard, anything a community does to foster and create a healthy economy can fall under the broad definition of "economic development".

Whereas the concept might encapsulate several meanings ranging from the creation of wealth to an investment in growing the economy, for purposes of this discussion, the most appropriate definition for "economic development" would be "the process whereby simple, low-income national economies are transformed into modern industrial economies".[22]

---

[17] Ussor (2011).

[18] UNDP (1992).

[19] Sen (1999), p. 3.

[20] Sen (1999), p. 3.

[21] Preamble to the Declaration.

[22] Myint and Krueger (2016).

In that sense, the relationship between economic development and human rights becomes quite important, and the interdependence and inextricability between the two become clearer. It is in that context that a human-rights-based approach to economic development should be seen and defined. It ought to be pointed out, however, that since economic development is a specific and important context of development, reference to a human-rights-based approach to development will encapsulate economic development. Accordingly, the Office of the High Commissioner for Human Rights sees the rights-based approach to development as "a conceptual framework for the process of human development that is normatively based on international human rights standards and operationally directed to promoting and protecting human rights".[23] It is "an approach [that] integrates the norms, standards and principles of the international human rights system into the plans, policies and processes of development".[24] Furthermore, according to Kofi Annan, the rights-based approach to development "describes situations not simply in terms of human needs, or of developmental requirements, but in terms of society's obligation to respond to the inalienable rights of individuals".[25]

A lot has been said and written about the relationship between human rights and development generally. Not much research, however, has been done regarding the relationship between human rights and economic development specifically. It could be said, though, that such a relationship applies to economic development specifically as much as it applies to development generally. In that regard, a golden thread in the literature is the interdependence and mutually reinforcing nature of the two following concepts: human rights and development. In short, you cannot achieve one without a reasonable level of achievement of the other. Indeed, it has been argued that "human rights and development can and should be integrated … there can be no doubt that the two overlap substantially and a number of international frameworks have begun to recognize the connections".[26] As mentioned earlier, the relationship between human rights and development was formally recognised by the United Nations in 1986, with the adoption of the Declaration of the Right to Development whose preamble expresses concern "at the existence of serious obstacles to development … constituted, *inter alia,* by the denial of civil, political, economic, social and cultural rights". Article 1 of the Declaration states:

> The right to development is an inalienable human right by virtue of which every human person and all peoples are entitled to participate in, contribute to, and enjoy economic, social, cultural and political development, in which all human rights and fundamental freedoms can be fully realized.

Since the adoption of the UN Declaration of the Right to Development, there have been many developments and shifts in thinking and in practice. In the particular context of Africa, it is important to note that the African Charter on Human and

[23] OHRHC (2010).

[24] OHRHC (2010).

[25] DMCDD, note 9 above.

[26] Mcinerney-Lankford (2009), p. 52.

People's Rights is the only regional/continental human rights instrument that incorporates the right to development. Article 22 of the Charter states:

1) All peoples shall have the right to their economic, social and cultural development with due regard to their freedom and identity and in the equal enjoyment of the common heritage of mankind.
2) States shall have the duty, individually or collectively, to ensure the exercise of the right to development.

What this implies is that not only is development a human right, but the full attainment of human rights requires the support of economic, social and cultural development. It also implies that such development is the basis for the realisation of all human rights. It is against that background that the current approaches to integrating human rights with development in Africa are now highlighted.

3 Integrating Human Rights in Development

In order to understand the current approaches to integrating human rights into economic development, it is important to distinguish between civil and political rights on one hand and social, economic and cultural rights on the other. This is because of the theoretical gaps that exist between the two generations of rights. As one commentator has opined: "… a rights-based approach to development bridges theoretical gaps between political, civil, social and economic rights by understanding how they are interconnected in practice".[27]

3.1 *Civil and Political Rights*

Although there are a number of specific rights that fall under this category, the mainstay of civil and political rights is equality and non-discrimination. Many aspects that are relevant to development fall directly or indirectly under this broad genre. These include gender equality (the rights of women), the rights of minority groups, the rights of poor and marginalised communities, the advancement of historically disadvantaged groups, equal benefit and protection of the law, equal access to resources and opportunities, and mutual respect and dignity among all people.

The other genre of civil and political rights consists of those rights that form the basis of a democratic society. These broadly include freedom of expression, freedom of association, right to make political choices, fair labour practices and religious freedom, to mention but a few. It may well be argued that strengthening these rights

---

[27] Offenheiser and Holcombe (2003), p. 268.

is a basis for good governance, which, in turn, is a basis for development. Moreover, these rights have become increasingly significant in decisions relating to development aid and donor funding. Non-compliance with civil and political rights has increasingly become a reason for withholding development aid. According to one commentator, for example, although the World Bank "does not endorse democratic development in the traditional sense, on occasion the Bank's loan practices take into account civil and political rights".[28]

It should also be pointed out that underlying the realisation of civil and political rights are notions of transparency and accountability. In many African states, public transparency and holding government officials accountable have been a rallying call for civil society organisations. Indeed, it has been argued that "accountability is the key to improved effectiveness and transparency of action".[29] In that regard, in its *Draft Guidelines for a Human Rights Approach to Poverty Reduction Strategies*, the Office of the UN High Commissioner for Human Rights expressed the importance of the notion of accountability as follows:

> Perhaps the most important source of added value in the human rights approach is the emphasis it places on the accountability of policy-makers and other actors whose actions have an impact on the rights of people. Rights imply duties, and duties demand accountability.[30]

It is in that context that the approaches of African countries towards integrating human rights with development have to be understood. The African Charter on Human and Peoples' Rights incorporates all internationally recognised civil and political rights. All African states that have constitutions have done the same. It is the level of protection, implementation and realisation of those rights that is in issue. No wonder then that in states where these rights are not respected, the level of economic development is concomitantly low.

3.2 Social and Economic Rights

There is no doubt that social and economic rights are central to the issue of economic development. However, the extent to which such rights should and can be enforced and protected has always been a source of controversy and debate.[31] Indeed, some countries, particularly in Africa, regard these rights as secondary priorities. This is because they have important social and economic dimensions—as most of them reflect specific areas of basic needs or the delivery of particular goods and services.[32] Socio-economic rights include rights to education, health care, food, water, social

---

28 Forsythe (1997), p. 346.

29 Filmer-Wilson (2005), p. 218.

30 OHCHR (2002).

31 Mubangizi (2013), p. 130.

32 Mubangizi (2013), p. 130.

security and housing. Clearly, claims in such areas require a level of availability of resources—an excuse that several African states have used to contest and even undermine the legitimacy of these rights. Many African countries pretend to promote social and economic rights while systematically undermining them. As a result, the rhetoric of these rights is not necessarily reflected in policies, programmes and budgetary allocations.

Although the African Union (AU) has stressed the importance of social and economic rights in achieving development, only a handful of African countries have included them in their constitutions. Even those that have attempted to do so have done it in such a way that makes them non-justifiable and, therefore, unenforceable. The notable exceptions are South Africa and Kenya. Indeed, South Africa is a leader in this respect as it not only has comprehensively included socio-economic rights in its Constitution, but also the courts, particularly the Constitutional Court, have so far decided cases in favour of the protection of these rights. The Kenyan Constitution also contains a Bill of Rights, which incorporates a section on economic and social rights. The Kenyan courts have begun to rise to the occasion in terms of interpreting and enforcing these rights much in the same way that the South African judiciary has done. This is illustrated in cases such as *Mathew Okwanda v The Minister of Health and Medical Services*[33] and *Satrose Ayuma & 11 Others v. The Registered Trustees of Kenya Railways Staff Retirement Benefits Fund Scheme and Others.*[34]

As mentioned above, most African countries do not include social and economic rights in the bills of rights of their constitutions. Some constitutions do not even contain bills of rights at all. What some countries have done, however, is to acknowledge such rights (or some of them) as the goals and objectives of government or the principles of state policy (for example, the Constitutions of Namibia, Ghana and Uganda). As such, they can be categorised not as constitutional rights but rather as policy or societal goals, which have no force of law.[35]

Integrating human rights into development efforts in Africa requires an approach that acknowledges the complex sociopolitical and economic landscape of the continent. In that regard, adopting and implementing robust legal frameworks aligned with international human rights standards is, firstly, crucial. However, merely having laws in place is not sufficient; there must be effective enforcement mechanisms and institutions capable of ensuring compliance at both national and regional levels. Secondly, economic development strategies should prioritise poverty alleviation and inclusive growth, aiming to uplift disadvantaged communities while ensuring the equitable distribution of resources and opportunities. Access to education, healthcare and decent work are fundamental rights that contribute to human development and should be prioritised. Thirdly, integrating human rights into development requires respecting indigenous land rights, promoting sustainable resource management

[33] Petition 94 of 2012 [2013] eKLR.

[34] Petition No. 65 of 2010 [2011] eKLR.

[35] Mubangizi (2007), p. 100.

practices and mitigating the adverse impacts of industrial activities on local communities and ecosystems.

Cognisance should also be taken of the conflict and instability that undermine development efforts and perpetuate human rights abuses. Therefore, investing in conflict prevention, peace building and promoting the rule of law are essential for creating an enabling environment for sustainable development. Moreover, ensuring the accountability of governments, businesses and development actors is critical for protecting human rights in development processes. Transparency in decision-making, access to information and mechanisms for grievance redressal are necessary to hold stakeholders accountable for their actions and decisions. It is for the above reasons that a human-rights-based approach is proposed.

A human-rights-based approach requires that social and economic rights be taken seriously as human rights. This is mainly because of the principles of universality, indivisibility, interdependence and interrelatedness of human rights—the consequence of which is that one or a few rights cannot be fully achieved in isolation from other rights. Attempting to realise civil and political rights while ignoring social and economic rights can only be futile. Moreover, the diverse human rights (civil and political on one hand and social and economic on the other) can be mutually reinforcing and complementary, and due to these complementarities, "the struggle to achieve economic and social rights should not be separated from the struggle to achieve civil and political rights … the two need to be pursued simultaneously".[36]

4 Opportunities

There are many opportunities through which a human-rights-based approach to economic development can be enhanced in Africa. The AU (and its predecessor, the Organization of African Unity (OAU)) has, for some time now, seen development and human rights as inseparable.[37] This view has its genesis in the 1981 African Charter on Human and Peoples Rights, on which the African system for the promotion and protection of human rights is primarily based. It is important to note that the Charter provides for not only traditional civil and political rights but also traditional social, economic and cultural rights. In the specific context of development, Article 22 provides for the right to economic, social and cultural development, and Article 23 provides for the right to "a general satisfactory environment favourable to … development". Also provided for is the right to self-determination, which includes people's right to "freely determine their political status and … pursue their economic and social development according to the policy they have freely chosen.[38]

[36]UNDP 2000.

[37]Murray (2004), p. 237.

[38]Article 20.

Together with the African Charter on Human and Peoples' Rights, there are two human rights implementation organs: namely, the African Commission on Human and Peoples' Rights and the African Court of Justice and Human Rights. The African Commission on Human and Peoples' Rights has had an opportunity to pronounce on the right to development. In *Centre for Minority Rights Development (CEMIRIDE) (on behalf of the Endorois) v Kenya*,[39] decided in 2009, the Commission held that by virtue of Article 22 of the African Charter on Human and Peoples' Rights, the right to development is a legal right that should be fulfilled by states parties. In *Sudan Human Rights Organisation & Centre on Housing Rights and Evictions (COHRE) v Sudan*,[40] also decided in 2009, the Commission held that in targeting the civilian population instead of the combatants while fighting the armed conflict, the state had violated the Sudanese people's right to development under Article 22 of the African Charter.

Unfortunately, the Commission has no legal enforcement procedure. There are no provisions requiring the enforcement of the Commission's recommendations, and therefore compliance primarily depends on the will of the member states. This lack of legal enforcement mechanisms is largely responsible for the popular view that the Commission has served as a limited means of control over human rights abuses. Moreover, according to one commentator,

> …the ability of the African Commission to monitor State compliance with human rights obligations under the African Charter has been largely limited by the fact that most States have not taken their reporting obligations seriously.[41]

The African Court of Justice and Human Rights was established in 2008 as a merger between the African Court on Human and Peoples' Rights (established in 1998) and the Court of Justice of the African Union (established in 2003). On its establishment, the merged court was seen to have the potential to develop into an important instrument for human rights protection on the continent.[42] Although it is difficult to assess the success (or otherwise) of this court, it may be argued that the African human rights system, which revolves around the Charter and the two implementation organs, presents a significant opportunity through which a human-rights-based approach to development can be adopted and realised.

Another important mechanism, through which a human-rights-based approach to economic development in Africa can be achieved, is the New Partnership for Africa's Development (NEPAD). NEPAD was conceived and adopted as an initiative for a more integrated approach to sustainable development. In that regard, NEPAD "has, as one of its foundations, the expansion of democratic frontiers and the deepening of the culture of human rights".[43] It acknowledges that its objectives

[39] Communication 276/2003.

[40] Communication 279/03-296/05.

[41] Ssenyonjo (2018), p. 30.

[42] Ugiabe (2010).

[43] Para 181.

will only be achieved if African leaders take joint responsibility for, among other things, "promoting and protecting democracy and human rights in their respective countries and regions, by developing clear standards of accountability, transparency and participatory governance at the national and subnational levels".[44] NEPAD also acknowledges that "peace, security, democracy, good governance, human rights and sound economic management are conditions for sustainable development"[45] and that "development is impossible in the absence of true democracy, respect for human rights, peace and good governance".[46]

In addition to the above statements, reference is also made—*inter alia*—to good governance, the rule of law, education, health and food. However, I consider that NEPAD was a missed opportunity for adopting a human-rights-based approach to economic development in Africa. It could have made a more explicit contribution in this regard not only by acknowledging the importance of human rights but also by making it an integral part of the NEPAD framework. Mere references to human rights are, in my view, insufficient. It is no wonder then that NEPAD has lost momentum and that the strength and drive with which it was adopted and initiated seems to be fizzling away.

All African countries have an opportunity to adopt a human-rights-based approach to economic development through constitutional and judicial means. Constitutionally, this should and can be done by including bills of rights in their constitutions and by incorporating all categories of human rights, including socio-economic rights. As mentioned earlier, South Africa has been particularly successful in doing this. Indeed, South Africa is said to have one of the most progressive constitutions in the world. Not only does it incorporate all categories of human rights, but it also provides for controversial socio-economic rights in a way that makes them justifiable. Moreover, the South African Constitution also establishes human rights institutions such as the South African Human Rights Commission and the Public Protector. It also provides for an independent judiciary, which, through innovation and creativity, has been able to give meaning and dignity to the Constitution and the rule of law. This is particularly so with respect to the Constitutional Court. Other African countries can learn a great deal from South Africa.

An important opportunity for adopting a human-rights-based approach to development in Africa is through the framework of the 2030 Agenda for Sustainable Development. Adopted by the United Nations General Assembly in September 2015, the 2030 Agenda provides a comprehensive and universal framework that brings together the environmental, social and economic dimensions of sustainable development. It was adopted with 17 Sustainable Development Goals (SDGs) and their 169 targets, which have now become the basis for the post-2015 global development agenda. It should be remembered that the SDGs followed up on the Millennium Development Goals (MDGs), which had been adopted by the United

---

[44]Para 49.

[45]Para 71.

[46]Para 79.

Nations General Assembly in September 2000. The main differences between the MDGs and SDGs are, firstly, that the SDGs have a broader scope and cover more issues than the MDGs. Secondly, whereas the MDGs applied to poor countries only, the SDGs are universal and relevant to all countries, and thirdly, unlike the MDGs, SDGs tend to take a more integrated approach to social, economic and environmental issues to ensure sustainability. As such, they are more focused on building productive capacity and giving more weight to economic and environmental factors.[47]

It is important to note that in terms of the human-rights-based approach, the SDGs and human rights share several characteristics, and each Goal can be linked to specific rights. For example, Goal 1 (end poverty in all its forms everywhere) links to the right to an adequate standard of living. Goal 2 (end hunger, achieve food security and improved nutrition…) links to the right to adequate food. Goal 3 (ensure healthy lives and promote well-being for all) links to the right to health. Goal 4 (ensure inclusive and equitable quality education…) can be linked to the right to education. Goal 5 (achieve gender equality and empower all women and girls) links to the right to equality. These linkages apply to all the 17 SDGs.

Although most of the SDGs directly or indirectly address economic growth and development, it is SDGs 8 and 9 that are quite specific. SDG 8 calls for the promotion of "sustained, inclusive and sustainable economic growth, full and productive employment and decent work for all", and SDG 9 calls for the building of "resilient infrastructure, promoting inclusive and sustainable industrialization and fostering innovation". Some of the targets of SDG 8 are

- Sustain per capita economic growth in accordance with national circumstances and, in particular, at least 7 per cent gross domestic product growth per annum in the least developed countries.
- Achieve higher levels of economic productivity through diversification, technological upgrading and innovation, including through a focus on high-value-added and labour-intensive sectors.
- Promote development-oriented policies that support productive activities, decent job creation, entrepreneurship, creativity and innovation, and encourage the formalisation and growth of micro-, small- and medium-sized enterprises, including through access to financial services.
- Improve progressively, through 2030, global resource efficiency in consumption and production and endeavour to decouple economic growth from environmental degradation, in accordance with the 10-year framework of programmes on sustainable consumption and production, with developed countries taking the lead.
- By 2020, substantially reduce the proportion of youth not in employment, education or training.
- By 2030, devise and implement policies to promote sustainable tourism that creates jobs and promotes local culture and products.
- Strengthen the capacity of domestic financial institutions to encourage and expand access to banking, insurance and financial services for all…

[47] Wall (2014).

A detailed discussion of the above targets is beyond the scope and depth of this chapter. Suffice it to say that in terms of the human-rights-based approach, SDG 8 can be linked to the right of development and the right to work, whereas SDG 9 can be linked to the right to enjoy the benefits of scientific progress and its application.

It is in the context of those shared characteristics and linkages between SDGs and human rights that a human-rights-based approach to economic development should be seen. It is also in that context that it is argued that the framework of the SDGs has provided and continues to provide an ideal opportunity for adopting a human-rights-based approach to development in Africa.

The same arguments can be made in relation to Africa's Agenda 2063. Adopted in January 2015 by the 24th African Union (AU) Assembly of Heads of State and Government, Agenda 2063 is "the continent's strategic framework that aims to deliver on its goal for inclusive and sustainable development".[48] It was developed through a people-centred consultative process over a period of 18 months. Among the main aspirations on which Agenda 2063 is based are these three, which are relevant to this discussion:

- A prosperous Africa based on inclusive growth and sustainable development;
- An Africa of good governance, respect for human rights, justice and the rule of law; and
- An Africa whose development is people-driven, relying on the potential of African people, especially its women and youth, and caring for children.

Agenda 2063 behoves African leaders "to prioritise inclusive social and economic development, continental and regional integration, democratic governance and peace and security amongst other issues aimed at repositioning Africa to becoming a dominant player in the global arena".[49] In so doing, Agenda 2063 presents yet another opportunity through which a human-rights-based approach to economic development can be realised.

It is clear from the foregoing discussion that there are many opportunities through which a human-rights-based approach to economic development in Africa can be achieved. That said, it has to be acknowledged, however, that there are several challenges in this regard, and these are now discussed.

5 Challenges

For purposes of clarity, and in the context of this discussion, "challenges" should be understood to mean the limitations and constraints that impede the effectiveness and ability to adopt a human-rights-based approach to economic development in Africa. In essence, these are the very same challenges that impact the full realisation and

[48] African Union (Agenda 2063).

[49] African Union (Agenda 2063).

enjoyment of fundamental human rights—albeit in the specific context of economic development. In highlighting these challenges, cognisance has to be taken of the relationship between human rights and economic development, discussed earlier.

There can be no doubt that the biggest challenge to a human-rights-based-approach to development in Africa is poverty. In discussing the relationship between poverty and human rights, the famous statement of Mary Robinson immediately comes to mind:

> I am often asked what is the most serious form of human rights violations in the world today, and my reply is consistent: extreme poverty.[50]

It is in that context that many have argued that not only is poverty an impediment to the enjoyment and realisation of human rights, but—in itself—it is also a violation of human rights.[51]

The levels of poverty in Africa and the facts verifying them are well documented. It is estimated that 490 million people in Africa are living in extreme poverty.[52] This translates to about 36% of Africa's total population.[53] Although there is evidence that sub-Saharan Africa is growing at a strong pace, poverty remains one of the most serious challenges to a human-rights-based approach to development on the continent. Indeed, it is no wonder that eradicating extreme poverty tops the list of targets of the SDGs, as seen earlier. It is also perhaps because of this that progress is currently being made in reducing poverty in Africa, and in the most recent past. That said, however, there is no doubt that the COVID-19 pandemic, which started spreading onto the continent in 2020, has had a significant impact on any progress in reducing poverty. Indeed, the economic impact of the COVID-19 shock in sub-Saharan Africa has been severe. Economic activity on the continent was estimated to have contracted by 2% in 2020 and plunged the region into a recession.[54]

Poverty affects the enjoyment of human rights in different ways—including the realisation of socio-economic rights. It also undermines democracy as many poor people are more preoccupied with the daily struggles of survival than with issues of democracy. Indeed, the low levels of democracy and good governance across Africa are another major challenge to a human-rights-based approach to development. I have previously argued elsewhere that human rights are a necessary component of any democratic society and that one of the tenets of democracy is a form of government that encourages, allows, promotes and protects the rights of its citizens.[55] By extension then, it could be argued that democracy is a critical and essential requisite for development. Unfortunately, democracy and good governance

[50] Mary Robinson – former UN High Commissioner for Human Rights and President of Ireland, quoted as an opening statement in UNDP "Poverty Reduction and Human Rights – A Practice Note" June 2003.

[51] See, for example, Pogge (2007).

[52] Human (2021).

[53] Human (2021).

[54] World Bank (2021).

[55] Mubangizi (2013), p. 8.

are a huge problem on the African continent. According to the Economist Intelligence Unit's 2020 Democracy Index, only one African country, Mauritius, is ranked as a "full" democracy.[56] The rest are ranked as flawed democracies, hybrid regimes, authoritarian regimes or failed states. The lack of democracy is usually accompanied and compounded by other factors, such as poor governance, mismanagement, corruption and nepotism. All these have a significantly negative impact on development. They also present a formidable challenge to a human-rights-based approach to development—particularly in Africa, where they are prevalent.

It must be pointed out, however, that democracy and good governance require a politically stable and socially peaceful environment. Unfortunately, several parts of Africa are currently experiencing political instability, armed conflicts and social strife. Currently, there are high-intensity armed conflicts in Nigeria, Somalia, the Democratic Republic of Congo (DRC), Burkina Faso, Mali, South Sudan and Cameroon. There are a number of low-intensity, sub-national armed conflicts in several other countries. There is no doubt that all these conflicts and instabilities do compromise the struggle for human rights and, therefore, present a significant challenge to a human-rights-based approach to development.

Mention was made earlier of the significant economic impact of the COVID-19 pandemic. In addition to COVID-19, however, Africa is home to diseases and epidemics such as human immunodeficiency virus (HIV)/acquired immunodeficiency syndrome (AIDS), malaria and tuberculosis, all of which have an impact on the right to health—an important socio-economic right. Although several factors—including access to anti-retroviral medication—have reduced the HIV/AIDS death rate, it still has a significant impact in terms of human suffering and health care. The concomitant impact on development cannot be overemphasised. So too is the impact on the adoption of a human-rights-based approach to development.

One important challenge relates to African cultural and traditional practices, which not only violate human rights but also have the effect of marginalising certain groups of people, such as women. Among the more common repugnant African cultural practices are female genital mutilation (FGM), virginity testing, marriage by abduction, bride price, polygamy and primogeniture (the right of the eldest surviving male to inherit the estate of the parents). Whereas many might argue that cultural rights are protected by international law and domestic constitutional systems, there is no doubt that many cultural practices do clash with human rights norms. Most of these traditional and cultural practices violate the right to equality, the right to human dignity and, in some cases, even the right to life. It must also be pointed out that most African cultural practices are gender related and, therefore, often result in human rights abuses that function as instruments of socialising women into prescribed gender roles within the community. Such practices are also linked to the unequal position of women in the political, social and economic structures of societies where they are practised.[57] This has the effect of marginalising women and denying them

[56] The Economist Intelligence Unit (2020).

[57] Mubangizi (2012), p. 14.

full participation in economic and other development activities of their communities. Therein lies the challenge of adopting a human-rights-based approach to economic development—in the face of such marginalisation, discrimination and abuse.

6 Conclusion

Peculiar conditions that prevail in Africa—and the assorted challenges highlighted above—are not the only inhibiting factors to the adoption of a human-rights-based approach to economic development. There are, for example, challenges facing African human rights implementation organs (the African Commission on Human and Peoples' Rights and the African Court of Justice and Human Rights). Other factors include low levels of education, widespread unemployment, natural disasters and crime. It is submitted that (perhaps) because of those challenges and obstacles, the need for adopting a human-rights-based approach to economic development is even more urgent and critical. It has been shown that there are opportunities through which this can be done. Not only is there a continental human rights framework—with instruments such as the African Charter on Human and Peoples Rights—but there are also other continental and international frameworks, such as NEPAD and the UN SDGs. Moreover, opportunities also exist through national constitutional and judicial frameworks. The South African experience, over the last two and a half decades—though not without its own shortcomings—is an example that could be emulated, and there are many lessons that can be learnt from it.

This chapter sought to highlight the opportunities and prospects for promoting a human-rights-based approach to economic development in Africa, on the one hand, and the challenges of doing so, on the other. Based on the discussion, it is recommended that the international legal and institutional framework play a more meaningful role in this endeavour. In particular, the African Charter on Human and Peoples Rights, the African Commission on Human and Peoples' Rights and the African Court of Justice and Human Rights can provide a legitimate starting point in establishing the processes for and the principles of adopting a human-rights-based approach to development. It is also recommended that the opportunities provided by the NEPAD framework and the Sustainable Development Goals be exploited. Finally, it is recommended that African countries take advantage of the opportunities to adopt a human-rights-based approach to economic development through constitutional and judicial means. The South African experience, though not exactly perfect, has shown that this is possible.

References

African Union. Agenda 2063: The Africa We Want. https://au.int/en/agenda2063/overview

CIFEDHOP (2012) The human rights-based approach: a field of action for human rights education. http://www.ciel.org/Publications/HR_Approach_Climate_2012.pdf

D'Hollander D, Marx A, Wouters J (2013) Integrating human rights in development policy: mapping donor strategies and practices. https://doi.org/10.2139/ssrn.2286204
Danish Mission Council Development Department, Position paper on a rights-based approach to development. https://videncenter.org/wp-content/uploads/2020/07/Position_paper_on_RBA-002.pdf
Filmer-Wilson E (2005) The human rights-based approach to development: the right to water. Neth Q Hum Rights 32(2):213–241
Forsythe DP (1997) The United Nations, human rights, and development. Hum Rights Q 19(2): 334–339
Human JH (2021) African countries continue to have the highest poverty rates in the world. https://www.developmentaid.org/#!/news-stream/post/84943/highest-poverty-rates-in-africa
Mcinerney-Lankford S (2009) Human rights and development: a comment on challenges and opportunities from a legal perspective. J Hum Rights Pract 1(1):51–82
Mubangizi JC (2007) The protection and enforcement of socio-economic rights in Africa: lessons from the South African experience. Afr Yearb Int Law 15:87–106
Mubangizi JC (2012) Building a human rights culture in the face of cultural diversity: context and conflict. Afr J Leg Stud 5(1):1–20
Mubangizi JC (2013) The protection of human rights in South Africa: a legal and practical guide, 2nd edn. Juta and Company Ltd, Claremont
Murray R (2004) Human rights in Africa: from the OAU to the African Union. Cambridge University Press, Cambridge
Myint H, Krueger AO (2016) "Economic development", Encyclopaedia Britannica. https://www.britannica.com/topic/economic-development
Offenheiser R, Holcombe S (2003) Challenges and opportunities in implementing a rights-based approach to development: an Oxfam America perspective. Non-profit Volunt Sect Q 32(2): 68–301
OHCHR (2002) Draft guidelines: a human rights approach to poverty reduction strategies. https://www.refworld.org/docid/3f8298544.html
OHCHR (2006) Frequently asked questions on a human-rights-based approach to development cooperation. https://www.ohchr.org/documents/publications/faqen.pdf
OHRHC (2010) Applying a human rights-based approach to climate change negotiations, policies and measures. https://www.unccleam.org/wp-content/uploads/library/infonotehrba1.pdf
Pogge T (2007) Severe poverty as a human rights violation. In: Freedom from poverty as a human right: who owes what to the very poor? Oxford University Press, Oxford
Sen A (1999) Development as freedom. Oxford University Press, Oxford
SHRC, "Care about Rights: What is a Human Rights-Based Approach?" https://careaboutrights.scottishhumanrights.com/whatisahumanrightsbasedapproach.html
Ssenyonjo M (2018) Responding to human rights violations in Africa assessing the role of the African Commission and Court on Human and Peoples' Rights (1987–2018). Int Hum Rights Law Rev 7:1–42
The Economist Intelligence Unit, Democracy Index 2020: In Sickness and in Health? https://www.eiu.com/n/campaigns/democracy-index-2020/
Ugiabe TB (2010) The African Court of Justice and Human Rights: future political and jurisdictional realities and challenges. https://www.ideasforpeace.org/content/the-african-court-of-justice-and-human-rights-future-political-and-jurisdictional-realities-and-challenges/
UNDP, Human Development Report 1992. New York
UNDP (1998) Integrating human rights with sustainable development: a policy document. http://www.undp-aciac.org/publications/other/undp/hr/hr-susdev98e.pdf
UNDP (2000) Human Development Report 2000. New York

Ussor M (2011) Integration of the human rights-based approach to development policies: a guide to the new EU Member States. Minority Rights Group International, London

Wall T (2014) Sustainable Development Goals: new targets hold promise for Africa. Africa Renewal, December 2014. https://www.un.org/africarenewal/magazine/december-2014/sustainable-development-goals-new-targets-hold-promise-africa

World Bank. Africa: Overview (2021). https://www.worldbank.org/en/region/afr/overview

John C. Mubangizi LL.B (Makerere University), LL.M (University of Cape Town), LL.D (University of KwaZulu-Natal), Professor, Free State Centre for Human Rights, Faculty of Law, University of the Free State, Bloemfontein, South Africa. E-mail: MubangiziJC@ufs.ac.za.

The Roles of Environmental Rights in Fostering Economic Development in Africa

Vicent Bartholomew Mtavangu

1 Introduction

The past three decades have demonstrated the vigorous efforts of African countries to develop their economies by using environmental resources such as minerals, petroleum, oil and gas. Unlike some European Union (EU) Member States that depend on imported raw materials, most African states are endowed with unexploited variety of environmental resources.[1] Insufficient capital and the lack of advanced technologies to harness deposited resources prevent many African countries from exploiting their raw materials. Thus, one of the strategies to fuel Africa's economies is to attract foreign direct investments (FDIs).

The economies of many African states, including Republic of South Africa, Zambia, Ghana, the Democratic Republic of the Congo (DRC) and Tanzania, are heavily dependent on the extractive industry.[2] However, resources extraction has failed to drive sustainable economic development, largely due to the absence of democratic values such as the rule of law, transparency, public participation, good governance and accountability in both governments and businesses.[3] These values are deeply rooted in the protection of human rights. Thus, aligning the extraction of natural resources with human rights standards is essential for promoting

[1] See De Sadeleer (2014), p. 137.

[2] Olawuyi (2018), p. 5.

[3] Ibid.

V. B. Mtavangu (✉)
Mzumbe University Mbeya Campus College-Department of Legal Studies (DLS), Mbeya, Tanzania

I. Kajiru et al. (eds.), *Economic Development and Human Rights in Contemporary Sub-Saharan Africa*, Ius Gentium: Comparative Perspectives on Law and Justice 122, https://doi.org/10.1007/978-3-031-81400-6_2

economic development, as human rights serve as a critical bridge between development and environmental sustainability.[4]

The connection between human rights and the environment is well-established. This is reflected in a myriad of literature as well as human rights and environmental instruments.[5] It is from such a nexus that environmental rights are borne. There is no doubt that environmental rights are human rights. Despite the difficulties in construing what constitutes 'environmental human rights' or 'environmental rights', it is indisputable that these concepts play a significant role in the economic growth of African states as they embody most of the democratic values. Unlike other human rights, environmental rights are more directly linked to economic aspect of sustainable development. This explains partly why the framers of the African Charter on Human and People Rights, 1981,[6] merged environmental rights with development. However, little has been studied and written on the role of environmental rights in fuelling the economic development of African countries.

Conversely, there is a belief that environmental rights conflict with the agenda of economic development. Certainly, neither environmental protection nor human rights hinder economic development.[7] This is because environmental rights are a yardstick for ensuring that development projects comply with certain values that put humankind into paramount consideration. For sure, a polluted environment cannot aid people in carrying out their economic activities. Also, the economic development of citizens may be hampered if they are not informed of pertinent environmental issues, if their right to participate in environmental decision-making is curtailed and if they are denied access to environmental justice. Moreover, the enjoyment of fundamental human rights depends on the existence of a conducive and favourable environment.[8]

Against this backdrop, this chapter highlights the importance of environmental rights in accelerating the economic growth of African states. The chapter starts by conceptualising key terms, *i.e.* human rights, the environment and environmental rights. It then examines African human rights and environmental instruments containing environmental rights. Further, the chapter discusses the enforcement of environmental rights by institutions established under the said instruments. Thereafter, the chapter underscores the role of substantive and procedural environmental rights in economic development. The next part accentuates the challenges and possibilities of enforcing environmental rights in Africa, followed by the conclusion.

---

[4] Leib (2011), p. 122.

[5] For details, see Lewis (2012), p. 36. See also Kotze and Daly (2019), p. 1047.

[6] 21 ILM 58 (1982).

[7] See Boyle (2012), p. 631.

[8] *Fuel Retailers Association of Southern Africa v. Director-General Environmental Management, Department of Agriculture, Conservation and Environment, Mpumalanga Province and Others*, Case No. CCT 67/06; ILDC 783 (ZA 2007), para. 102.

2 The Concept of Human Rights, the Environment and Environmental Rights

Human rights as a non-legal concept can sometimes be interpreted in various ways depending on one's perspective. This implies that there is no agreeable and universal definition of the concept of human rights. What can be considered a human right in a given society may not necessarily be so in another. This means that 'human rights' is a versatile concept. At their core, human rights are entitlements grounded in principles of morality, justice and fairness, values upon which the nations of the world have collectively agreed that all individuals are inherently entitled.[9] This definition implies that there are basic entitlements common to all humankind around the globe. They are codified in human rights instruments like the Universal Declaration of Human Rights (UDHR), 1948;[10] the International Covenant on Civil and Political Rights (ICCPR), 1966;[11] the International Covenant on Economic, Social and Cultural Rights (ICESCR), 1966;[12] and the Convention on the Rights of the Child (CRC), 1989.[13] Despite the fact that the above instruments are widely ratified by states and clearly provide human rights provisions, some human rights may not be common to all nations in the world. Cultural norms and practices contribute to the particularism of human rights.

Generally, human rights consist of apex demands that an individual or group of individuals make to society. These rights aim to promote, protect and improve human conditions.[14] Given their immutable nature, human rights are universally regarded as automatically belonging to every individual within a society, and no one has the authority to strip them away. The state is not the source of these rights rather it serves as the crucial entity responsible for safeguarding, enforcing and promoting them. Regardless of whether fundamental human rights are explicitly enshrined in the Constitution, the state bears responsibility to recognise and enforce them for the benefit of all, as they are essential to achieve development.[15]

There are three groups of human rights, namely the first, second and third generations. The first generation comprises civil and political rights, whereas the second generation focuses on economic, social and cultural rights.[16] The third generation of rights is sometimes referred to as collective, solidarity or people's rights. They consist of rights that can be enjoyed not only by an individual but also

---

[9] Beder (2006), p. 91.

[10] See the UN General Assembly Resolution 217 A (III) of 10 December 1948.

[11] See the UN General Assembly Resolution 2200 A(XXI) of 16 December 1966.

[12] Ibid.

[13] See the UN General Assembly Resolution No. 44/25 of 20 November 1989.

[14] Karan (2004), p. 33.

[15] Cullet (1995), p. 30.

[16] See Nanda and Pring (2013), p. 597.

by the community at large. A person enjoys them as part of a group or a community and not merely as an individual.

Third-generation rights, such as the right to a clean and healthy environment and the right to development, are distinct from the right outlined in the first and second generations. Nevertheless, environmental rights intersects with those of other generations of human rights.[17] It is because the enjoyment of other rights squarely depends on the existence of this right. Thus, the stand-alone environmental right may be considered the cornerstone of all human rights, highlighting that the environment is a cross-cutting issue in human rights discourse.

Economic growth and the eradication of poverty are among the goals of third-generation human rights.[18] It is for this reason that the implementation and enforcement of group rights are significant for the economic development of third-world countries, some of which are in Africa. This explains further why the struggle to include the third generation of human rights in the list of the world's human rights was spearheaded by the developing countries, *inter alia,* due to the socio-economic marginalisation experienced by them.[19] Thus, the realisation of collective rights, especially environmentally related rights, is a prerequisite for the economic development of African states.

However, defining precisely the notion of 'environment' is a daunting task. The challenge in precisely defining the term 'environment' arises from its overlap with various concepts, such as ecology, nature, biodiversity and sustainable development, among others.[20] This indicates that the environment is not only a very open concept but also a catch-all concept. Shanthakumar defines the environment as 'everything surrounds you, including the air, the land, the oceans, and all living things'.[21] This definition is focused on the surroundings. A definition of the environment that focuses only on the surroundings is not adequate. It is because the environment includes everything—human beings, invisible and intangible objects and known and unidentified phenomena.

Nhamo and Inyang[22] further conceptualise the term environment into two dimensions. The first dimension, according to them, is biophysical (natural), which constitutes elements such as climate (temperature, rainfall, wind and evaporation), air, topography, geology, soil, vegetation (flora), fauna (animals), groundwater (hydrogeology) and surface water (hydrology). The second dimension is the human dimension (socio-economic and political dimension), which is composed of elements like people, land tenure and use, and archaeological, social, cultural, political and economic aspects. This description is comprehensive as it captures all

---

[17] De Sadeleer (2014), p. 96. See also Ruppel (2011), p. 221.

[18] Leib (2011), p. 122.

[19] See LHRC and ZLSC (2017), p. 310.

[20] De Sadeleer (2014), p. 7.

[21] Shanthakumar (2007), p. 2.

[22] See Nhamo and Inyang (2011), p. 1.

aspects, *viz.* human beings and surroundings, although it does not cover unseen objects.

As can be gathered from the above definitions, the environment includes human beings, natural elements as well as man-made features or surroundings. The surroundings include living and non-living things. The non-living components of the environment are comprised of land, water, air atmospheric temperature, and wind and its velocity, whereas the living components constitute germs, plants and animals. Therefore, the environment is a complex interplay of various, features and conditions that influence life, encompassing both human-made and natural elements.

Akin to the term environment, it is fraught with complexity to precisely define the concept of 'environmental human rights' or 'environmental rights'. Given their complexities, much of the literature on environmental law and human rights tend to avoid defining and outlining the contents of environmental rights. There are diverse understandings of the concept either concerning substantive environmental rights, procedural environmental rights or a combination of the two.[23] Essentially, environmental human rights represent a distinct approach that extends traditional human rights to address environmental concerns. This approach seeks to strength the protection of the environment, which is the fundamental to the survival of humankind and other living things.

Shelton,[24] for instance, describes environmental rights with the reference 'to any proclamation of a human right to environmental conditions of a specified quality'. This description refers to substantive environmental rights only, such as the stand-alone right to a clean, decent, safe or healthy environment. Some authors also describe environmental rights as all rights related to human environmental issues, such as the right to life, the right to food and the right to health, just to mention a few.[25] These scholars assert that any right with a bearing on a human-environmental interest, whether a political, socio-economic or procedural right, is an environmental right.

Consequently, there is yet to be unanimous agreement in international environmental law on which rights are encompassed within the definition of environmental rights.[26] This is perhaps due to the fact that rights related to environmental protection are considered newer than civil and political rights. Additionally, the contents and scope of environmental rights are uncertain as they differ from one state to another depending on the variation of the time.[27] Essentially, both international environmental instruments and domestic laws lack a precise definitions of what 'environmental rights' encompas. Therefore, the lack of a common understanding of the phrase 'environmental rights' is among the factors that hinder their enforcement internationally and under national laws.[28]

[23] See Atapattu and Schapper (2019), p. 4.

[24] Shelton (2010a), p. 89.

[25] See Atapattu and Schapper (2019), p. 4. See also Kotze and Daly (2019), p. 1046.

[26] Sunkin et al. (2002), p. 746.

[27] Amsalu (2020), p. 266.

[28] Otubu (2012), p. 17.

In this chapter, environmental rights would mean the substantive and procedural rights related to the protection and conservation of environmental components such as minerals, water, air and natural forests, just to mention a few. Put differently, environmental rights consist of human rights relating to the governance of natural resources. They comprise the right to a clean and healthy environment, the right to environmental information, the right to public participation in environmental decision-making and access to environmental justice.

3 Environmental Rights in the African Normative Framework

Environmental rights are embedded in many African human rights and environmental instruments. For example, the African Charter on Human and Peoples' Rights entrenches in Article 24 recognises the right to a general satisfactory environment as part of collective rights. While the exact nature, scope and enforceability of this right remain somewhat vague, its inclusion makes the Charter the first binding international instrument to explicitly address this substantive environmental right. The Charter states that 'all peoples shall have the right to a general satisfactory environment favourable to their development'. This means that a clean and decent environment is not only a fundamental condition for enjoying other human rights but also a crucial driver of economic development in African states.[29] This is why the framers of the Charter intentionally connected this substantive environmental right with the right to development. In contrast, in regions such as Europe and America, a substantive environmental right is are directly linked to the right to health.

Nevertheless, it is argued that comprehending exactly Article 24, especially the phrase 'satisfactory environment favourable to their development', is problematic as it contains a range of different components, such as socio-economic rights as well as civil and political rights.[30] This leaves to the African Court and the Commission the obligation to interpret the concept based on the facts of each case. Furthermore, linking environmental rights with the right to development is argued to have the effect of weakening the former right in case of conflict between the two rights.[31] This implies that socio-economic development may sometimes outweigh environmental rights, especially in developing countries, which strive to grow economically. It is further argued that framing a substantive environmental right as a group right, as distinguished from an individual right, is a weak formulation as it prevents the right from being easily enforced.[32] The point here is that it is sometimes relatively easy for

[29] See Amechi (2009), p. 62. See also Addaney et al. (2020), p. 13.

[30] Lumina (2020), pp. 36 & 52.

[31] See Amechi (2009), p. 61.

[32] See Sunkin et al. (2002), p. 747.

an individual to enforce his rights rather than his group rights because of divergent ideas and philosophies.

The Charter is also criticised for not being clear as to the extent to which environmental pollution would be considered a violation of human rights.[33] This is because there are no uniform environmental standards across all African countries. A breach of certain environmental standards in one country may not necessarily entail a violation of environmental rights in another.

Besides the Charter, there is also the African Convention on the Conservation of Nature and Natural Resources, 2003. The Convention is guided by several principles, including the right of all peoples to a satisfactory environment that is favourable to their development.[34] This provision is a replica of the African Charter. Thus, the Convention unequivocally recognises substantive environmental rights. Like in the Charter, environmental rights in the Convention are ingrained in the right to development. This indicates the indivisibility of the two rights. As noted earlier, the challenge for African states striving to grow economically through reliance on environmental goods is how to balance the two rights.

The Protocol to the African Charter on Human and Peoples' Rights on the Rights of Women in Africa also recognises environmental rights, especially the right to a healthy and sustainable environment.[35] The Protocol mostly encompass substantive environmental rights, as distinguished from procedural environmental rights. Particularly, it calls for states parties to protect the right of women to live in a healthy and sustainable environment by promoting its preservation as well as providing for the regulation, management, processing and proper storage and disposal of both domestic and toxic wastes.[36] Largely, this Protocol aims at empowering women by promoting gender equality and increasing their participation in economic development. However, for most African women, the realisation of environmental rights contained in the Protocol is far from reality. This is because African women are still considered unequal partners in many spheres of environmental management.[37]

Apart from regional normative frameworks, the Constitutions and national laws of many African countries also recognise environmental rights. It is believed that more than half of the Constitutions of African states contain the said rights. This is plausible as the Constitution of a state is the highest law of the land. If a Constitution is silent on environmental rights, there is a danger of an act of parliament to narrow the *locus standi* and thus limit their enforceability. Kenya,[38] Uganda,[39] the Republic

[33] Sands et al. (2015), p. 778.

[34] See Art. III (1)

[35] See Art. 18. The Protocol was adopted on 1 July 2003 and entered into force on 25 November 2005. See also Keetharuth (2009), p. 187, and Boshoff (2020), p. 117.

[36] See Art. 18(1)(2)(c)(d).

[37] See Keetharuth (2009), p. 187. See also Boshoff (2020), p. 117.

[38] See Arts. 42 and 70(1) of the Constitution of Kenya, 2010.

[39] See Art. 39 of the Constitution of Uganda, 1995.

of South Africa,[40] Ethiopia[41] and the DRC[42] provide good examples of countries with constitutionally protected environmental rights.

The questions to ponder at this juncture are whether there is a correlation between development and entrenched environmental rights and also whether there is an effective execution of these rights by these countries since recognition is one thing while enforcement is another. National courts must construe existing rights, such as the right to life, in order to enforce environmental rights, even in African countries whose Constitutions are silent about it. The High Court of Tanzania, for instance, ingeniously construed the right to life, as provided by Article 14 of the Constitution, to include the right to a clean and healthy environment.[43]

It is also interesting that in some countries, environmental rights have been formulated to reflect unique environmental situations facing African countries.[44] For instance, the South African environmental right entrenched in the Constitution is said to reflect its revolutionary anti-apartheid struggle.[45] The Kenyan formulation of constitutional environmental rights takes into account indigenous knowledge of the protection and conservation of the environment,[46] whereas the Ethiopian Constitution's provision on environmental rights reflects the drought conditions and ecological disasters the country experiences.[47] Despite the embodiment of environmental rights in those Constitutions, the implementation and enforcement of those rights is still a great challenge among many African states. The lack of political will by some African governments and the incapacity of environmental enforcement institutions to deal with environmental polluters, like giant mining companies, are among the contributory challenges.[48]

[40] See Art. 24 of the Constitution of the Republic of South Africa, 1996.

[41] See Art. 44 of the Constitution of Ethiopia, 1995.

[42] See Art. 53 of the Constitution of DRC, 2006. This constitutional provision reiterates what is stated in Article 24 of the African Charter by linking the environment and development.

[43] See *Joseph D. Kessy and Others v. The City Council of Dar es Salaam*, High Court of Tanzania at Dar es Salaam, Civil Case No. 299 of 1988 (unreported), and *Festo Balegele and 794 Others v. Dar es Salaam City Council*, High Court of Tanzania at Dar es Salaam Misc. Civil Case No. 90 of 1991 (unreported).

[44] Kotze and Daly (2019), p. 181.

[45] Kotze (2015), p. 180.

[46] Ibid. Article 162 of the Kenyan Constitution also establishes the environmental specialised court, *viz.* the Environment and Land Court of Kenya.

[47] Kotze (2015), p. 181.

[48] Boyd (2012), p. 149.

4 Institutional Enforcement of Environmental Rights in Africa

Apart from the national courts and environmental enforcement agencies, there are also regional institutions that can implement and enforce environmental rights in Africa. The African Commission on Human and Peoples Rights (hereinafter referred to as 'the Commission') is one of them. Several disputes related to environmental rights have been determined by the Commission.[49] *Social and Economic Rights Action Centre (SERAC) and Centre for Economic Social Rights (CESR) v. Federal Republic of Nigeria*[50] is a seminal example. In this communication, Nigeria was alleged to violate, *inter alia*, Article 24 of the African Charter related to substantive environmental rights. The claimants further contended that the victims were denied the environmental procedural right to information regarding the danger of oil exploitation and also were not involved in the environmental decision-making concerning Ogoniland. The Commission ruled in favour of the complainants. In construing Article 24, the Commission stated that the right to a healthy environment

> imposes clear obligations upon a government … to take reasonable and other measures to prevent pollution and ecological degradation, to promote conservation, and to secure an ecologically sustainable development and use of natural resources.[51]

Particularly, the Commission remarked that the Government of Nigeria not only failed to protect its people from the violation of their rights by the oil consortium but also assisted in the devastation of Ogoniland.[52] Unfortunately, this decision was not a panacea for environmental pollution in Nigeria. This is exacerbated by the fact that the Commission's decisions have no legal force other than persuasive authority. The decision is significant because it clarified the substantive content of Article 24 of the Charter. The substantive part of the environmental right, as stipulated by the Charter, comprises, *inter alia*, the prevention of environmental pollution and ecological degradation.[53]

Centre for Minority Rights Development (Kenya) and Minority Rights Group International (on Behalf of Endorois Welfare Council) v. Kenya[54] is another complaint determined by the Commission. Although the Commission interpreted not Article 24 but rather Article 22 of the Charter on the right to development, it is still a

---

[49] See, for example, *Front for Liberation of the State of Cabinda v. Republic of Angola*, Communication No. 328/06 decided during the 54th Ordinary Session of the Commission held from 22 October to 5 November 2013, and *Centre on Housing Rights and Evictions v. the Sudan*, Communication No. 296/05 decided in the 39th Ordinary Session of the African Commission on Human and Peoples' Rights held from 11 to 25 May 2006.

[50] Communication No. 155/96, delivered at the 30th Ordinary session held in Banjul, Gambia, from 13 to 27 October 2001.

[51] Ibid.

[52] Ibid, para. 58.

[53] See Amechi (2009), p. 65.

[54] Application 276/03.

relevant decision as it impliedly linked the right to the environment and development. In this communication, the Endorois people claimed that their right to access the natural environment, its resources and ancestral land was deprived by the Government of Kenya through an eviction order. The Commission decided in favour of the Endorois people, and the Kenyan Government was declared to have violated, among others, the right to development.

The African Court on Human and Peoples' Rights (ACHPR) is another enforcement institution that was established in 1998 to supplement the Commission.[55] It is the only continental judicial institution established by the African Union (AU) to strengthen the protective mandate of the African Commission. The court was envisaged to be a coercive enforcement apparatus for all rights enshrined in the Charter. Except for the decision in *The African Commission on Human and Peoples' Rights v. Republic of Kenya*,[56] there is no other relevant dispute that has been tested before the court regarding environmental rights. The brief facts of that case are that in 2009, the Kenyan Government issued a notice to evict the Ogiek indigenous minority community of the Mau forest. As per the government, the eviction was intended to protect the Mau forest and water catchment area. The Ogiek people argued that such an eviction was contrary to the Charter and other international human rights instruments. The African Court entered a judgment in favour of the Ogiek people.

There is also the East African Court of Justice (EACJ), a sub-regional judicial body of the East African Community whose task is to enforce the rights and duties of the citizens of the Member States. *The Attorney General of the United Republic of Tanzania v. African Network for Animal Welfare (ANAW)*[57] is the landmark decision regarding environmental rights that was delivered by the EACJ. In this case, the EACJ interpreted the EAC Treaty in line with the obligations of the Member States to protect the environment. This judgment indicates that sometimes environmental concerns prevail over the socio-economic development of a given society.[58]

The Court of Justice for the Economic Community of the West African States (ECOWAS) also plays a significant role in interpreting and enforcing environmental rights in West Africa. *The Socio-Economic Rights and Accountability Project (SERAP) v. Nigeria*[59] is a good illustration of this. In this case, the applicants argued, *inter alia*, that the right to a clean and healthy environment was violated by petroleum companies due to oil spillage. The court ordered the Nigerian Government to restore the damaged environment in the Niger Delta for the satisfaction of

---

[55]The ACHPR was established by the Protocol to the African Charter on Human and Peoples' Rights on the Establishment of an African Court on Human and Peoples' Rights, 1998.

[56]See Application No. 006/2012, decided on 26 May 2017.

[57]The Appellate Division of the EACJ, Appeal No. 3 of 2014.

[58]Mtavangu (2017), p. 181.

[59]Judgment No. ECW/CCJ/JUD/18/2012.

human beings living there and to ensure sustainable development, as well as to prevent the occurrence of any other damage.[60]

The common problem facing the above institutions is the refusal or failure of some states parties to comply with their decisions or the delay in their compliance with such decisions. One of the reasons for the non-implementation by some African states of the environmental decisions rendered by continental and regional institutions is the lack of a legal framework among states parties for the recognition of international judgments.[61] Most of the countries have domestic laws concerning the recognition of the foreign judgments of other states only and not of international tribunals and judicial bodies. This practice makes these institutions ineffective in enforcing the environmental rights stipulated in various international, regional and national instruments. Consequently, their credibility is undermined. Furthermore, the victims of violations of environmental rights obtain no remedy.

5 The Roles of Environmental Rights in Economic Development

The economic development of a country is sometimes achieved through the realisation of human rights obligations. This is because human rights are the highest entitlement of rights for humankind. Environmental right as a human right is a public good that is a desideratum for economic growth. This explains the necessity of putting the environment as a forethought rather than as an afterthought for all development strategies.[62] As was noted earlier, in the African context, substantive environmental rights are closely associated with the right to development. However, this does not guarantee the concurrent enforcement of these two rights by states parties. It only entails that sustainable development is the fruit of a clean and healthy environment.[63] This may offer insight into paradox that African countries perceive human rights discourse as instrumental in attaining sustainable economic growth.

Explaining the importance of environmental rights, Leib remarks that 'Environmental rights equip human rights activists, environmentalists and victims of environmental degradation with a powerful tool with which to overcome the "sovereignty wall" often raised as a barrier to any form of state liability'.[64] Thus, environmental rights create solidarity among stakeholders in fighting against environmental injustice, which sometimes acts as a barrier to economic growth. In guaranteeing environmental rights, concerted efforts are needed from the citizens,

---

[60] Ibid, para. 101.

[61] Coalition for an Effective African Court on Human and Peoples' Rights (2021), p. 35.

[62] Karan (2004), p. 36.

[63] See Addaney et al. (2020), p. 14.

[64] Leib (2011), p. 2.

corporations, governments as well as the international community because the effects of environmental pollution know no boundary.[65]

The promotion and enforcement of environmental procedural rights enable citizens to actively take part in environmental democracy. This means that citizens can fully participate in, influence and challenge environmental law and policy.[66] The reason is that procedural environmental rights intensify government accountability and support transparency. The consequence of the enforcement of environmental procedural rights in Africa is the introduction of democratic practices. In the long run, this would enhance the economic development of a given state as democracy is a fundamental instrument for the promotion of the development process of a given country.[67] The truth is that there is mutual dependency between democracy and development. In its core, democracy requires the economic priorities and needs of the people to be clearly defined through public involvement.

In the same vein, it is believed that economic development achieved through a democratic framework is sustainable compared to one obtained through the command of an individual or a few people.[68] It is for this reason that in a democratic context, there will be a sense of involvement in development programmes among the people. In essence, procedural environmental rights, as part of good governance, carry aspects such as openness and accountability.[69]

A state that fully enforces procedural environmental rights complies with the principle of good governance, which is among the catalysts for economic development. In sum, the sustainability of the environment is likely to be improved when marginalised people, like women, minorities and the poor, are able to access environmental information and justice and are involved in environmental decision-making processes. The next sections discuss in detail the contribution of substantive and procedural environmental rights in the economic development of African countries.

5.1 Reinvigorating Africa's Economy via Substantive Environmental Rights

Substantive environmental right or the right to a clean and healthy environment entails 'the prevention of pollution and ecological degradation, promotion of conservation, and securing an ecologically sustainable development and use of natural resources'.[70] This right is directly associated with environmental protection and

---

[65] Ibid, 56.

[66] See Addaney et al. (2020), p. 9.

[67] Leib (2011), p. 124.

[68] Karan (2004), p. 51.

[69] Razzaque (2010), p. 293.

[70] Amechi (2009), p. 65.

conservation of unique species, a variety of biological diversities and precious gemstones found in the environment. The availability of natural resources or environmental products also depends on the advancement of the right to a clean and healthy environment. This means that the enforcement of environmental rights entails preventing environmental degradation, thereby ensuring the availability of natural resources crucial for sustaining a country's that are necessary to boost the economic growth. Consequently, the stand-alone environmental right serves as a is a legal benchmark for assessing development initiatives in Africa.[71] This is because the rigorous economic governance of environmental resources is indispensable for the reduction of poverty among African countries.

Put simply, the substantive environmental right promotes the responsible and sustainable use of natural resources to improve per capita income and gross domestic product (GDP).[72] It further compels the state to take necessary measures to enforce environmental laws and regulate environmental risks to enhance sustainable economic development. Besides, the imposition of liability or accountability on the part of the government for failure to control environmental pollution is among the ways to promote a responsible government and the rule of law.[73] Thus, the right is an essential instrument for alleviating poverty by fostering economic growth.

Substantive environmental right usually aims to promote an environment that is favourable to development.[74] Additionally, it plays a key role in regulating the overuse and depletion of natural resources supporting sustainable development. Natural resources are the backbone of the economies of African countries as they contribute to a great extent to the stimulation of other sectors such as manufacturing, fishing and mining.[75] Tourism, for example, is one of the economic activities that flourish in a clean and healthy environment. Given that the economies of many African countries also rely on tourism, it is evident that governments have a responsibility to protect and conserve the environment - not only to safeguard this right but also to stimulate economic development. The revenue generated through environmental conservation may play a significant role in achieving this objective.

Responsible and sustainable economic development may be achieved, *inter alia*, when there is conservation and safeguarding of the natural resources or biodiversity against any kind of pollution or squandering for the benefit of the present and future generations.[76] Similarly, the robust enforcement of a substantive right to a healthy environment acts as an incentive and a critical factor in driving the economic growth of African states, provided other development factors remain constant. This is because well-conserved and protected biodiversity in a given locality provides an opportunity for local economic growth.

---

[71] Soyapi (2019), p. 152.

[72] De Sadeleer (2014), p. 14.

[73] See Boyle (2012), p. 613.

[74] Amechi (2009), p. 62.

[75] See LHRC and ZLSC (2017), p. 317.

[76] See De Sadeleer (2014), p. 472.

There are many indigenous communities in Africa whose livelihood entirely depends on the environment by means of hunting and gathering. The Maasai, Tindiga and Hadzabe in Tanzania provide a good example of this. Furthermore, the cash income of some communities in sub-Saharan Africa depends on forest products like wild fruit, firewood, honey and mushrooms, to mention a few. Therefore, without a decent environment, these communities may suffer economic loss due to missed environmental opportunities. Conversely, Contrariwise, the extraction of forest products such as charcoal and firewood can lead to deforestation and environmental degradation.

For Africans to achieve sustainable economic growth and realise the right to development, governments must guarantee unquestionable and inalienable environmental rights, especially the right to natural wealth or resources.[77] All the same, citizens must actively protect and conserve the environment, as its destruction directly hinders economic development.

In safeguarding the state's natural resources for economic growth, Tanzania, for instance, has recently enacted legislation containing the principle of permanent sovereignty over natural resources.[78] The purpose of this principle is to ensure that all natural resources are controlled and governed by the state in which they are situated for the benefit and development of the people within a particular state. Nonetheless, the pursuit of economic development under this principle should not undermine environmental protection and its sustainability.[79]

The stand-alone environmental right also insists on controlling and curbing environmental pollution. This is because pollution has many economic effects, like damage to property and land, reduction in crop production and the dwindling and extinction of plants and animals of economic importance.[80] Governments sometimes need to spend public money to neutralise the effect caused by pollution rather than directing the said money to economic development projects, especially in a situation where the polluter pays principle (PPP) is partially implemented. This sometimes compels environmental enforcement agencies to spend public funds to clean part of the polluted environment.[81] The economic effect of the non-internalisation of environmental externalities, such as pollution, is the passing of external costs to the consumers or society generally.

There is a clear connection between the low-income status and living in close proximity to polluting industrial facilities.[82] Since the substantive right to the environment promotes unpolluted environment, thus, it assists in improving the quality of the environment and stimulates economic growth. Principally, this

---

[77] See LHRC and ZLSC (2017), p. 311.

[78] The Act of Parliament enacted is called the Natural Wealth and Resources (Permanent Sovereignty) Act, No. 5 of 2017.

[79] Boyle (2020), p. 186.

[80] Shanthakumar (2007), p. 24.

[81] Ibid.

[82] Finger and Zorzi (2013), p. 226.

environmental right has been formulated, *inter alia*, to curb the problems of environmental degradation facing the world.[83]

Substantive environmental right is also closely related to other rights, such as the right to life, the right to property and the right to health, to mention a few. On this ground, the promotion of this right helps to safeguard many other rights which are vital catalysts of economic development. A healthy person, for instance, is sound in many multiple dimensions that extends beyond mere physical appearance. This is because the right to health encompasses intellectual, moral, cultural, spiritual, political and social well-being,[84] which all depend on one's environment. Therefore, one may argue that substantive environmental rights improve the quality of life of humankind.

As noted earlier, the substantive environmental right cuts across all generations of human rights. The significance of the first and second generations of human rights in global economic growth cannot be overstated. Since environmental rights are embedded within both generations, their promotion and enforcement clearly contribute to economic growth. Conversely, the failure to observe of environmental rights can hinder the economic development of a given jurisdiction.

Zimbabwe, for example, is among the African countries whose Constitution is silent on environmental rights, and for some years now, its economic development has been in a quagmire. Furthermore, the country has unprecedented records of violations of civil and political human rights. To revamp the country's economy, it is suggested to include environmental rights in the reform process of the Zimbabwean Constitution.[85] It is because environmental rights are crucial not only for promoting, protecting, and fulfilling civil, cultural, political and socio-economic rights, but also for ensuring their enjoyment.

5.2 *Environmental Right to Information's Contribution to Economic Growth*

Information is powerful. This is why the right to information is often compared to oxygen, essential for the well-being of any individual.[86] This right is reflected in most instruments governing human rights and the environment in Africa. The right to information is also entrenched in the Constitutions of many African countries. It is the index for measuring the growth and development of a state.[87]

[83]See Nanda and Pring (2013), p. 596.

[84]See *Advocates Coalition for Development and Environment v. Attorney General*, Misc. Cause No. 0100 of 2004 (HCU) at Kampala.

[85]Murombo (2011), p. 135.

[86]Laskar (2016), p. 216.

[87]Ibid.

A person who is denied access to information cannot advance in all spheres, that is, economically, socially, politically and culturally. Equally, an individual who lacks environmental information, *e.g.* on climate change, is not likely to achieve robust personal economic growth. For example, a farmer who has no information about the weather forecast can be expected to incur a loss in his farming activities, that play a crucial role in economic development. This is because such information can help the farmer make an informed decision.

The right to environmental information is relevant to investors and the public at large. A foreign investor cannot blindly inject his capital in agricultural activities in a particular area, for example, without possessing any information related to the environment in that area. Therefore, this right avails an opportunity for investors and business partners to get relevant environmental information, which, in the long term, fosters economic development. Additionally, this right strengthens the exchange of ideas and environmental information. As a result, significant drivers of economic development, such as creativity and innovation, are nurtured in a situation where people are availed of free access to environmental information.[88] Without access to environmental information, it is difficult to achieve sustainable development. The reason is that the non-disclosure of pertinent information regarding the environment leaves the public ignorant of issues crucial to their economic development.

The ability to access relevant environmental information and participating actively in environmental dialogues also empower citizens to influence decisions that affect the environment and their lives.[89] Thus, the right to environmental information is a crucial tool for advancing the principles of good governance, including transparency, accountability, predictability and participation. The government and its environmental regulators or enforcement agencies need to possess these criteria, which may be realised through the exercise of the right to environmental information.[90]

Most environmental information today may be accessed on the Internet. The issue is whether African governments have adequate investment in this area and can ensure that Internet services are freely available or can be accessed at a low cost. In DRC, for example, not many people have electricity or access to Internet services; hence, they are denied the right to environmental information.[91] This problem is also common in many other African states.

Language barrier is one of the hindrances to accessing relevant environmental information from the government and businesses. For instance, in Ghana, it is said that the most useful information on the environment is in English, a language that is not common to many poor Ghanaians.[92] This calls for the need to interpret or

---

[88] See Cole 2016), p. 379.

[89] See Leib (2011), p. 87.

[90] Laskar (2016), p. 220.

[91] The Access Initiative et al. (2022), p. 17.

[92] Ibid.

translate environmental information into local dialects that are readily available to the local communities. It is important to do so as this procedural right supports a more rightful sharing of natural resources.

Although the right to information is reflected in many African Constitutions, in Tanzania, for instance, the government and public authorities-the custodians of vital environmental information- are often reluctant to release it. Withholding relevant environmental information or not ensuring the timely sharing of such information is sometimes coupled with providing misleading information to citizens.

5.3 *The Effect of Participating in Environmental Decision-Making on Economic Growth*

The right to environmental information is closely linked to the right to participation specifically in decision-making. Participation in environmental decision-making represents the second stage, following the receipt of relevant environmental information. The participation of the public in environmental matters that affect their lives is fundamental to any democratic state.[93] It is among the well-known tenets underpinning the discourse of development policy.

Sustainable economic development normally encompasses the principle of leaving no one behind. Everyone regardless of his social or economic status is equally entitled to be involved in the development agenda. It is because equality principles are normally contained in the development dialogues.[94] Similarly, participation in environmental decision-making embodies the principle of equality, a core tenet in most constitutions and human rights instruments.

The right to participate in and contribute to environmental decision-making is a crucial component of the right to development.[95] Conversely, marginalising the participation of people, especially those outside the government, poses a significant challenge to achieving this goal. This indicates that this procedural environmental right enhances the rule of law and government accountability to the citizens. It further improves the quality and increases the legitimacy of the environmental decisions made by the public.[96]

The environmental impact assessment (EIA) and social environmental impact assessment (SEIA) are the most notable environmental exercises that require people's participation. Most projects that fully comply with the two instruments and adequately involve the public are sustainable. This is because these tools give poor, local and marginalised people the voice and an opportunity to take an active role in deciding pertinent environmental issues affecting their lives. Moreover, these tools

[93] See Toxopeus and Kotze (2017), p. 56.

[94] Lankford (2009), p. 54.

[95] See LHRC and ZLSC (2017), p. 311.

[96] Toxopeus and Kotze (2017), p. 56.

are crucial economic instruments for internalising externalities like environmental pollution.[97] Specifically, EIA is an essential tool in balancing economic development and people's anticipations for a descent environment.[98] On the other hand, conflicts between the citizens and the government or project developers hinder the economic development of a given area. Actually, the cost of environmental management is lower when the public is actively engaged in environmental issues.[99]

Participation and consultation of stakeholders are among the necessary and prominent tenets in the mainstream of development policy.[100] African governments have to ensure that all people participate in policy decisions and are consulted, *inter alia*, through public meetings, which are held in accessible areas. Participation and consultation are also signs of good governance. They form a central theme of the policies and agenda of most development agencies such as the World Bank (WB) and the United Nations Development Programme (UNDP).[101] A country that either lacks those tenets in its normative frameworks or fails to enforce them is likely to forfeit economic development grants from major international institutions and renowned funding bodies.

This procedural right is implemented by allowing stakeholders to participate or be consulted in all decisions related to development that affects their communities.[102] The Superior Court of South Africa, in *The Director, Mineral Development Gauteng Region and Sasol Mining (Pty) Ltd v Save the Vaal Environment and Others*,[103] ruled that it is imperative for the government to listen to people who might be affected by a permit authorising a private company to conduct mining activities. Some African governments allow people to participate, but ultimately, their views may not be taken into consideration.

Participation, especially of the private sector in environmental decision-making has also the advantage of assisting in generating financial resources.[104] This indicates that economic development is bedevilled, among others, by the passive participation of all people, regardless of their gender or social status in society. Women in non-western worlds, particularly in Africa play a pivotal role in driving economic development.[105] They are responsible for the production and marketing of most environmental products. Particularly, in rural areas where agriculture is a dominant economic activity, women are the key decision-makers in all farm works.[106] Nonetheless, due to cultural practices and stereotypes, most African

[97] Faure and Partain (2019), p. 16.
[98] See De Sadeleer (2014), p. 216.
[99] Razzaque (2010), p. 293.
[100] Lankford (2009), p. 53.
[101] Ibid.
[102] *SERAC v. Nigeria*, para. 53.
[103] 1999 (2) SA 709 (A).
[104] Razzaque (2010), p. 293.
[105] See Karan (2004), p. 36.
[106] Ibid., 499.

societies do not allow women to participate in environmental decision-making processes. In Cameroon, like many other African countries, the right to participate in environmental decision-making is just a myth and not a reality and only exists on paper.[107]

Absence of consultation by the government with the local communities, indigenous people or all stakeholders affected by the decisions constitutes a violation of the right to development. A good example to illustrate this assertion is the *African Commission on Human and Peoples' Rights v. Republic of Kenya.*[108] In this case, the court ruled that the eviction order issued by the Government of Kenya against the Ogieks without consulting and involving them in the environmental decision concerning the Mau forest violated Article 22 of the African Charter related to the right to development.[109]

5.4 *Significance of Accessing Environmental Justice to Economic Growth*

Access to justice is the central component of the rule of law. The rule of law ensures, *inter alia*, that a state benefits from its environment.[110] The primary objective of accessing environmental justice is to defend and be able to claim compensation for violated rights, including environmental rights. It ensures that the benefits of natural resources are accessed by all people. The concept of environmental justice is broadly understood as

> a mechanism of accountability for the protection of rights and the prevention and punishment of wrongs related to the disproportionate impacts of growth on the poor and vulnerable in society from rising pollution and degradation of ecosystem services, and from inequitable access to and benefits from the use of natural assets and extractive resources.[111]

Access to environmental justice largely depends on the common law doctrine of *locus standi*. Widening the *locus standi* in environmental matters may enable people to knock on the court's door to seek environmental remedies. This is because environmental justice requires individuals and communities to freely access the courts to defend against the wasteful and unjust exploitation of natural resources.[112] Particularly, citizens may be able to legally challenge and block some projects that degrade the environment through court injunctions. The enforcement of environmental justice enables the public to challenge the decisions by either the government

[107] See Ashukem (2019), p. 370.
[108] Application No. 006/2012, decided on 26 May 2017.
[109] Ibid., paras. 210 and 211.
[110] See Faure and Partain (2019), p. 297.
[111] UNDP (2022), p. 5.
[112] See Razzaque (2009), p. 119.

or businesses that are detrimental to economic and social welfare and those that do not comply with environmental laws.[113] All the same, costly environmental court proceedings are among the bottlenecks for many Africans in accessing environmental justice.

Environmental remediation and compensation of victims are among the remedies that may be ordered by a tribunal, commission or court of law following successful access to environmental justice, *e.g.* in pollution cases. While compensation aims to bring back the victim to his economic status before the event in question, environmental remediation entails

> bringing a part of the natural environment from a state of decay, injury or loss back to its original self-sustaining condition, so that it will support all the forms of life which formerly inhabited it.[114]

Therefore, environmental restoration aims to turn a degraded environment into a productive and economically useful environment. The two environmental remedies, if effectively enforced and implemented, assist in the economic development of the victims of environmental degradation.

Access to environmental justice also helps in the protection of the environment and the governance of natural resources.[115] The reason is that it helps to control unsustainable consumption and the overuse of natural resources, while also correcting the damage to public property. Tensions that may arise between investors and the public may be reduced if there is unimpeded access to justice by both parties either for mediation or adjudication. Where disputes are swiftly resolved, there is a likelihood of achieving economic development. For low-income populations, especially those who reside near potentially polluting facilities, to benefit from economic development originating from investments, they must have access to environmental justice.[116] On this ground, specialised environmental courts may play significant roles in ensuring that people get unimpeded access to environmental justice.

Further, access to environmental justice contributes to eliminating legal discrimination, poverty and inequality, which are among the hindrances to economic growth.[117] Most of the poor or low-income societies, such as the indigenous people, do not have equal access to the natural resources found in their localities. This right is important, especially in ensuring that vulnerable groups and disadvantaged members of society whose lives entirely depend on natural resources take part in the development regime.[118]

---

[113] Razzaque (2010), p. 284.

[114] Saxe (1992), p. 78.

[115] Crawhall and Silverman (2016), p. 6.

[116] Finger and Zorzi (2013), p. 226.

[117] See Karan (2004), p. 36.

[118] Crawhall and Silverman (2016), p. 9.

6 Challenges and Possibilities in Implementing and Enforcing Environmental Rights

Since the stand-alone right to the environment is linked to the right to development, states are sometimes put in limbo when deciding which right should take precedence in case the two rights conflict. The reason is that African countries are striving to develop their economies. Economic activities, such as industrialisation or mining, are sometimes the main causes of environmental degradation, which may directly curtail substantive environmental rights. Striking a balance between the two rights is not easy for most states; hence, economic activities that lead to development are sometimes given priority over environmental rights.[119]

The political challenge of enforcing environmental rights, especially against large private corporations, can often be attributed to the significant economic influence these entities hold within a country. In many cases, they are major sources of government income and employment.[120] This dilemma is further exacerbated by the government's lack of political will to address environmental issues. Consequently, many businesses pay insufficient attention to environmental concerns and rights, despite the requirement-outlined in the Guiding Principles on Business and Human Rights- for companies to implement policies that, among other things, focus on the prevention, mitigation, and remediation of the negative impacts of their operations.[121]

Another challenge to implementing and enforcing environmental rights is how to overcome the public's ignorance of these rights. Awareness by the public of the protection of the environment against polluters is of utmost importance. An individual cannot enforce his environmental rights unless he is aware of the same. Similarly, knowledge by the public of the institutions and procedures governing the enforcement of environmental rights and laws is also vital.[122] A well-informed public assists business entities in complying with environmental laws. Not only that, but a public that is well knowledgeable on environmental policies, laws and rights also engages actively in protecting the environment.

Besides entrenching environmental rights in their Constitutions, African states need to develop effective environmental legal frameworks and strengthen environmental regulators or agencies. These are significant institutions that may play a role in speeding up the country's economy, upholding environmental quality and ensuring environmental benefits.[123] Though the judiciary in several African countries has been robust in protecting environmental rights by invoking constitutional provisions related to the right to life, public interest litigation (PIL) remains to be an

[119] See Addaney et al. (2020), p. 43.

[120] Shelton (2010b), p. 278.

[121] See Principle 15.

[122] Twinomugisha (2007), p. 258.

[123] See Faure and Partain (2019), p. 297.

indispensable tool in enforcing environmental rights. This tool assists the illiterate, mediocre and indigent people in challenging violations of their environmental rights before the courts of law.

All in all, environmental rights, by themselves, are not a panacea for the problems hindering the economic growth of African countries. As noted earlier, DRC's Constitution, for example, is embedded with the substantive right to a clean and healthy environment. This right is not fully implemented, among others, because of political instability between the ruling government and a Congolese rebel military group, popularly known as the March 23 Movement (M23). This conflict has resulted in the plundering of the mineral resources and wealth of the nation and does not benefit the local communities where these natural resources are extracted.[124] Thus, there is a necessity for amalgamating environmental rights with civil and political rights in African states such as the DRC in order to guarantee the sustainable economic growth of the nation and the flourishing of good governance and the rule of law.

7 Conclusion

This chapter has demonstrated that there is a close nexus between environment, environmental rights and economic development. Thus, the enforcement and implementation of environmental rights is a prerequisite for economic growth. As has been noted above, sustainable economic development may be achieved when environmental rights go in tandem with civil and political rights. The chapter has also revealed that environmental rights are adequately entrenched in the African environmental and human rights legal framework, which also establishes various institutions to enforce them. The legal framework reviewed indicates that environmental rights and economic development are inseparable.

The chapter further noted that environmental rights, like other human rights, are significant drivers of the economic development of African countries. They hold certain promises for economic growth since they incorporate some democratic tenets associated with sustainable development. Procedural environmental rights, for instance, besides providing the means for attaining substantive environmental rights, also promote democratisation and good governance, which are important values for speeding up economic growth.[125] This explains the importance of not only expressly entrenching these rights in the national Constitution but also adequately promoting and enforcing them. This is because human rights law is not about stopping all human activities but about recognising that they utilise scarce resources.[126] This understanding aligns with the principles underlying economics and development.

---

[124] Murombo (2011), p. 142.

[125] Kotze and Daly (2019), pp. 1044–1072.

[126] Shelton (2010a), p. 119.

Furthermore, reconciling economic development and environmental protection is imperative in safeguarding environmental rights in Africa, especially when the two strategies conflict with each other. Environmental and economic laws are some of the instruments that may be used prudently to reconcile the two competing interests towards achieving sustainable development. Balancing these two interests is essential, at it is unrealistic to pursue economic growth while the citizens suffer from the consequences of environmental pollution.[127] Indeed, economic growth and environmental protection are not foes; rather, they complement each other.

References

Addaney M, Moyo G, Ramakhula T (2020) Human rights, regional law and the environment in Africa: legal and conceptual foundations. In: Addaney M, Jegede A (eds) Human rights and environment under African Union law. Palgrave Macmillan, Cham, pp 3–24

Amechi E (2009) Enhancing environmental protection and socio-economic development in Africa: a fresh look at the right to a general satisfactory environment under the African Charter on Human and Peoples' Rights. LEAD J 5(1):61–71

Amsalu D (2020) Implementing human rights-related environmental obligations in Ethiopia. In: Addaney M, Jegede A (eds) Human rights and environment under African Union law. Palgrave Macmillan, Cham, pp 263–286

Ashukem J (2019) Public participation in environmental decision-making in Cameroon- myth or reality? In: Mbote P et al (eds) Law and environment in Africa. Konrad Adenauer Stiftung, Baden-Baden, pp 315–348

Atapattu S, Schapper A (2019) Human rights and the environment: key issues. Routledge Taylor & Francis Group, London

Beder S (2006) Environmental principles and policies: an interdisciplinary approach. University of South Wales Press Ltd, Sydney

Boshoff E (2020) Women's environmental human rights in Africa with reflections on key provisions of Maputo Protocol. In: Addaney M, Jegede A (eds) Human rights and environment under African Union law. Palgrave Macmillan, Cham, pp 107–136

Boyd D (2012) The environmental rights revolution: a global study of constitutions, human rights, and the environment. University of British Columbia Press, New York

Boyle A (2012) Human rights and environment: where next? Eur J Int Law 23(3):613–642

Boyle A (2020) Climate change, sustainable development and human rights. In: Kaltenborn M, Krajewski M, Kuhn H (eds) Sustainable development goals and human rights. Springer, Cham, pp 171–187

Coalition for an Effective African Court on Human and Peoples' Rights (2021) Booklet on the Implementation of Decisions of the African Court on Human & Peoples' Rights, 2nd edn. Arusha

Cole W (2016) The effects of human rights on economic growth, 1965 to 2010. Sociol Dev 2(4): 375–412

Crawhall N, Silverman A (2016) Access to justice and right to sustain nature. Working Paper

Cullet P (1995) Definition of an environmental right in a human rights context. Neth Q Hum Rights 13:25–40

[127] See *Asiimwe & Others v. Leaf Tobacco & Commodities (U) Ltd & NEMA*, Misc. Case No. 43 of 2013 (High Court of Uganda).

De Sadeleer N (2014) EU environmental law and the internal market, 1st edn. Oxford University Press, Oxford

Faure M, Partain R (2019) Environmental law and economics: theory and practice. Cambridge University Press, Cambridge

Finger M, Zorzi F (2013) Environmental justice. UFRGS Model UN J 1:222–243

Karan P (2004) The non-western world: environment, development and human rights. Routledge, New York

Keetharuth S (2009) Major African legal instruments. In: Bosl A, Diescho J (eds) Human rights in Africa: legal perspectives on their protection and promotion. Konrad-Adenauer-Stiftung, Windhoek, pp 163–231

Kotze L (2015) Human rights, the environmental and the global south. In: Alam S et al (eds) International environmental law and global south. Cambridge University Press, New York, pp 171–191

Kotze L, Daly E (2019) A cartography of environmental human rights. In: Lees E, Vinuales J (eds) The Oxford handbook of comparative environmental law. Oxford University Press, Oxford, pp 1044–1072

Lankford S (2009) Human rights and development: a comment on challenges and opportunities from a legal perspective. J Hum Rights Pract 1:51–82

Laskar S (2016) Importance of right to information for good governance in India. Bharati Law Rev: 216–229

Legal and Human Rights Centre (LHRC) and Zanzibar Legal Services Centre (ZLSC) (2017) Tanzania human rights report

Leib L (2011) Human rights and environment: philosophical, theoretical and legal perspectives. Martinus Nijhoff Publishers, Leiden

Lewis B (2012) Environmental right or right to the environment? Exploring the nexus between human rights and environmental protection. Macquarie J Int Comp Environ Law 8(1):36–47

Lumina M (2020) The right to a clean, safe and healthy environment under the African Human Rights System. In: Addaney M, Jegede A (eds) Human rights and environment under African Union law. Palgrave Macmillan, Cham, pp 25–54

Mtavangu V (2017) Order of permanent injunction against sovereign state on the execution of a socio-economic program. Tanzania Lawyer J 1(2):181–188

Murombo T (2011) The utility of environmental rights to sustainable development in Zimbabwe: a contribution to constitutional reform debate. Afr Hum Rights Law J 11:120–146

Nanda V, Pring G (2013) International environmental law and policy for the 21st century, 2nd revised edn. Martinus Njihoff Publishers, Leiden

Nhamo G, Inyang E (2011) Framework and tools for environmental management in Africa. CODESRIA Book Series, Dakar

Olawuyi D (2018) Extractive industry law in Africa. Springer, Cham

Otubu A (2012) Environmental protection and human rights: an overview of current trend. https://papers.ssrn.com/sol3/papers.cfm?abstract_id=1718380

Razzaque J (2009) Participatory rights in natural resource management: the role of communities in South Asia. In: Ebbeson J, Okowa P (eds) Environmental law and justice in context. Cambridge University Press, Cambridge, pp 284–302

Razzaque J (2010) Human rights to a clean environment, procedural rights. In: Fitzmaurice M, Ong D, Merkouris P (eds) Research handbook on international environmental law. Edward Elgar Publishing Ltd, Cheltenham, pp 284–302

Ruppel O (2011) Human rights and the environment. In: Ruppel O, Schlichting K (eds) Environmental law and policy in Namibia. Orumbonde Press & Welwitschia Verlag Dr. A. Eckl, Essen, Windhoek, pp 219–240

Sands P et al (2015) Principles of international environmental law, 3rd edn. Cambridge University Press, Cambridge

Saxe D (1992) Reflection on environmental restoration. J Environ Law Pract 2:74–95

Shanthakumar S (2007) Introduction to environmental law, 2nd edn. Wadhwa and Company Law Publisher, New Delhi

Shelton D (2010a) Developing substantive environmental rights. J Hum Rights Environ 1(1): 89–120

Shelton D (2010b) Human rights and the environment: substantive justice. In: Fitzmaurice M, Ong D, Merkouris P (eds) Research handbook on international environmental law. Edward Elgar Publishing Ltd, Cheltenham, pp 265–283

Soyapi C (2019) The courts and the constitutional right to a clean and healthy environment in Uganda. Rev Eur Comp Int Environ Law 28:152–161

Sunkin M, Ong D, Wight R (2002) Sourcebook on environmental law, 2nd edn. Cavendish Publishing Ltd, London

The Access Initiative et al (2022) The road to realize environmental rights in Africa. https://accessinitiative.org/resource/the-road-to-realizing-environmental-rights-in-africa-moving-from-principles-to-practice/

Toxopeus M, Kotze L (2017) Promoting environmental justice through civil-based instruments in South Africa. LEAD J 13(1):49–72

Twinomugisha B (2007) Some reflections on judicial protection on the right to clean and healthy environment in Uganda. LEAD J 3(3):246–225

UNDP (2022) Environmental justice: comparative experiences in legal empowerment. https://www.google.com/search?q=UNDP%2C+Environmental+Justice+Comparative+pdf&ei=XuO5YOCxIc2Ml

Vicent Bartholomew Mtavangu LL.B (UDSM), LL.M (MU), PhD in Law (UDSM): Lecturer in laws at Mzumbe University Mbeya Campus College; Advocate; founder member and Partner at Primo Attorneys, the law firm based in Mbeya-Tanzania.

Mining Companies' Legal Duty to Safeguard Local Communities Against COVID-19: A South African Perspective

John S. Ombella and Julius Cosmas

1 Introduction

Health concerns in the mineral sector are not new. According to the literature, the mining sector has long been linked to health issues because either it is a direct source of chronic diseases or it contributes to the wide spread of epidemic and pandemic diseases. The first category, i.e. mining as a direct source of diseases, is connected to mining workplaces, termed occupational diseases,[1] such as those affecting the respiratory organs, like lung diseases, cancer, and tuberculosis (TB).

In the second category, there is the indirect contribution of the mining sector to the wide spread of diseases. This can be explained twofold. Firstly, mines contribute to the spread of communicable diseases among employees and local communities. Such communicable diseases include TB, Ebola, COVID-19, human immunodeficiency virus (HIV) and other sexually transmitted diseases. Commonly, diseases easily spread due to interactions between mine employees and local communities. It is shown, for example, that the South African mining industry draws its workers from not only within South Africa but also beyond its borders, such as Zimbabwe, Botswana, Lesotho and Mozambique, to name but a few countries.[2] Secondly, mining activities also contribute to the eruption and spread of non-communicable diseases due to environmental destruction, subjecting local communities to degraded

[1] Osburn (1969), p. 1312; Cookson et al. (1974), p. 2317; Lurie and Stuckler (2010), p. 1206; Stuckler et al. (2013), p. 43; Schrecker et al. (2018), p. 138; Loewenson et al. (2016), para 3.2; 'Extractive Industry and Health' https://www.ghwatch.org/sites/www.ghwatch.org/files/C6_0.pdf, para 3.2.

[2] Stuckler et al. (2013), p. 43.

J. S. Ombella (✉) · J. Cosmas
Private Law Department, Faculty of Law, Mzumbe University, Morogoro, Tanzania
e-mail: john.ombella@mu.ac.tz

I. Kajiru et al. (eds.), *Economic Development and Human Rights in Contemporary Sub-Saharan Africa*, Ius Gentium: Comparative Perspectives on Law and Justice 122, https://doi.org/10.1007/978-3-031-81400-6_3

environments. Common diseases under this category are stress, asthma, mental health problems and substance abuse, to name but a few.[3]

Notably, the contribution of the mining sector to the wide spread of diseases poses a challenge to the health systems in developing countries, more so in many natural-resource-rich developing countries where health services are already overburdened by epidemic and pandemic diseases such as Ebola, HIV, TB and malaria.[4] Currently, COVID-19 is a global threat. Although many countries locked down most economic activities and restricted people's movements, the mining sector in South Africa was declared an essential service and was, consequently, not closed.[5] It is argued that African countries that are able to adopt effective legal and policy measures to secure their communities will be better equipped to combat COVID-19.[6] This is because some of the legal measures, for example mandatory quarantine and movement restrictions, may impede other human rights, such as access to food by vulnerable members of communities. This chapter conducts a documentary review of the legal measures adopted by South Africa in the mining sector, with a view to obliging mining companies to safeguard local communities' health from COVID-19. The chapter focuses on the period between 2020 and 2021, which covers the time when there was no COVID-19 vaccination. The choice of this period is based on the fact that discussions on vaccination are regulated by other laws, such as the laws on contract and intellectual property, at both international and local levels.

This chapter is organised into six major sections, including this introduction. Section 2 presents a background to the problem, while Sect. 3 provides a brief description of the international legal framework on companies' duty to safeguard local communities' health. Section 4 presents a critical discussion of the legal measures taken in South Africa to oblige mining companies to safeguard local communities' health. Section 5 expounds on the discussion in Sect. 4 by identifying and analysing the impediments to the full realisation of the efforts to safeguard local communities' health against COVID-19. Section 6 provides a conclusion and recommendations.

2 Background to the Problem

Responding to COVID-19 as a means to safeguard local communities' health is crucial for a number of reasons. Generally, the response aims to guarantee protection not only for the local communities, from which most of the employees come and/or with whom they interact, but also for the mining workers themselves. In particular,

---

[3]Bench Marks Foundation and Bench Mark Centre for CSR (2015), para 8.3; Gomezulu et al. (2018), pp. 116–121; Schrecker et al. (2018), p. 42.

[4]Eriamiatoe (2020), pp. 32–33; Okonofua et al. (2020), p. 11.

[5]Republic of South Africa (2020a, b, c), para 3; Ramdoo (2020), p. 7.

[6]Tinti (2020).

the rationale for imposing a duty on mining companies to safeguard local communities' health against COVID-19 can be explained as follows.

2.1 *Nature and Quality of Health Services and Their Ability to Curb Pandemics*

The capability of health services in many natural-resource-rich African countries to guarantee the right to health for all is reportedly challenged. According to The Economist, there is an inadequate number of physicians and surgeons in African countries.[7] And despite the availability of health equipment, a considerable number of such equipment is out of order; hence, inaccuracies in the diagnosis of diseases are not uncommon.[8] Additionally, Tinti has highlighted challenges such as inadequate testing equipment and insufficient intensive care equipment, such as ventilators and intensive care beds, which are essential for combating COVID-19.[9] Accordingly, the African Commission on Human and Peoples' Rights (ACHPR) is aware that

> …millions of people in Africa are not enjoying the right to health maximally because African countries are generally faced with problem of poverty which renders them incapable to provide necessary amenities, infrastructure and resources that facilitate the full enjoyment of this right…[10]

In particular, it is reported that South Africa suffers from inadequate health staff and a challenging hospital infrastructure, leading to congestion in hospitals.[11] Furthermore, health services in local communities are inadequate due to their unreliability, the lack of water and electricity services and inaccessibility due to poor road infrastructure, to name but a few.[12] Consequently, it is crucial to safeguard the health of local communities and mine workers against pandemics, given the challenged health service. However, unlike mine workers who under employment contract impose a legal duty to their employers, (mining companies) to safeguard their health, local communities' relation with the mines does not create such a duty.[13]

As noted earlier, epidemics and pandemic diseases, such as Ebola, HIV/AIDS and TB, threaten not only local communities but also the mining sector. Meanwhile, COVID-19 is reportedly a pandemic disease and a global health threat. If not properly managed, it may cause devastating impacts on mining employees and

[7]The Economist (2018), p. 9.

[8]The Economist (2018), pp. 3 and 9.

[9]Tinti (2020).

[10]*Purohit and Another v The Gambia* (ACHPR), para 81.

[11]Republic of South Africa, Department of Health (2020d), para 7.7.

[12]Bench Marks Foundation and Bench Mark Centre for CSR (2015), para 8.3.

[13]The Mine Health and Safety Act No. 29 of 1996, sections 5–10.

local communities in many resource-rich developing countries.[14] In particular, the prevalence of other pandemics, such as HIV, TB and malaria, coupled with underprivileged socio-economic and environmental conditions in most local communities, may exacerbate the spread of COVID-19 if not properly regulated.[15]

2.2 *Nature of the Spread of COVID-19*

As noted in the introduction above, COVID-19 is pronounced as a global pandemic. It threatens not only developing countries but also global economic giants. The threats lie in the nature of its spread and the significant number of people's lives it claims. COVID-19 spreads from one person to another through contamination with mucus and/or droplets from the nostrils and/or mouth of an affected person.[16] The mucus and/or droplets are commonly expelled when one sneezes and/or coughs.[17] Consequently, if one touches an affected person or a surface contaminated with these droplets and then touches his face (nose or mouth), he also becomes infected. Although it is not scientifically proven, COVID-19 is not considered an airborne disease like TB.[18]

In light of the above, it is required to regularly maintain social distancing between persons, cover the nostrils and mouth with a mask and wash hands with clean, flowing water and soap in order to protect oneself from contamination with COVID-19.[19] In case one has been diagnosed with COVID-19, he has to be isolated for a minimum of 14 days.[20] The mining sector, therefore, has to reform some of its routines to comply with these new requirements. Indeed, these requirements seem to be new to the mineral sector, as they are to other sectors that did not have guidelines to this effect.

2.3 *Vulnerability to COVID-19 Among People of Various Age and Health Conditions*

Given the nature of the spread of COVID-19, everyone is at risk of contracting it. However, the risk of contamination with COVID-19 and the ability to endure it vary from one person to another. There are a number of factors that contribute to low

[14] ICMM (2020).

[15] The National Environmental Management Act No. 107 of 1998, the Preamble.

[16] WHO (2020).

[17] Hakim (2020), p. 41.

[18] WHO (2020).

[19] Hakim (2020), pp. 41–42.

[20] Hakim (2020), pp. 41–42.

endurance and, hence, high risk when contracting this disease. According to the World Health Organization (WHO), people aged 60 and above; those with chronic diseases such as HIV/AIDS, cancer, hypertension and diabetes; and individuals with more than one chronic disease are more prone than others to COVID-19.[21]

According to statistics from the Minerals Council South Africa, people with more than one chronic disease are likely to be most vulnerable to COVID-19.[22] While the death rate of those with more than one chronic disease is estimated at 66%, that of individuals with only one chronic disease such as diabetes is 34%.[23] Additionally, the Minerals Council South Africa reports that between the years 2009 and 2014, more than 80,000 employees suffered from one or more chronic diseases.[24] Consequently, the need to protect local communities that host mine employees who are also dependent on them becomes paramount.

2.4 Nature of the Interaction Between Local Communities and Mine Employees

Interaction between local communities and mine employees is hardly avoidable. This part presents two perspectives—social and economic—which signify such interaction and the risk associated with contracting COVID-19. Socially, some of the mine workers reside within the local communities, indicating the first point of interaction. According to Linda Starke, local communities are also a source of labour for mines in natural-resource-rich countries.[25] This signifies movement to and from the mines by employees who reside in the vicinity of the mines. Starke further states that due to the nature of the mineral sector, there is a high demand for specialised skills that may not be obtained from the local communities. In most cases, these skilled labourers are procured from other countries, often the developed ones.[26] Consequently, interaction between local and foreign experts within the mineral sector is unavoidable. Given the widespread nature of COVID-19, the use of foreign experts necessitates regulation since the disease did not originate in South Africa. In the case of *Association of Mine Workers and Construction Union vs Minister of Mineral Resources and Energy and others*,[27] the concern was that employees returning from their communities to the mine site after lockdown might be infected

[21] Temperoni et al. (2021), p. 8.

[22] Republic of South Africa (2020a, b, c), p. 5.

[23] Republic of South Africa (2020a, b, c), p. 5.

[24] Republic of South Africa (2020a, b, c), p. 6.

[25] Starke (2002), p. 200.

[26] Starke (2002), p. 200.

[27] *Association of Mine Workers and Construction Union v Minister of Mineral Resources and Energy and Others, The Labour Court of South Africa* [2020] Labour Court J.427/, para 35.

with COVID-19. Equally, the local communities were concerned about the potential risks posed by returning employees who might be infected by COVID-19.[28]

In addition, it is shown that local communities benefit from some of the infrastructure established by mining companies, such as water and health facilities installed for mine workers.[29] If not properly regulated, the shared use of these infrastructures would also create interaction points, where COVID-19 may spread to local communities from the employees or vice versa.

Economically, local communities supply commodities to the mines for use by mine workers. Mining companies have showcased their involvement with local communities through sustainable initiatives. Among these initiatives are involving local communities in diversified activities like agriculture to feed the mining sector population, including mine workers. Consequently, mine workers consume some of the produce of the local communities, such as chickens, vegetables and fruits.[30] The meeting of mine workers and local community is propeleld by economic force that compels the meeting of the two groups as they seem to be mutually dependent. Although this signifies an indirect interaction, vegetables and fruits, if not properly handled, may contribute to the spread of COVID-19.

Apparently, there is a need to safeguard local communities. Although there have been other health threats, such as HIV/AIDS, Ebola and TB, COVID-19 brings a new challenge to the mining industry due to the mode of its spread, which calls for a new approach to counter it. Indeed, a divided approach, such as focusing only on mine employees, will defeat the purpose, owing to the interwoven nature of interactions between mine employees and local communities.[31] Before analysing the nature and extent to which mining companies protect local communities' health in South Africa, a snapshot of the international frameworks on multinational companies' obligation to safeguard local communities' health is presented below.

---

[28] *Association of Mine Workers and Construction Union v Minister of Mineral Resources and Energy and Others, The Labour Court of South Africa* [2020] Labour Court J.427/, para 38.

[29] Thomashausen (2015).

[30] Natural Resource Governance Institute (2015), p. 3.

[31] The discussion on the duty of mining companies to safeguard the health of mine workers is provided under the Mine Health and Safety Act. No. 29 of 1996, where mining companies, as employers, are duty bound to safeguard the health of their employees. Unlike employees whose legal relation creates such a duty, local communities do not enjoy such a status; however, they are prone to the wide spread of COVID-19 due to the presence of mines in their locality. Consequently, the need for a review of the mining companies' duty to safeguard their health against COVID-19 is inevitable.

3 International Legal Frameworks on Companies' Duty to Safeguarding Local Communities' Health

Generally, there is no international legal instrument that regulates the rights and duties of multinational corporations (MNCs).[32] According to Blanco and Razzaque, the regulation of MNCs is a complex issue.[33] The complexity arises from jurisdictional issues, such as where the MNCs are established and where they operate, the form of their operations (e.g. subsidiary companies) and the place where the majority of their shareholders resides.[34] According to Loewenson, Henricher and Papamichai, there is no express statutory provision in the mining laws of East and Southern African countries requiring mining companies to safeguard the health of local communities.[35] This is despite the fact that a number of countries in the East and Southern Africa provide for the right to health as one of the human rights under their municipal laws.[36]

In particular, with regard to binding international frameworks, there is a negative duty on the part of mining companies not to contribute towards activities that impair the health of local communities. Such a negative duty is founded on human rights, where everyone has a right to health.[37] According to the African Commission on Human and Peoples' Rights (ACHPR) Guideline, the right to health also entails the ability of health services to meet the needs of the population by delivering relevant medicines and materials for the prevention and treatment of diseases, among others.[38] However, the negative duty owed by companies relates to the requirement to respect human rights in all their dealings. Consequently, unlike the state, which has a dual obligation to respect and protect, mining companies will only be held accountable if poor state regulations on companies' activities result in human rights violations.[39]

Generally, commentators on the duty of MNCs to safeguard local communities' health seem to indicate that such a duty is more negative than positive. According to

---

[32]Starke (2002), p. 219.

[33]Blanco and Razzaque (2011), p. 230.

[34]Blanco and Razzaque (2011), p. 230.

[35]Loewenson et al. (2016), paras 3.4 and 6.1.

[36]See, for example, the Constitutions of Kenya, DRC Congo, Zimbabwe and South Africa.

[37]Universal Declaration of Human Rights 1948.; International Covenant on Social, Economic and Cultural Rights 1966.; African Charter on Human and Peoples' Rights 1986, to name but a few.

[38]See ACHPR, 'Principles and Guidelines on the Implementations of Economic, Social and Cultural Rights in the African Charter on Human and Peoples' Rights', para 67(i).

[39]*Sudan Human Rights Organisation and Centre on Housing Rights and Eviction (COHRE) v Sudan* [2005] African Commission on Human and Peoples' Rights 279/03-296, paras 148 and 210; *Social and Economic Rights Action Centre (SERAC) and Centre for Economic Social Rights (CESR) v Nigeria* [2001] ACHPR 155/96, para 57; OHCHR, 'CESCR General Comment No. 14: The Right to the Highest Attainable Right Standard of Health (Art. 12) Adopted at the Twenty-Second Session of the Committee on Economic, Social and Cultural Rights, on 11 August 2000 (Contained in Document E/C.12/2000/4)' OHCHR (2000), para 51.

Villiani *et al.*, mining companies are only able to control disease outbreaks within their compound.[40] Furthermore, it is stated that mining companies do not have control over issues such as hygiene and the ability of local communities to curb disease outbreaks.[41] After all, mining companies are argued to pay taxes to the countries where they operate.[42] Consequently, it is the duty of the respective country to make use of these taxes to guarantee the good health of its population (including local communities). If at all companies are to be involved, their involvement is based on corporate social responsibility (CSR) rather than a positive legal duty.[43]

Blanco and Razzaque note that MNCs possess vast resources (finance, technology, skilled human resources) compared to the countries in which they invest.[44] Through lobbying, they also influence the manner in which laws and policies are framed and enforced in their areas of investment.[45] The combination of all these factors makes MNCs powerful organs incapable of being regulated in many developing countries; instead, they are relied upon by governments to assist them in providing social services such as education and health.[46] On this basis, there is a global move to attain Sustainable Development Goals (SDGs), particularly Goal 3, which aims to address and bring an end to pandemic diseases by 2030, which can only be realised if both states and other stakeholders, such as mining companies operating in various areas, work jointly to achieve it.[47] However, the effectiveness of these efforts depends on whether such provisions are reflected in the domestic laws of many African countries. Evidence of weak frameworks is noted in resistance movements and/or the proliferation of litigation against MNCs in areas such as the ecosystem and/or health.[48] Indeed, the absence of binding international frameworks for the regulation of MNCs' rights and duties, coupled with local resistance due to the significant impacts of MNCs' operations in developing countries, dictates the need for a new approach.

CSRs become the model principle to restore MNCs ruined reputation through apportioning more socio-economic benefits (education and health services) to locals. Western African states, for example, are required to enact laws that will make CSR compulsory.[49] This calls for mainstreaming CSR into mineral regulatory codes in a

---

[40] Villian et al. (2016), p. 8.
[41] Villian et al. (2016), p. 8.
[42] Osewe (2015).
[43] Osewe (2015).
[44] Blanco and Razzaque (2011), pp. 230–231.
[45] Blanco and Razzaque (2011), pp. 230–231.
[46] Blanco and Razzaque (2011), p. 231.
[47] General Assembly Resolution (2012) Gola 3.3; African Union and Commission (Agenda 2063), para 10.
[48] Blanco and Razzaque (2011), p. 229.
[49] ECOWAS, Directive on the Harmonisation of Guiding Principles and Policies in the Mining Sector (2009), Article 11(2).

manner that makes them a condition precedent to issuing mineral rights.[50] In addition, to benefit from CSR, the programmes, plans and strategies for drafting, implementing, monitoring and evaluation must involve local communities.[51] The Mining Code in Sierra Leone, for example, makes it mandatory for mining companies to contribute to, among other things, health and education infrastructures in areas where they operate.[52] The Southern African Development Community (SADC) incorporates CSR into so-called socio-economic empowerment initiatives for historically disadvantaged communities (HDCs), which include women, disabled individuals and indigenous peoples.[53] For example, it is shown that the involvement of business firms, such as mining companies, in the reconstruction of communities affected by COVID-19 not only aims to achieve SDG 3 but also serves as a tool to improve their reputation in the areas where they operate.[54] It is shown above that given the noted challenges facing the health sector in most natural-resource-rich developing countries, if mining companies do not take a proactive role in curbing pandemics, the sector will be significantly impacted.[55]

Taking note of the above lacunae on companies' positive duty to protect the health of local communities, recourse to non-binding initiatives may be sought. It appears that the duty of mining companies to safeguard local communities' health is widely covered under international soft laws, save for a few practices like in the Sierra Leone case above.[56] Soft laws include guidelines, resolutions and frameworks issued by global and regional institutions such as the World Bank Group (WBG),[57] the Organisation for Economic Co-operation and Development (OECD),[58] the United Nations (UN) and the Natural Resource Governance Institute (NRGI),[59] which do not have a binding effect on states. Consequently, these initiatives create a non-binding duty on companies to safeguard local communities' health. Mining companies under such initiatives are generally required to respect human rights in the course of their business. According to the UN, respect for human rights requires companies to:

(a) Avoid causing or contributing to adverse human rights impacts through their own activities, and address such impacts when they occur;

[50] ECOWAS (2009), Article 11(2–3).

[51] ECOWAS (2009), Article 11(2).

[52] The Mines and Minerals Act No. 12 of 2009, section 140(2)(b).

[53] Protocol on Mining 1997, Articles 1 and 2(8).

[54] Alvares-Rico and Del-Aguila-Arcentales (2022), p. 157.

[55] See Sect. 2 on the background to the problem in this chapter.

[56] See the immediate paragraph above.

[57] International Finance Corporation (2012).

[58] OECD (2011).

[59] Natural Resource Governance Institute (2014).

(b) Seek to prevent or mitigate adverse human rights impacts that are directly linked to their operations, products or services by their business relationships, even if they have not contributed to those impacts[60]

Additionally, the mining industry is known for its contribution not only to revenue but also to supporting other social issues in the countries and/or communities where they operate.[61] As such, private sector businesses are considered to be properly functioning if they address, among other things, the health concerns in the area where they operate. Given the fact that many MNCs may be operating in countries with weak legal frameworks, the business sector is called upon to not only respect but also support the realisation of internationally recognised human rights, such as contributing to preserving the health not only of its labour force but also the country at large.[62] The Ten Principles of the UN Global Compact, for example, recognise the need for MNCs to protect the health of the communities in the vicinity of their economic activities.[63] Particularly, MNCs involved in the mining sector are expressly called to address the health concerns of the communities surrounding them.[64] As noted above, this obligation, though expressly provided, is founded on non-enforceable instruments and is not reflected in the domestic laws of many mineral-resource-rich African countries.

Similarly, at the African regional level, the ACHPR issued a call to all natural-resource-rich African countries to enact laws that would compel mining companies to respect human rights as provided under the African Charter on Human and Peoples' Rights.[65] In particular, laws should compel mining companies, among other things, to contribute towards the health needs of local communities.[66] According to the Office of the High Commissioner for Human Rights, the realisation of the right to health is not a one-man show; other stakeholders, such as business entities (MNCs), are also duty-bound to contribute to the realisation of such rights.[67] States are required to put in place relevant regulations to engage the private sector in the realisation of human rights, including the right to health.[68] Consequently, it may be seen here that mining companies do owe a positive duty to protect the health of the local communities where they operate by contributing to improving the health system in terms of the detection, prevention and treatment of diseases.

---

[60] UN (2011), para 13.

[61] General Assembly Resolution, the Future We Want, para. 228.

[62] UNGA Resolution, 'Addis Ababa Agenda of the Third International Conference on Financing for Development (Addis Ababa Action Agenda) A/RES/69/313' (2015), para 37.

[63] UN (2000), principles 1–2.

[64] United Commission on Sustainable Development (2002), para 46; UN Commission on Sustainable Development (2010), p. 10.

[65] African Commission on Human and Peoples' Rights (2017), para 2.

[66] See para 2(d).

[67] OHCHR (2000), paras 42 and 55.

[68] OHCHR (2000), paras 42 and 55.

In addition, under the OECD, International Finance Corporation (IFC) and NRGI frameworks, mining companies are required to safeguard the health of the local communities where they operate. Under the WBG framework for example, MNCs duty to preserve human rights is preconditioned in the financing of mining projects.[69] Under the OECD and the NRGI frameworks, MNCs and states are also called to take into consideration health aspects of the communities where mineral extraction takes place.[70]

All in all, MNCs, as a non-state actor, owe local communities a negative duty to ensure the preservation of their health. MNCs are therefore not duty bound to provide for the right to health apart from respecting such a right and refrain from impacting local communities health negatively. As such, companies collaborate with the state in a bid to curb diseases that may also impact their activities if the government's ability is overwhelmed by epidemics such as Ebola and pandemics such as HIV, TB, malaria and COVID-19. The discussion below reviews this position from a South African legal perspective.

4 Legal Measures Adopted to Safeguard Local Communities Against COVID-19

The right to health in South Africa is guaranteed under the Constitution as one of the internationally recognised human rights. The Constitution reads as follows:

> Everyone has the right to have access to—(a) health care services, including reproductive health care; (...)[71]

Such a right creates obligations for both the state and MNCs operating in South Africa. While the state is duty-bound to respect, protect and fulfil human rights, including the right to health, MNCs are bound only to respect such rights.[72] The state is required to guarantee the progressive realisation of the right to health, among other rights.[73] In order to achieve this, legislative and administrative measures, such as the passing of laws, regulations, plans, policies and strategies, are inevitable. The right to health is also recognised under environmental law, which requires MNCs and states to guarantee that such a right is mainstreamed in the life cycle of their activities.[74] To achieve this, prior to large-scale development projects such as mining, various impact assessments on environmental, social and human

[69] See World Bank, International Finance Corporation, performance standard 4.

[70] OECD (2011), para VI (3); Natural Resource Governance Institute (2015), p. 2, precepts 5 and 7.

[71] Constitution of the Republic of South Africa No. 108 of 1996, Article 27(1)(a).

[72] Constitution of the Republic of South Africa, Article 7.

[73] Constitution of the Republic of South Africa, Article 27(2).

[74] National Environmental Management Act No. 107 of 1998, preamble and principle 2(2).

rights are expected to be carried out.[75] Arguably, the state cannot rely only on its laws and/or guidelines to guard against any violations of human rights, especially when MNCs' large-scale development projects significantly impact local communities.

In addition, South Africa's mineral-related laws seem to have adopted the CSR measures noted above.[76] As such, they call for the broad-based socio-economic empowerment of HDCs.[77] Indeed, this approach resonates with the above-noted requirement under the SADC protocol on mining. However, notably, the emphasis seems to be focused on socio-economic empowerment, which is to be evidenced by the percentage of locals hired and/or trained by MNCs and the percentage of goods and/or services procured from local communities.[78] Particularly, the health aspect seems to be implied than express. Arguably, when one is economically empowered, it becomes easier to realise their human rights, such as the right to health, owing to the fact that health services have financial implications. Without financial resources, many people will not be able to access such a right. However, apart from the fact that the right to health seems implied, it is argued that even with all these legal initiatives, CSR in South Africa suffers due to inadequate coordination, limited stakeholder involvement and poor monitoring and evaluation.[79] It is also noted that MNCs' compliance with empowerment schemes is relatively low due to less deterrent penalties compared to the profit margins of non-complying companies.[80]

In particular, a number of legal measures, apart from CSR, have been taken in response to the concerns about COVID-19 in the South African mining industry (SAMI). These measures include declaring COVID-19 as a national disaster and issuing regulations, guiding principles and guidelines, among others. Of all the measures taken, three seem to be relevant to the mining companies' duty to safeguard local communities' health against COVID-19. These are the declaration of COVID-19 as a national disaster, the issuance of a regulation compelling mining companies to safeguard local communities' health and the mandatory requirement for mining companies to prepare and effectively use guidelines to curb COVID-19 at the workplace. The details of these measures are analysed below.

Firstly, as concerns the declaration of COVID-19 as a national disaster, according to the Disaster Management Act,[81] the term disaster is defined and explained at different levels. At the national level, for example, the term is described to mean any calamity that impacts more than one of the provinces beyond their effective control. Due to the widespread and severe impacts of COVID-19, the South African

[75] National Environmental Management Act, principle 2(4).

[76] See para 4 above.

[77] Mineral and Petroleum Resources Development Act No. 28 of 2002, section 12.

[78] The Broad-Based Black Economic Empowerment Act No. 53 of 2003; Republic of South Africa (2016, 2017, 2018a, b).

[79] Siyobi (2015), p. 4.

[80] Diale (2014), pp. 24–25.

[81] Disaster Management Act No. 57 of 2002. section 23(6)(b).

President declared it a national disaster on 23 March 2020.[82] Under the Disaster Management Act 2002, once a national disaster is declared, the government is duty-bound to develop guidelines and principles for disaster management as well as strategies for the prevention and mitigation of the risks arising from it.[83]

In addition, it is the government's duty to guide the public sector, the private sector, communities and individuals, subject to available resources, on how to prevent and mitigate the potential risks accompanying the disaster. Notably, government resources can hardly contain a calamity as huge as COVID-19, a fact that calls for collaboration between the government and the private sector in the fight against COVID-19. To reiterate the statutory provision, here is the quote:

> The National Centre must promote formal and informal initiatives that encourage risk-avoidance behaviour by organs of state, the private sector, non-governmental organisations, communities and individuals...[84]

Consequently, since COVID-19 was declared a national disaster, the private sector (including the mining industry) is a key player in the fight against it, under the guidance and in collaboration with the government.

Available records indicate that mining companies are actively collaborating with the government and local communities to curb the spread of COVID-19. According to the International Council on Mining and Metals (ICMM), mining companies in South Africa contributed to increasing the number of classrooms in surrounding communities to enable social distancing among the students.[85] In parallel with that, schools were connected to Internet services to allow distance learning during the lockdown.[86] These measures are relevant to avoid congestion in local schools, given the need for social distancing as a means to curb the spread of COVID-19. Notably, these measures are carried out by mining companies as part of their CSR initiatives. Differently from South Africa, in Colombia, a special legal decree was issued that aimed to implement education through digital platforms all over the country as a measure to curb the spread of COVID-19.[87] Moreover, mining companies are also shown to have contributed funds to the central and local governments through the Solidarity Fund, which can help in the fight against COVID-19.[88] Additional support to local communities, for example, is pledged by the South Deep Mining Company in case there will be a need for isolation camps.[89]

---

[82] Republic of South Africa (2020a, b, c), paras 1–2.

[83] Disaster Management Act No. 57 of 2002, section 19(e).

[84] Disaster Management Act, section 20(2).

[85] ICMM (2020), p. 3.

[86] ICMM (2020), p. 3.

[87] Acosta et al. (2020).

[88] Preece (2020).

[89] Preece (2020).

Secondly, the regulations issued under section 27 (2) of the Disaster Management Act, 2002,[90] categorically impose a duty on mining companies to safeguard local communities against COVID-19. Such a duty requires every mining company to provide personal protective equipment (PPE) to its employees, who by the nature of their operations, come into contact with the public.[91] Other obligations under the regulations include regulating congestion in their facilities where they offer services, such as health centres and transport, and providing PPE to those who visit their offices as a means to protect both the members of the local communities and the mine workers.[92] The nature of the obligations created by this regulation seems to be positive than negative. Here, mining companies have to take positive actions, such as providing PPE to local community members visiting their facilities and limiting the number of passengers in their transport facilities to avoid congestion.

Thirdly, the Guideline for the Compilation of Mandatory Code of Practice for the Mitigation and Management of COVID-19 Outbreak (Guideline)[93] is also relevant to safeguarding local communities' health against COVID-19. The Guideline is structured into three major segments. Segment A contains the guideline itself, while segment B provides assistance to authors on how to prepare their respective employers' guides. Part C, which is the final part, outlines the expected content of the employers' guide. The main purpose of the Guideline is to help employers in the SAMI prepare their own guides for the mitigation of COVID-19 at the mines.[94] Notably, the objective of the Guideline seems to be narrower than its scope. According to the Guideline, the employers' guide will be applicable to all its employees as well as the local communities:

> The aim is to ensure that mine employees returning to work and any other person/s at mines, are protected from transmission of the Corona virus at the work place, and where reasonably practicable, in the community, whilst providing guidance to all stakeholders regarding their roles and responsibilities in the management of COVID-19 outbreak…[95]

To emphasis on the mining companies' wide scope of safeguarding local communities against COVID-19, part B requires among the content of the employers' guide to categorically state that, mitigation of COVID-19 will not only be on the mine site but also in the local communities.[96] Consequently, it is shown in this part that despite the absence of a direct legal obligation on the part of mining companies to safeguard the health of local communities, the fight against COVID-19 seems to necessitate a different approach owing to the above justifications.[97]

---

[90] Disaster Management Act No. 57 of 2002; see Regulations issued under section 27(2).

[91] Disaster Management Act, section 5(3); Regulations issued under section 27(2).

[92] Disaster Management Act, section 5(4)(a–d) Regulations issued under section 27(2).

[93] Republic of South Africa (2020a, b, c).

[94] Republic of South Africa (2020a, b, c), para 5.1.

[95] Republic of South Africa (2020a, b, c), see para 5.2.

[96] Republic of South Africa (2020a, b, c), see para 3.1(i).

[97] See para 2 above.

5 Challenges to Be Addressed

The discussion above shows the legal measures adopted to curb COVID -19 in the mineral sector. However, a number of challanges are noted when the relation a between local community, mining and diseases are concerned. These challenges include access to clean water in local communities, material support for members of the local communities under isolation, provision of remedies for local communities in case of a widespread outbreak of COVID-19 and the regulation of congestion in local communities.

Starting with the first challenge—access to clean water—South Africa is known among Southern African nations to be a water-scarce country.[98] Water scarcity in South Africa is generally caused by several factors, such as the natural distribution of both surface and underground water, the impacts of climate change, demographic increases, and increased economic activities demanding water, such as industries, mining and agriculture, as well as poor water infrastructures.[99] Mining industry is however, regareded to be the prime contributor to water stress in South Africa. Mining-induced water stress happens when improperly regulated mining activities impair the quality and quantity of water. Regarding water quality, on the one hand, acid mine drainage is reported to contribute to more than 80% of all water pollution in South Africa.[100] This is mainly caused by the presence of numerous abandoned mines, which are approximated to be around 600, which are scattered all over the country.[101] On the other hand, water quantity is diminished due to variations in the water table, which is impacted by over-abstraction and other activities, such as underground mining operations.[102]

It is shown above that running clean water is vital in maintaining hygiene as a means to curb the spread of COVID-19.[103] In highlighting the value of water to one's health, the ACHPR once stated that the failure of the government to supply its population with clean water and electricity, among other needs, violates the right to health.[104] In South Africa, the provision of clean water may not escape holding mining companies accountable for polluting water sources by requiring them to provide clean water to communities that are affected. A number of government

---

[98] Republic of South Africa (2018a, b), para 1.

[99] Republic of South Africa (2018a, b), paras 1 and 8.2; UNEP (2010), p. 285; Loubser et al. (2021), p. 8.

[100] Hoadley et al. (2002), para 3.5.3; CSIR (2009), p. 1; Mhlongo and Amponsah-Dacosta (2016), p. 280.

[101] Mhlongo and Amponsah-Dacosta (2016), p. 283; Republic of South Africa (2018a, b), para 3.6.1.4.

[102] Republic of South Africa (2018a, b), para 3.6.1.2.

[103] See Sect. 2 above on the background to the problem.

[104] *Free Legal Assistance Group, Lawyers Committee for Human Rights, Union Interafricaine des Droit Del' Homme, Les Te'Moins de Jehova vs Zaire Communication No 25/89, 47/90, 56/91, 100/93* (ACHPR), para 47.

initiatives have been put in place to guarantee local communities' access to clean water, including the supply of water through water storage tanks and water tanker trucks from 2016 to 2020.[105] However, despite such efforts, access to water remains irregular and intermittent for a considerable portion of the population in South Africa.[106]

In addition, among the legal measures adopted above, there are no provisions relevant to the supply of clean water to local communities as a means to curb the COVID-19 pandemic. However, mining companies are required to provide clean water, sanitisers, and soap to their employees at the mining site.[107] Experiences from Colombia and India show that special legal measures were adopted to guarantee access to water for local communities, including the installation of water and sanitiser kiosks in various localities during COVID-19.[108] Although such measures are not confined to mining companies, at least the right to access to clean water and sanitisers in these countries is given primacy in the fight against COVID-19, given that water is vital for one's hygiene.

Second, it is noted above that mining companies merely collaborate with the government to safeguard the health of local communities as it is not their legal duty to do so. The absence of a positive duty requiring mining companies to safeguard the health of local communities diminishes the chance for local communities to hold them accountable and/or to claim remedies for the breach of such a duty. As already mentioned, some companies have pledged to offer isolation camps to local communities whenever needed.[109] However, given the widespread and increasing infections, in the absence of a legal duty, mining companies may simply withdraw from such a pledge without any legal consequences at the expense of local communities' lives.

The third challenge relates to the material support of members of the local communities under isolation or quarantine. As noted above, the southern African region and South Africa, in particular, are overwhelmed by socio-economic underprivilege.[110] The socio-economic underprivileged status is mainly caused by the historical racial and economic discrimination policies that were adopted under the Such a apartheid regime. Despite a new era bringing an end to the apartheid regime, the majority of the black community still lives on a subsistence economy. Consequently, subjecting the members of local communities to isolation/quarantine as a means to curb the spread of COVID-19 signifies a dwindling income per person. According to William,

[105] Loubser et al. (2021), p. 8.

[106] Loubser et al. (2021), p. 8.

[107] Republic of South Africa (2020a, b, c), para 4.1(d–e).

[108] Acosta et al. (2020); Kurian (2020), p. 65.

[109] See para 4 above for details.

[110] See para 2 above for details.

> Lockdowns related to COVID-19 have been particularly challenging for the poorest of the poor in the urban areas of lower-income countries, because these populations depend on casual labour and informal market activity to make the money they need to buy food.[111]

Notably, the adopted legal measures seem silent on the material support for local community members who will be diagnosed with COVID-19 and be subjected to isolation or quarantine. A similar concern is also true with respect to mining companies that pledged to offer support for isolation facilities, as the pledge does not mention other material support to those who will be isolated. According to Bright Nkrumah, even before the COVID-19 outbreak, about 22% of South Africans went to bed hungry.[112] Consequently, subjecting members of local communities to isolation/quarantine without material support, such as food and clean water, may not yield the expected result of curbing the spread of COVID-19.[113] According to Precious Eriamitoe, restrictions on movement and mandatory quarantine will drive people into hunger and, potentially, death before they could even contract the coronavirus.[114] Experiences from India and the Dominican Republic show that vulnerable groups within local communities were provided with subsidised food during the COVID-19 pandemic.[115] The absence of clear measures on access to necessities, like food, sparks riots and instability related to COVID-19 lockdowns and/or isolation.[116]

6 Conclusion and Recommendations

Generally, the above discussion shows that mining companies do not have a positive legal duty to safeguard local communities' health in areas where they operate. Such a legal position is shown to have its foundation in binding international laws. At the national level, South Africa recognises such a legal position in its laws. Notably, the eruption of pandemics such as HIV/AIDS and COVID-19 dictates the need for adopting special measures to curb their spread. Mining companies, therefore, seem to be assigned a positive legal duty to safeguard the health of local communities against COVID-19. Among such duties are the provision of PPE and isolation camps and the decongesting of their facilities, such as health centres and transport facilities, to name but a few. Such legal measures may be adopted by any other resource-rich developing country in its bid to curb the spread of COVID-19 to local communities.

Despite the good intentions of the government and mining companies to safeguard the health of local communities against COVID-19, a number of limitations

[111] Moseley (2020), p. 44.

[112] Nkrumah (2018), p. 4.

[113] Nkrumah (2018), p. 4.

[114] Eriamiatoe (2020), pp. 29–30.

[115] Kurian (2020), p. 66; Belique (2020), p. 46.

[116] Evans and Steven (2020), p. 29; Moseley (2020), p. 45.

remain, such as the inaccessibility of clean water, the absence of guaranteed material support for those under isolation/quarantine and the lack of a legal remedy in case mining companies breach the established positive duty to supply PPE, provide isolation camps and decongest their facilities. Perhaps these limitations stem from the fact that no specific law compels MNCs operating in the South African mineral sector to safeguard the health of communities in their vicinity. Even where the right to health is implied, inadequate compliance defeats the good intentions of the lawmakers.

In order to improve efforts to curb the wide spread of COVID-19 in local communities, mining companies' positive duties ought to be expressly provided under mineral laws. Also, their positive duties should be extended to include the following: supplying clean water to local communities in areas where mining has contributed to water stress, providing remedies to local communities in case mining companies fail to provide PPE, and, collaborating with the government to provide material support (such as food) to members of local communities under isolation/ quarantine. In particular, given the above-discussed socio-economic underprivileged situations among the members of local communities, the provision of food to those under isolation also translates to the right to food, which is also guaranteed under the South African Constitution.[117]

References

Acosta A, Zia M, Sanchez N (2020) Confronting COVID-19 in Colombia, Gender Justice and Security. <lse.ac.uk/gender-justice-security>

Alvares-Rico A, Del-Aguila-Arcentales S (2022) Multinational enterprises and global strategies to collaborate with SDG 2 and SDG 3. In: Mcntyre J, Ivanaj S, Ivanaj V (eds) The role of multinational enterprises in supporting the United Nations' SDGs. Edward Elgar, Cheltenham

Belique A (2020) Invisible in the face of COVID-19 pandemic in the Dominican Republic. In: Villamil J, Morris M (eds) Pandemic inequality: civil society narratives from the Global South. Dejusticia, Bogota, pp 40–48

Bench Marks Foundation and Bench Mark Centre for CSR (2015) Floating or Sinking Social License to Operate (SLO) Kumba Iron Ore Ltd, Policy Gap 10. Potchefstroom

Blanco E, Razzaque J (2011) Globalisation and natural resources law: challenges, key issues and perspectives. Edward Elgar, Cheltenham

Cookson JB, Samuels BL, Gome NF (1974) Cancer of the lung in Rhodesian Blacks. S A Med J 48: 2314–2318

CSIR (2009) CSIR Briefing Note: Acid Mine Drainage in South Africa

Diale A (2014) Corporate Social Responsibility in the South African Mining Industry: necessity, conformity or convenience? Int J Bus Econ Dev 2:16–32

Eriamiatoe P (2020) No Corona Virus in Nigeria? In: Villamil J, Morris M (eds) Pandemic inequality Civil Society narratives from the Global South. Dejusticia, Bogota, pp 28–34

Evans A, Steven D (2020) Building trust, confidence and collective action in the age of COVID-19. World Polit Rev

[117] Constitution of the Republic of South Africa.

Gomezulu E, Mwakaje A, Kitima J (2018) Heavy metal and cyanide distribution in the villages surrounding Buzwagi Gold Mine in Tanzania. Tanzania J Sci:107–123
Hakim E (2020) Preventing the spread of COVID-19 in South Sudan. South Sudan Med J 13:40–43
Hoadley M, Liptlaw D, Weaver A (2002) MMSD Southern Africa-Mining, Minerals and Sustainable Development in Southern Africa. International Institute for Environment and Development. <https://pubs.iied.org/sites/default/files/pdfs/migrate/G00607.pdf>
ICMM (2020) ICMM-Briefing: Covid19: Mining with Principles to Address a Health and Social Crisis
IFC (2012) Performance Standard on Environmental and Social Sustainability
Kurian N (2020) COVID Mahamaari: grassroots experience from Kerala, India. In: Villamil J, Morris M (eds) Pandemic inequality: civil society narratives from the Global South. Dejusticia, Bogota, pp 64–70
Loewenson R, Henricher J, Papamichai A (2016) Corporate responsibility for health in the extractive sector in East and Southern Africa. Regional Network for Equity in Health in East and Southern Africa: Discussion Paper No 108
Loubser C, Chimbanga B, Jacobs H (2021) Intermittent water supply: a South Africa perspective. Water SA 47:1–9. https://doi.org/10.17159/wsa/2021.v.47.i1.9440
Lurie M, Stuckler D (2010) The role of mining in the spread of TB in Africa: policy implication. Expert Rev Anti-infective Ther 8:1205–1207. https://doi.org/10.1586/eri.10.120
Mhlongo SE, Amponsah-Dacosta F (2016) A review of problems and solutions of abandoned mines in South Africa. Int J Min Reclam Environ 30:279–294. https://doi.org/10.1080/17480930.2015.1044046
Moseley W (2020) The geography of COVID-19 and vulnerable global food system. World Polit Rev
Natural Resource Governance Institute (NRGI) (2014) Natural Resources Charter 2nd Edition.
Natural Resource Governance Institute (2015) NRGI Reader: local content strengthening local economy and work force. Natural Resource Governance Institute
Nkrumah B (2018) Food protest in South Africa: them belly full, but we are hungry. ESR Rev 4:4–7
OECD (2011) Guideline for Multinational Enterprises
OHCHR (2000) CESCR General Comment No. 14: The Right to the Highest Attainable Right Standard of Health (Art.12) Adopted at the Twenty-Second Session of the Committee on Economic, Social and Cultural Rights, Contained in Document E/C.12/2000/4)
Okonofua F et al (2020) COVID-19: addressing healthy system deficits and peculiarities in the African region. Afr J Reprod Health 24:11–16. https://doi.org/10.29063/ajrh2020/v24i2s.1
Osburn H (1969) Lung cancer in a mining district in Rhodesia. S A Med J 43:1307–1312
Osewe P (2015) Better health in mines and mining communities: a shared responsibility. WORLD BANK BLOGS. <https://blogs.worldbank.org/health/better-health-mines-and-mining-communities-shared-responsibility>
Preece M (2020) South deep support efforts to alleviate impacts of COVID-19 (Brief to the People of South Deep). http://www.overend.co.za/download/south-deep-brief-from-martin-new.pdf
Ramdoo I (2020) The impacts of COVID-19 on employment in mining. International Institute for Sustainable Development. https://www.iisd.org/system/files/publications/covid-19-employment-mining-en.pdf
Republic of South Africa (2016) Broad-Based Black Socio-Economic Empowerment Charter for the South African Mining and Minerals Industry. Department of Mineral Resources
Republic of South Africa (2017) Broad-Based Black Socio-Economic Empowerment Charter for the South African Mining and Minerals Industry. Department of Mineral Resources
Republic of South Africa (2018a) Broad-Based Black Socio-Economic Empowerment Charter for the South African Mining and Minerals Industry. Department of Mineral Resources
Republic of South Africa (2018b) National Water and Sanitation Master Plan. Department of Water and Sanitation
Republic of South Africa (2020a) Guidance on COVID-19and Vulnerable Populations. Mining Council South Africa

Republic of South Africa (2020b) Guideline for the Compilation of Mandatory Code of Practice for the Mitigation and Management of COVID-19 Outbreak. South Africa Mining Industry
Republic of South Africa (2020c) Guiding Principles on Prevention and Management of COVID-19 in SAMI. Department of Mineral Resources and Energy
Republic of South Africa (2020d) Department of Health, 'National Infection, Prevention and Control Strategic Framework, Department of Health
Schrecker T, Aguilera M, Birn A (2018) How extractive industries affect health: political economy underpinnings and pathways. Health Place 52:135–147. https://doi.org/10.1016/j.healthplace.2018.05.005
Siyobi B (2015) Corporate Social Responsibility in South Africa's Mining Industry: an assessment. South African Institute of International Affairs. https://saiia.org.za/wp-content/uploads/2015/09/Policy-Briefing-142.pdf
Starke L (2002) Breaking New Ground: Mining, Minerals, and Sustainable Development: The Report of the MMSD Project, Volume 1. IIED. <http://pubs.iied.org/pdfs/9084IIED.pdf>
Stuckler D et al (2013) "Dying for Gold": the effects of mineral mining on HIV, TB, silicosis and occupational diseases in Southern Africa. Int J Health Services 43:639–649. https://doi.org/10.2190/HS.43.4.c
Temperoni C et al (2021) Clinical characteristics, management and health related quality of life in young to middle age adult with COVID-19. BMC Infect Dis 21:1–10. https://doi.org/10.1186/s12879-021-05841-1
The Economist (2018) Special Report: Universal Health Care: An Affordable Necessity
Thomashausen S (2015) Shared-use mining infrastructure in Sub-Saharan Africa: challenges and opportunities. Colombia Centre on Sustainable Investment. https://scholarship.law.columbia.edu/sustainable_investment_staffpubs/128
Tinti P (2020) Can Africa continue to fend off the worst of COVID-19? World Polit Rev. <https://www.worldpoliticsreview.com/articles/28763/can-african-countries-continue-to-fend-off-the-worst-of-covid-19>
UN the Office of the High Commissioner (2011) Guiding Principles on Business and Human Rights
United Nations Environment Programme (2010) Africa: Water Atlas
Villian F et al (2016) Mining and emerging infectious diseases: results of the Infectious Diseases Risk Assessment and Management (IDRAM) Initiative Pilot. Extr Ind Soc 4:251–259. https://doi.org/10.1016/j.exis.2016.08.009
WHO (2020) Modes of transmission of virus causing COVID-19: implications for IPC precaution recommendations. <https://www.who.int/news-room/commentaries/detail/modes-of-transmission-of-virus-causing-covid-19-implications-for-ipc-precaution-recommendations>

John S. Ombella LLB (MU-2005) Tanzania, LL.M (UWC-2007) South Africa, LL.D (OUT-2023) Tanzania, Certificate of Sustainable Development and Human Rights Law (SUSTLAW) Antwerp University-Belgium (2017), Certificate on Climate Change International Legal Regime (UNITAR/UNEP-2024), Lecturer Economic Law Department, Faculty of Law Mzumbe University, and an advocate of the High Court. The author can be reached via: majaliwaj.sinato@gmail.com.

Julius Cosmas LL.B (UDSM) Tanzania, LL.M (SU) South Africa, PhD (UWC) South Africa, HoD, Private Law Department, Senior Lecturer, Private Law Department, Faculty of Law, Mzumbe University, An advocate of the High Court. The author may be reached via swigo2003@gmail.com.

Investment Protection Vis-à-Vis the Protection of Environmental Rights in Tanzania

Elia Mwanga and Justina M. Danda

1 Introduction

Investments, particularly foreign direct investments (FDIs), play a vital role in the development of countries. Many developing countries heavily rely on foreign investors to exploit their natural resources, such as minerals, oil, and gas, and for the transfer of technology.[1] Developing countries anticipate generating revenue from foreign investments. Local communities in host states expect to enhance their quality of life through opportunities brought by foreign investments, which include employment creation, income generation, and wealth.[2] On the other hand, foreign investors aim to make significant profits from their investments in developing countries, and this sometimes trigger conflicts of interest. These conflicts may result in environmental degradation, tax evasion, and violations of the rights of local communities. Walwa argues that because FDIs operate under liberal market principles and focus on competition and profit making, environmental concerns are often overlooked. Investors typically do not prioritize environmental conservation due to their lack of property rights over the environment.[3] Foreign investors often neglect the environmental impact of their activities since they are rarely direct victims of environmental pollution.[4]

[1] Ibe (2021), p. 126.

[2] Tamo (2016), p. 152.

[3] Walwa (2016), p. 9.

[4] Ibid.

E. Mwanga (✉) · J. M. Danda
School of Law, University of Dodoma, Dodoma, Tanzania
e-mail: elia.mwanga@udom.ac.tz

I. Kajiru et al. (eds.), *Economic Development and Human Rights in Contemporary Sub-Saharan Africa*, Ius Gentium: Comparative Perspectives on Law and Justice 122, https://doi.org/10.1007/978-3-031-81400-6_4

In order to attract FDIs, states often relax their regulations, which may lead to violations of human rights in states with weak governance policies.[5] Developing countries often lower their standards to attract FDIs with the hope of integrating their economies into the global economy.[6] To balance the competing interests of investment protection and environmental rights, effective legal and regulatory frameworks are necessary to govern foreign investments. These frameworks must take into account environmental considerations as the benefits of foreign investments to host states depend on investors complying with environmental standards. Given the current global and national focus on environmental issues, it is clear that investment laws should not only prioritize economic concerns. Social issues such as environmental rights should be adequately addressed. This chapter examines the legal and regulatory frameworks in Tanzania that govern investments, and the aim is to determine how these frameworks contribute to the protection of environmental rights, particularly the right to a clean, safe, and sustainable environment. The chapter is divided into five sections. The first section provides an overview of FDIs and their historical background in Tanzania. The second section explains the development and interpretation of environmental rights. The third section examines the legal and institutional framework governing FDIs. The fourth section analyzes the protection of investment in relation to the protection of environmental rights by assessing the legal and regulatory frameworks. The final section concludes the chapter.

2 Understanding FDIs and Their Historical Background in Tanzania

This chapter focuses on FDIs, which are a type of investment where the natural resources and wealth of a host country are utilized through the investment of technology and financial resources by foreign entities. It is also defined as a business investment in another country, often by setting up local production facilities or purchasing existing businesses.[7] In developing countries, FDIs typically utilize their natural resources with the expertise and financial support provided by foreign entities.

Historically, Tanzania saw a significant increase in FDIs following the government's decision to liberalize the economy in the 1980s.[8] In the period following the Arusha Declaration of 1967, Tanzania's socialism and self-reliance policy failed, leading to a severe economic crisis. Between 1976 and 1986, the country experienced a notable decline in real per capita income, falling by more than 15 per cent.

[5] Khan and Khan (2017), p. 76.

[6] Lopez (2020), p. 345.

[7] Diyamett et al. (2011), p. 22.

[8] Kitonka (2023), p. 97.

This downturn was primarily driven by a trade imbalance and deficits in public finances. The weakening economy was largely attributed to the decreasing prices of primary commodities in the international market, alongside rising costs for manufactured imports and oil. Furthermore, the 1979 war between Tanzania and Uganda significantly stalled the country's economic growth, leading to a serious downturn. To address this, Tanzania underwent significant economic restructuring aimed at transforming its economy from socialist to capitalist. Various projects, both domestically and donor sponsored, were implemented to assist Tanzania in liberalizing its economy. Key projects included the National Economic Survival Program, the International Monetary Fund and World Bank's Structural Adjustment Programme, and the Economic Recovery Programme.[9] The above programs generally opened doors for private investments in Tanzania and, in particular, encouraged foreign investors to invest in the country.

The reforms mentioned above have resulted in foreign investors benefiting more from their investments at the expense of Tanzania's sustainable development. For example, the implementation of the Mining Act of 1998 has led to negligible contributions to gross domestic product (GDP) from the mining sector, tax evasion, and the inadequate integration of the mining sector with other sectors of the economy.[10]

Therefore, to address the deficiencies of previous laws, especially during the period of liberalization, the government has constantly been introducing amendments to the existing investment laws and policies.

3 Development of Environmental Rights and Their Reflection in Tanzanian Laws

On 8 October 2021, the United Nations Human Rights Council, a body dedicated to promoting and protecting human rights globally, adopted a resolution that directed "the right to a clean, healthy and sustainable environment to be a human right that is important for the enjoyment of human rights."[11] Ten months later, the United Nations General Assembly (UNGA) unanimously adopted a resolution recognizing "the right to a clean, healthy and sustainable environment as a human right."[12] The resolution further calls upon states and other stakeholders to "scale up efforts to ensure a clean, healthy and sustainable environment for all."[13]

Even before such express recognition of the right by the UNGA, the two primary international human rights instruments, the Universal Declaration of Human Rights

[9]Magai and Márquez-Velázquez (2021), p. 2.

[10]Walwa (2016), pp. 107–115.

[11]See UNGA, HRC (2021).

[12]See UNGA (2022).

[13]UNGA (2022).

(UDHR)[14] and the International Covenant on Civil and Political Rights,[15] played a significant role in developing the environmental rights we know today. The legal documents cited above safeguard both procedural and substantive rights, which have been utilized to indirectly protect environmental rights. Procedural rights encompass the right to access information, the right to participate in decision-making, the right to access justice, and the right to free, prior, and informed consent.[16] On the other hand, substantive rights, such as the right to life, freedom of association, right to health, access to adequate food and living standards, and the right to access religious sites, have also been leveraged indirectly to protect environmental rights.[17] In addition, judicial bodies and tribunals have used their powers creatively to interpret protected basic human rights more broadly, ensuring the protection of environmental rights and granting people the right to a healthy environment.[18]

The African Charter on Human and Peoples Rights (ACHPR),[19] to which Tanzania is a party, is among the early regional human rights treaties to protect the right to a healthy environment explicitly. In its Article 27, the Charter states that "All peoples shall have the right to a satisfactory general environment favourable to their development." The existing international human rights treaties that explicitly protect the right to a clean, healthy, and sustainable environment, such as the African Charter, are relatively scarce compared to the overall number of international human rights instruments. This can be attributed to the underdeveloped state of environmental rights during the time many of these treaties were drafted. It is highly probable that if these treaties were being drafted today, they would explicitly include environmental rights.[20] Notwithstanding the deficiencies present in international human rights treaties, the right to a clean, healthy, and sustainable environment is progressively gaining protection within various national legal frameworks.

Generally, this right covers the right to live in an environment that fosters life and growth without causing harm. Additionally, it necessitates a healthy human habitat that includes uncontaminated water, air, and soil, devoid of toxins or hazards that pose a threat to human well-being.[21] This right is acknowledged for its significance in both life and the general human habitat. In the absence of a healthy environment, individuals are incapable of realizing their ambitions or attaining a standard of living congruent with the basic requisites of human dignity.[22] Moreover, this right

---

[14] Adopted on 10 December 1948, 217 A (III).

[15] U.N.T.S 999 (December): 171.

[16] Turner (2019), p. 20. See also UNEP, p. 7.

[17] Ibid.

[18] Turner discusses intensively how courts and treaty bodies have been interpreting basic human rights to cover environmental rights. See Turner (2019), pp. 1–40.

[19] See CAB/LEG/67/3 rev. 5, 21 I.L.M. 58 (1982). Other regional treaties that recognize the right to clean, safe, and healthy environment are the Aarhus Convention on Access to Information, Public Participation, and Access to Justice in Environmental Matters, the San Salvador Protocol, and the Arab Charter on Human Rights.

[20] Atapattu (2019), p. 21.

[21] Okpara (2012), p. 5.

[22] Ibid.

necessitates the protection of the environment for the benefit of both current and future generations. Additionally, it empowers victims to legally pursue and protect this right in the event of any violations.

In Tanzania, the Constitution of the United Republic of Tanzania (CURT) of 1977 does not expressly protect the right to a healthy environment. However, this has not prevented the courts from acknowledging and protecting environmental rights, including the right to a clean, healthy, and sustainable environment. For instance, in the case of *Joseph Kessy and Others v Dar-es-Salaam City Council*,[23] the respondents had been disposing of various forms of waste, including garbage and refuse collected from across the city, in Tabata, a residential area. The applicants brought the matter before the High Court of Tanzania, contesting the dumping of waste in their residential area on the ground that it posed a threat to their lives. The High Court, in its ruling, associated the right to life with the right to a clean, healthy, and sustainable environment. The Court held that by polluting the environment, the lives of the affected individuals were endangered, thereby violating their constitutional right to life.

Another relevant case is *Festo Balegele and 794 Others v Dar es Salaam City Council*,[24] where the High Court of Tanzania broadened the interpretation of the right to life to include the right to a clean, safe and healthy environment. In the Environmental Management Act,[25] the right to a clean, healthy and sustainable environment is explicitly stated in the unenforceable provision of the Act. Section 4 of the above Act states:

(1) Every person living in Tanzania shall have a right to clean, safe and healthy environment.
(2) The right to clean, safe and healthy environment shall include the right of access by any citizen to the various public elements or segments of the environment for recreational, educational, health, spiritual, cultural and economic purposes.

To give significance to the aforementioned, section 5 of the same Act confers *locus standi* to initiate legal proceedings for the enforcement of the right to a clean, healthy, and sustainable environment. However, sections 4 and 5 do not fall within the enforceable provisions of the Act. Consequently, the incorporation of the right to a clean, healthy, and sustainable environment in the Act signifies a non-binding obligation of the State to ensure the accessibility and enjoyment of the right.

[23] See Civil Case No. 299 of 1988, High Court of Tanzania at Dar-es-Salaam.

[24] See Miscellaneous Civil Cause No. 90 of 1991, reported in UNEP/UNDP/Dutch Government Joint Project on Environmental Law in Africa, Compendium of Judicial Decisions on Matters Related to Environment, National Decisions, Volume I, p. 87.

[25] Act No. 20 of 2004.

4 Legal and Institutional Frameworks Governing FDIs in Tanzania

The primary legal documents that significantly regulate FDIs in Tanzania are the Constitution of the United Republic of Tanzania,[26] the Tanzania Investment Act,[27,] the Land Act,[28] the Village Land Act,[29] and the Environmental Management Act.[30] Other legal documents are sectoral-oriented laws, such as laws regulating mining, petroleum, special economic zones, and tax laws. There are also bilateral investment agreements (BITs) between Tanzania and other countries. These laws have guaranteed certain rights and privileges to investors.

The Investment Act, which was revised in 2022, regulates investments in Tanzania, including FDIs. The Act offers various benefits to investors. It also imposes obligations on investors and the government. The Tanzania Investment Act reiterates the position of the Constitution[31] on nationalization.[32] The Act explicitly prohibits the government from nationalizing businesses owned by investors. Furthermore, it requires that in the event of an acquisition of an investor's business, such action must adhere to the law, guaranteeing just compensation and affording the investor the right to pursue legal recourse or arbitration to ascertain their rights and the sum payable subsequent to the government's decision to nationalize their assets.[33]

Access to land is subject to restrictions with regard to foreign individuals. Foreign investors are permitted to access and take possession of land solely for investment purposes, and the land allocated to them is in the form of a derivative right.[34] The government has the power to compulsorily acquire any land that is needed for the public interest.[35]The exercise of the power to compulsorily acquire land is contingent upon the provision of prompt, fair, and equitable compensation. This principle extends to land occupied by foreign investors. Unless foreign investors are in breach of conditions associated with their right of occupancy, the government is precluded

[26]Cap, 2 R.E. 2002.

[27]No. 10 of 2022.

[28]Cap. 113 R.E. 2019.

[29]Cap. 114 R.E .2019.

[30]Cap. 191.

[31]See Art. 24 Constitution of Tanzania.

[32]See sect. 29 of Act No. 10 of 2022. Nationalization can be defined to mean "a conversion of property owned by natural persons or legal entities into state-owned property." See Okounev (1999), pp. 838–843.

[33]The Tanzania Investment Act, sect. 29.

[34]See sect. 20(1) of the Land Act, which provides that a foreigner can occupy land by way of a derivative right under the Tanzania Investment Centre (TIC). The derivative right is created out of the granted right of occupancy. This means that the land needed by a foreigner will first be granted to TIC, and the investor will then derive the right to occupy land from TIC and not from the Commissioner for Land.

[35]See sect. 3 of the Land Acquisition Act, Cap. 118 R.E 2002. See also the case of *AG v Lohay Akoonay & Joseph Lohay* [1995] TLR 80.

from the compulsory acquisition of such land without adhering to the requirements for prompt, fair, and equitable compensation.

Foreign investments also enjoy several tax/fiscal and nonfiscal incentives. The Tanzania Investment Act defines incentives as "tax reliefs, concessional tax rates or any other benefits which may be accessed by an investor under any law for the time being in force."[36] In Tanzania, investment incentives are delineated across various statutes. To be eligible for the incentives outlined in the Tanzania Investment Act, an investor must obtain a certificate of incentives as per section 19 of the Act. Typically, tax incentives available to investors encompass zero-rated import duties, value-added tax benefits, and tax exemptions[37] and tax holidays.[38] Apart from fiscal incentives, investors are also granted nonfiscal incentives, such as receiving facilitation from the Tanzania Investment Centre (TIC) and unconditional transferability of profits[39] and an opportunity to access arbitral tribunals in case of dispute between the investor and the government. This must be done in accordance with the arbitration laws of Tanzania or the "rules of procedure for arbitration of the International Centre for the Settlement of Investment Disputes" or in accordance with "bilateral or multilateral agreement on investment protection agreed to by the Government of the United Republic and the government of the country where the investor originates."[40]

The Tanzania Investment Act provides supplementary incentives for investments deemed strategic or specially strategic. Strategic investments are characterized by a substantial capital outlay, requiring a minimum of USD 20,000,000 for Tanzanian-owned investments and USD 50,000,000 for foreign-owned investments.[41] Strategic investments should also have the capability of generating no less than 1000 employment opportunities for Tanzanians while simultaneously bolstering exports, diminishing imports, and facilitating the transfer of advanced technology.[42] Special strategic investments are required to have a minimum capital of USD 300,000,000 and are expected to provide employment opportunities for not less than 1500 Tanzanians. Moreover, these investments should contribute to generating foreign exchange and decreasing the importation of goods.[43] The minister responsible for investment is empowered to propose additional incentives for strategic and special strategic investments. It is essential to note that the Tanzania Investment Act does not extend to mining and petroleum operations, with the exception of sections 28 and 29, which ensure the transfer of capital, income, and dividends, as well as provide protection against nationalization.

---

[36] See sect. 3 of the Tanzania Investment Act.

[37] Second schedule to the Income Tax Act lists transactions exempted from taxation.

[38] For instance, a corporation newly registered under the Dar es Salaam enjoys a tax holiday of 5% off for 3 years.

[39] See sect. 28 of the Tanzania Investment Act.

[40] Ibid, sect. 33.

[41] Ibid, sect. 33.

[42] Ibid.

[43] Ibid.

FDIs are obligated to adhere to the laws of the country, protect consumer rights and environmental rights, and utilize raw materials or resources available in Tanzania.[44] Investment regulations comprise environmental laws. According to the Environmental Management Act, investors are obligated to register their projects with the National Environment Council (NEMC) in order to ascertain whether the project necessitates a mandatory environmental impact assessment (EIA) prior to implementation.[45] The list of projects that require mandatory EIA and those that do not need mandatory EIA is provided in the Environmental Management Act[46] and its regulations and the Environmental Impact Assessment and Audit Regulations, 2005, as amended in 2018.[47]

The Environmental Management Act stipulates that the acquisition of licenses and permits for a specific project does not confer the right to proceed with a project, so the investor must first obtain an environmental impact assessment (EIA) certificate.[48] The EIA Regulations take an additional step by prohibiting government authorities from granting licenses and permits to investors who commence projects necessitating mandatory EIA before obtaining EIA certificates.

Investors in sectors like mining and petroleum production, which pose serious threats to the environment, also need to provide environmental performance bonds, which act as security for adhering to environmental standards. In the event that any of the environmental requirements outlined in the Environmental Management Act are violated, the performance bond will be used to repair the damaged environment.[49] Environmental performance bonds further act as security to the effect that at the close of the project, the investor will implement safe decommissioning, site rehabilitation and ecosystem restoration.[50]

Tanzanian environmental laws incorporate international environmental principles, including the polluter pays principle, the precautionary principle, and the sustainable development principle. These international environmental law principles must be taken into consideration by courts, tribunals, and other agencies exercising their jurisdiction under the Environmental Management Act.[51]

Additionally, in order to fulfill the environmental standards outlined in the Environmental Management Act, any individual, in their own interest, the interest of a group of individuals, or the public interest, may file a lawsuit to ensure

[44] Ibid., sect. 26.

[45] See Environment Impact Assessment and Audit Regulations of 2005 GN No. 349 of 2004, as amended by the Environmental Management (Environmental Impact Assessment and Audit) (Amendment) Regulations, 2018, GN No. 474 of 2018, Regulations 8 and 9.

[46] See Third Schedule.

[47] See First Schedule.

[48] See sect. 81(3).

[49] See sect. 227 of the Environmental Management Act.

[50] Ibid., sect. 102.

[51] See sect. (3).

compliance with the environmental standards.[52] However, the Act does not provide procedures for implementing the above right and does not mention the court with the competent jurisdiction to entertain such action.

The Tanzania Investment Centre (TIC), which was founded in accordance with the Investment Act, is the principal government agency tasked with coordinating, encouraging, and promoting investment in Tanzania as well as providing policy advice to the government.[53] The agency helps investors get all the licenses and approvals they require. Note that TIC does not grant licenses, approvals, or permissions for investments. Licenses, permissions, and approvals are granted by the appropriate authorities, including the Mineral Commission, the Petroleum Upstream Regulatory Authority, the Commissioner for Land, the minister in charge of environmental matters, and other local government agencies. In order to obtain the required licenses, permissions, and approvals, TIC must liaise with the appropriate authorities.[54] Therefore, since most of the investment-related permits and licenses are not issued by TIC, the role of TIC in ensuring that environmental standards are observed is restricted.

However, a major factor influencing the execution of foreign investment projects is the National Environment Management Council (NEMC), which is in charge of ascertaining compliance with the Environmental Management Act. In addition to reviewing environmental impact statements, NEMC has the power to control the performance of EIA studies.[55] In practice, EIA is commissioned by the investor. It is the investor who hires and pays experts to conduct EIA. NEMC thereafter reviews the EIA statements produced by the experts and forwards its recommendations to the minister responsible for the environment, who approves the EIA studies and issues EIA certificates.[56] A person aggrieved by the decision of the minister may appeal to the Environmental Appeals Tribunal.[57] However, the Tribunal has never come into existence since the enactment of the Environmental Management Act in 2004. Therefore, there is no mechanism for controlling the exercise of the above discretionary powers vested in the minister.

NEMC is responsible for environmental audits and monitoring during project execution. Ensuring that the project is implemented in a way that does not violate national environmental standards is the ultimate goal of monitoring and auditing projects. When an established project violates applicable environmental standards, NEMC has the power to issue appropriate orders, such as imposing a ban on environmental pollution and ordering the investor whose project caused the pollution to repair the affected area.[58]

---

[52] See sect. 2022.

[53] See sect. 4.

[54] See sect. 18.

[55] See sect. 18 of the Environmental Management Act.

[56] Ibid., sects. 91 and 92.

[57] Ibid., sect. 95.

[58] Ibid., sects. b151, 195, 196, 197, and 198.

In contrast to TIC and NEMC, which serve multiple sectors and have broad tasks, other institutions that oversee foreign direct investments are focused on specific industries. Their capabilities are restricted to a specific investment industry. NEMC, however, is primarily responsible for ensuring that foreign investment conforms with environmental regulations.

Sector-specific institutions like the ministry in charge of minerals, the ministry responsible for petroleum, the Mining Commission, and the Petroleum Upstream Regulatory Authority are among the other institutions that oversee FDIs. Specialized fields are under their purview. The Cabinet also has the power to grant special mining licenses[59] and petroleum production sharing agreements.[60]

5 The Protection of Investment *Vis-à-Vis* the Protection of Environmental Rights: Observation on the Legal and Regulatory Frameworks

This part seeks to examine/evaluate the effectiveness of the legal and regulatory frameworks for investments in protecting the right to a clean, healthy, and sustainable environment. The aim is to underscore how the laws and relevant institutions regulating FDIs promote adherence to acceptable environmental standards.

It must be noted that both the positive and negative effects of FDIs can be felt by the host country. Particularly in cases where the legal and regulatory systems are inadequate, weak, or corrupt, the environment is most likely to suffer. On a positive note, FDIs are expected to provide jobs, tax income, technology transfers, expertise, and know-how acquisitions. From a negative perspective, the adverse effects of FDIs include food shortages brought on by land expropriation, the degradation of the environment, and abuse of human rights, such as the right to a safe, clean, and sustainable environment.[61]

Practical legal and regulatory frameworks should be put in place to regulate FDIs in order to maximize their positive effects and minimize the negative ones. Alongside protecting and enabling the enjoyment of environmental rights, such as the right to a safe, clean, and sustainable environment, the aforementioned frameworks should also ascertain that foreign investors observe the environmental protection standards set in place.

Tanzania, like many other developing countries, gives careful consideration to international investments. Developing states generally strive to heighten FDIs' activities within their states in an effort to strengthen their own national economies. Due to this, FDIs are protected by national laws, bilateral investment agreements, and investment contracts between host states and foreign investors, in addition to

[59] See sect. 42(1) of the Mining Act [Cap. 123 R.E. 2019].

[60] See Petroleum Act No. 21 of 2015.

[61] See Ibe (2021), p. 126, and Tamo (2016), p. 152.

international treaties. Additionally, governments occasionally compromise their national environmental standards in order to attract foreign investment by providing incentives to foreign companies without considering the impact of FDIs on the sustainable growth of their nations.[62]

Despite the recognition of the human right to a clean, safe, and sustainable environment, the CURT does not explicitly provide for this right. To address this anomaly, courts have subsequently broadened the interpretation of the existing rights to encompass the right to a clean, healthy, and sustainable environment. However, the challenge is that for an applicant to successfully establish a violation of the right to a clean, healthy, and sustainable environment, he must demonstrate that the effects of the act complained of threaten a human right that is protected in the CURT, such as the right to life.

Since there are no set guidelines for determining the degree of infringement, the applicant may have difficulty demonstrating how much his right to life has been violated. Because of this, proving the connection between the right to a clean, healthy, and sustainable environment and the right to life becomes more challenging. As such, enforcing the right to a healthy environment may be subjected to the position of the judge called upon to interpret the relevant provisions of the Constitution.

Additionally, the government, the private sector, and foreign investors may all violate the rights outlined in the Constitution, which may indirectly include the right to a healthy environment. When the state or an individual is being sued for violating procedural or substantive environmental rights guaranteed by the Constitution, questions pertaining to *locus standi* may arise. Anyone who can demonstrate that they are a direct victim of the breach may sue under the Basic Rights and Duties and Enforcement Act.[63] This means that other persons, such as civil society organizations or human rights defenders, cannot sue on behalf of the members of society unless they can prove that they suffered directly from the violation.[64] Considering that most victims of environmental rights violations are rural inhabitants, most of them are poor and ignorant of their rights. Therefore, many environmental rights violators often go unpunished.

Additionally, it should be noted that even while the Environmental Management Act expressly guarantees the right to a clean, healthy, and sustainable environment, it is unenforceable because it is not included in the Act's enforceable sections. Alternatively, the Environmental Management Act's provisions pertaining to EIA, monitoring, and auditing could be crucial in guaranteeing the right to a clean, healthy, and sustainable environment if Tanzania's EIA processes are to be stringently enforced. However, for an EIA to be effective enough to produce the underlying benefits, all stakeholders—including the local community and civil society organizations—must be actively involved in the process, and there must be

[62] Khan and Khan (2017), p. 76.

[63] See sect. 4(2), as amended by the Written Laws (Miscellaneous Amendments) (No. 3) Act, 2020.

[64] See Nyeko (2020).

a dedicated and effective institution overseeing its performance.[65] The above requirements are lacking with respect to EIA in Tanzania. Studies demonstrate that local communities, as well as civil societies, are not actively involved in the EIA process.[66]

The procedural challenges facing the authority vested with the power to approve environmental impact assessments and issue EIA certificates are some of the factors undermining the efficacy of EIA in Tanzania. The president appoints the NEMC's director, who oversees the organization's EIA reviews. Simultaneously, the minister, a political figurehead and a presidential appointee, is empowered to approve EIAs and issue EIA certificates.[67] Furthermore, when deciding whether to approve or disapprove the EIA study and thereby issue an EIA certificate, the minister is not bound by the recommendations of NEMC. Therefore, he may choose to approve the EIA study and issue an EIA certificate even when NEMC recommends otherwise.[68] It might be inferred from this that environmental protection standards for FDIs in which the government has an interest may eventually be lowered, eliminating even the slightest prospect of initiating legal action for violations.

It is also debatable whether NEMC can effectively and efficiently enforce compliance with the Environmental Management Act. Among other things, NEMC has the power to sanction pollution and to order that the damaged environment be repaired accordingly.

Even with the reestablishment of NEMC over 18 years ago, certain foreign companies have persisted in polluting the environment. So far, there has been no documented legal action taken against these companies. Reports have surfaced exposing several environmental damage incidents that have gone unpunished. For instance, protests against the environmental harm caused by the mine's effluents have been ongoing among nearby villages of Acacia Gold Mining's North Mara Gold Mine.[69] However, NEMC did not take any action until it was ordered by the President to probe the claim.[70] In spite of having complete power to penalize anyone who violates the environmental standards outlined in the Environmental Management Act, it is unclear why NEMC has been unable to respond to local communities' complaints for the past 10 years.

The protection of the right to a clean, safe, and sustainable environment is also affected by the exercise of discretionary powers. Experience from previous implementation of other laws suggests that there are dangers when discretionary powers

[65] Walwa (2016), p. 105.

[66] Ibid.

[67] Mwanga (2022b), p. 101.

[68] An example is when the Minister responsible for the environment approved an EIA objected to by the NEMC concerning the prawn farm project in the Rufiji River Delta. The project was opposed by both the NEMC and the public. Even though the NEMC's EIA review found that the project was likely to degrade the Rufiji Delta due to poisonous effluents and clearing mangroves, in 1997, the proposal was approved. Ibid., 106.

[69] See Xinhua (2019).

[70] Ibid.

are vested in an individual without proper mechanisms for regulating those powers. These powers are likely to be abused as some investors engage in corrupt practices to influence the exercise of discretionary powers in their favor.[71] For instance, when the Mining Act of 1998 existed, several mining projects were commenced without undertaking an EIA study. The discretionary powers granted to the mining minister to bar any investor from performing an environmental impact assessment (EIA) were a major setback in protecting the environment. The end consequence was severe environmental damage and a breach of the people's right to a safe, clean, and sustainable environment.[72]

The current rules pertaining to investments also grant specific individuals, such as the environment minister, discretionary authority without providing adequate controls over such powers. The risk lies in the increased possibility of misusing those powers. Amendments of the law introduced in 2017 through the Written Laws (Miscellaneous Amendments) Act No. 7 of 2017 reduced the discretionary powers of the minister responsible for minerals, including the power to negotiate and sign a development agreement on behalf of the government.[73]

The institutions set up by parliamentary acts regulate large foreign direct investments (FDIs) at the national level, including mining and petroleum enterprises. Consequently, local government officials in areas where these companies have been established do not have the authority to regulate the activities of the companies. As a result, they are unable to stop or take action against the environmental damage these investments cause. If the central government does not act or acts slowly to address the major environmental hazards, the local communities could be exposed to dangerous conditions that could endanger their health.

There are several different laws governing FDIs. Despite being the main piece of legislation, the Tanzania Investment Act does not apply to certain investments. Certain sector-specific laws governing mining and petroleum operations have the potential to negatively impact the environment. Additional rules that bind the parties are provided by development agreements that Tanzania and the investor sign. There is confidentiality surrounding these development agreements. Therefore, the public is unaware of their terms and conditions.

Nevertheless, the state's ability to enforce its laws, particularly those that safeguard the right to safe, clean, and sustainable development, may be restricted by these agreements.

---

[71] Cooksey (2011), p. 75.

[72] Mwanga (2022a), p. 84.

[73] See sect. 10 of the Written Laws (Miscellaneous Amendments) Act No. 7 of 2017. This Act repealed sect. 12, which empowered the minister to negotiate and sign development agreements on behalf of the government. The powers of the minister to grant mining licenses have also been abolished. Currently, it is the Mining Commission that is vested with the power to grant mining licenses. In the case of special mining licenses, the cabinet must approve such grants.

6 Conclusion

Developing countries rely heavily on FDIs due to the benefits that come along with FDIs. This has ultimately led to an unjust safeguarding of FDIs, a fact that has adversely affected the preservation of the right to a safe, clean, and sustainable environment. Tanzania greatly values foreign direct investments and actively works on safeguarding them. This paper recommends that the legal framework in Tanzania concerning FDI requires revision, as it is currently contributing to the violation of environmental standards. The weaknesses embedded in investment laws make it difficult to efficiently safeguard the aforementioned right. Lastly, the existence of weak institutions to enforce the country's laws exacerbates the problem.

References

Atapattu S (2019) Environmental rights and international human rights covenants: what standards are relevant? In: Turner SJ et al (eds) Environmental rights: development of standard. CUP, Cambridge

Cooksey B (2011) The investment and business environment for gold exploration and mining in Tanzania: Background paper 03. Overseas Development Institute. https://assets.publishing.service.gov.uk/media/57a08ad140f0b652dd00090e/20110606-appp-background-paper-03-brian-cooksey-june-2011.pd

Diyamett B, Ngowi P, Mutambala LM (2011) The role of foreign direct investment (FDI) in local technological capability building: the case of Tanzania

Ibe EC (2021) Responsibility of human rights violations by transnational corporations under international law. IJOCLLEP 3:125–133

Khan AM, Khan IU (2017) Making transnational corporations more responsible: a human rights approach. J Law Soc 48:73–90

Kitonka NH (2023) Balance between investment protection and sustainable development under Tanzania-Canada BITs: need for progressive domestic investment law. J Law Leg Reform 4:93–128. https://doi.org/10.15294/jllr.v4i1.60464

Lopez AF (2020) Contemporary responses to businesses' negative human rights impact. Braz J Int Law 17:341–362

Magai PS, Márquez-Velázquez AL (2021) Tanzania's mining sector and its implications for the country's development

Mwanga E (2022a) The state of the law on small scale mining in Tanzania: challenges and prospects from colonial period to present. J Afr Law Contemp Leg Issues 1:71–95

Mwanga E (2022b) Tanzanian environmental impact assessment laws and practice for projects in world heritage sites. J Environ Dev 31:88–107. https://doi.org/10.1177/10704965211073587

Nyeko O (2020) Public interest litigation under threat in Tanzania: latest in restrictions on political and civil rights

Okounev KV (1999) Guarantees against nationalisation, requisition and confiscation of foreign investments in Russia. SvJT:838–843

Okpara CI (2012) Right to a clean and healthy environment: the panacea to the Niger Delta struggle. J Polit Law 5:3–5. https://doi.org/10.5539/jpl.v5n1p3

Tamo A (2016) New thinking on transnational corporations and human rights: towards a multi-stakeholder approach. Neth Q Hum Rights 34:147–173. https://doi.org/10.1177/016934411603400

Turner SJ (2019) Introduction: a brief history of environmental rights and the development of standards. In: Turner SJ et al (eds) Environmental rights: development of standard. CUP, pp 1–10

UNEP Right to a Healthy Environment: Good practices, Report of the Special Rapporteur on the issue of human rights obligations relating to the enjoyment of a safe, clean, healthy and sustainable environment. https://wedocs.unep.org/bitstream/handle/20.500.11822/32450/RHE.pdf?sequence=1&isAllowed=y

UNGA (2022) The human right to a clean, healthy and sustainable environment, A/RES/76/300

UNGA, HRC (2021) The human right to a clean, healthy and sustainable environment, A/HRC/RES/48/13

URT, Ministry of Energy and Minerals (2009) The mineral policy of Tanzania. Ministry of Energy and Minerals

Walwa WJ (2016) Large-scale mining and the right to a clean, health and safe environment in Tanzania. Afr Rev 43:97–123

Xinhua (2019) Tanzania Fines Acacia Mining over Environmental Pollution: Official. http://www.xinhuanet.com/english/africa/2019-05/17/c_138067402.htm

Elia Mwanga LL.B (Hons); LL.M; PhD (Law) from the University of Dar es Salaam; Senior Lecturer of Law at the University of Dodoma; E-mail: elia.mwanga@udom.ac.tz.

Justina M. Danda LL.B (Hons); LL.M from Ruaha Catholic University; PhD candidate University of the Free State—South Africa, Assistant Lecturer in Law—School of Law at the University of Dodoma; Email: dandajustina@gmail.com.

Regulating Access to Proprietary Technological Information in Africa: Intellectual Property and Human Rights Perspectives

Saudin Jacob Mwakaje

1 Introduction

Policy and regulatory issues pertaining to access to information attract debates from various perspectives, including intellectual property rights (IPR), human rights, and the sustainable development agenda, as reflected in the current initiatives under the United Nations Sustainable Development Goals (SDGs).[1] Recently, the use of axiomatic expressions such as 'information is power', 'information age', and 'knowledge-based society' reaffirms the impact of the changing societal interface in various facets of human life. The shifting global landscape of information and knowledge systems, which play a crucial role in shaping socio-economic progression in contemporary societies, merits such nomenclature.[2] Consequently, policy and regulatory attention, among others, targets the informatisation of social life, with continual reference to the global information economy predicated on a conceptual paradigm shift, which values, equates, and treats proprietary information like other corporate assets.[3] As such, the control of and access to such information constitute one of the key agendas at various organisational levels and in supply chain management. In this chapter, the term 'proprietary technological information' broadly refers to any innovation, inventions, know-how, trade secret, systems, or specific tool that an organisation or an individual exclusively owns in addition to providing a competitive edge or advantage over others. Invariably, legal instruments dealing

[1] Saadoun (2024); Kaltenborn et al. (2020).

[2] Martin (1988), p. 303; Sigurdson (1993); Chiumbu (2006), p. 86; Vadi (2008), p. 347; Gopal et al. (2011), pp. 727–731; Zeng et al. (2020), p. 3337.

[3] Webster (2002), pp. 61–81.

S. J. Mwakaje (✉)
University of Dar es Salaam, School of Law, Dar es Salaam, Tanzania
e-mail: saudinj@udsm.ac.tz

I. Kajiru et al. (eds.), *Economic Development and Human Rights in Contemporary Sub-Saharan Africa*, Ius Gentium: Comparative Perspectives on Law and Justice 122, https://doi.org/10.1007/978-3-031-81400-6_5

with human rights have recognised the right of access to information as one of the fundamental human rights tenets embedded in national constitutions, regional treaties, and international conventions. In Africa, the key legal instruments on access to information, intellectual property rights, and human rights include the African Charter on Human and People's Rights of 1981,[4] the African Union's Model Law on Access to Information for Africa of 2013,[5] the Guidelines on Access to Information and Elections in Africa of 2017,[6] the revised Declaration of Principles on Freedom of Expression and Access to Information in Africa of 2019,[7] and the recently adopted African Continental Free Trade Area (AfCFTA) Protocol on Intellectual Property Rights of 2023.[8] Most of these instruments broadly define 'information' without necessarily specifying its various strata based on its nature and use context. Thus, this chapter discusses the perspectives of human rights in dealing with 'proprietary technological information' by situating the discourse in critically assessing the appropriate regulatory balance of IPR and human rights in accessing proprietary information. It focuses on the inherent regulatory tensions between restrictive private proprietary rights and liberal approaches advocating for public access to such information for human development.

Generally, the IPR legal system is structured to recognise and protect proprietary information and other intangible properties expressed in various formulations of creative ideas. IPR confers ownership or exclusive proprietary rights over such ideas or information, hence the term 'proprietary information'. Subject to prescribed statutory exceptions, the acquisition of IPR ownership grants statutory or contractual exclusive rights to certain classified information, such as patents, trade secrets, or copyrights.[9] However, in some cases, excessive protection of IPR coupled with the absence of clarified statutory parameters for IPR protection, particularly in cases of competing interests between owners of such information and the public rights of access, have resulted into regulatory tension as evidenced during the Covid-19 pandemic where developing and least developed countries complained against excessive patent restrictions on accessing the vaccination owned by multinational pharmaceutical companies. In contrast, the human rights regime adopts a cautious regulatory approach by striking a balance between ownership and the right of access to proprietary information.[10] As a regulatory compromise, there is a mounting drive

---

[4] Accessible at www.au.int/en/treaties/african-charter-human-and-peoples-rights.

[5] Accessible at www.achpr.au.int/en/node/873.

[6] Accessible at www.achpr.au.int/index.php/ar/node/894.

[7] Accessible at www.achpr.au.int/en/node/902.

[8] The Protocol was adopted on 19 February 2023 as per the AU's Communiqué of the 36th Ordinary Session of the Assembly of the Union (Assembly/AU/Dec.854(XXXVI), para. 14; also *The East African*, 'AU's Approval of AfCFTA Draft Protocols Paves Way for More Trade', 28 February 2023, https://www.theeastafrican.co.ke/tea/business/au-approves-afcfta-draft-protocols-4139080.

[9] Elkin-Koren and Netanel (2002).

[10] Article 27 of the UN Universal Declaration of Human Rights, 1948.

to reformulate the IPR system to capture human rights perspectives and optimise the regulatory balance between the contrasting interests of IPR holders and users of their works.[11] This regulatory tension is more evident in the ongoing debates centered on the need for calibrating the balance between private ownership rights and public right of access to such proprietary technological information.[12] Therefore, this chapter locate its discourse in the delicate regulatory tensions in balancing the right to protection or own against the right of access as briefly canvassed under article 27 of the UN Universal Declaration of Human Rights of 1948 by examining the regulatory efficacy of the IPR regime regulating access to proprietary technological information founded and inspired by human rights virtues in the context of Africa.

2 Issues for Review

The legal principles governing human rights and IPR system provides a useful platform for assessing suitable regulatory models for the protection and access regime of proprietary technological information. Under the IPR system, the legal protection framework under patents, copyrights, trade secrets, and plant breeders' rights are designed to protect such information. From its inception, the IPR system, buttressed by utilitarian theoretical construct, has been formulated and structured as an incentive regime to foster human ingenuity and creativity by conferring statutory exclusive rights on creative works and ideas.[13] The scope and rationale of IPR protection continue to evolve, influenced by both technological development and societal and public critique partly arising from widespread discontent over the perceived onerous and unjustified bias in protection, which disproportionately favours owners of proprietary information and thereby limits its contribution in achieving broader developmental impact. Consequently, the fundamental precepts governing the IPR system are mainly inclined towards facilitating private control of creative works, ideas, and information, while public access rights are peripherally captured in intellectual property statutes.

Exclusive IP rights enables owners of proprietary technological information to obtain economic and reputational gains through various transactional arrangements and attribution for their works. The public also benefit because the protection of creative ideas and information leads to discovery and introduction of new and better solutions to address various societal problems. However, one of the major concerns has been the existing asymmetrical and imbalanced relationship between the users and owners of rights, with the owners in some cases, excessively asserting rights to

[11] Mwakaje (2020), pp. 72–91.

[12] Arup and Plahe (2023); Sundaram (2018); UNDP (2014); Klug (2012); Haugen (2010), pp. 697–728.

[13] Mwakaje (2018), pp. 1–34; Adeleke (2013), pp. 83–105.

the detriment of broad public interests. Their divergent interests are contradictory based on the underlying usage motivation and objectives. Owners who are mainly driven by economic interests to recoup research and development costs are pressing for a stricter IP protection regime, while users prefer a moderate regulatory framework. Thus, tensions frequently occur when regulating access to products or technical solutions that are essential to addressing public needs given the fact that IPR protection tends to naturally limit their availability and affordability. For instance, the regulatory tension between IPR and human rights during the COVID-19 pandemic resulted in the widespread condemnation of excessive patent protection, which inhibited access to vaccination in low-income countries.[14] Similar concerns have emerged in connection with affordable access to proprietary information contained in scholarly publications,[15] as well as in the context of the negotiation imbalances in the North-South technology transfer and development agreements.[16]

This regulatory conundrum on how to balance public access rights and protection of proprietary technological information requires a re-examination of a suitable regulatory model in the context of the African Union Agenda 2023 sustainable and inclusive development. Towards this end, incorporating a human rights approach in formulating the IPR regulatory framework for access to such information could offer the needed balance that accommodate the contradictory interests of the holders and users of proprietary technological information. This chapter thus explores the extent to which human rights ramifications have or can influence the structure of IPR regimes pertaining to access to proprietary technological information to achieve broader developmental goals in the African context, taking into account the underlying specific national and regional variations.

3 Intellectual Property, Human Rights, and Development

The interface of intellectual property, human rights, and sustainable development has attracted extensive research, policymaking, as well as legal and regulatory interest. From the outset, the benchmarking of the IPR system has relied on the need to balance and accommodate public rights to access such works, as evidenced by the Venice Patent Act of 1474, which granted exclusive rights 'for a limited period of time', after which inventions would revert to the public domain. Moreover, the preamble to the Statute of Anne of 1710 states that its overriding objective is 'for the encouragement of learning', thus placing broader public interest above the private rights of authors of copyright. In huma rights terms, article 27 of the United Nations Declaration of Human Rights (UDHR) of 1948 attempts to balance the interest of the rights holders of creative works with the public's right to the

[14] Arup; Pogge et al. (2010).

[15] Makulilo (2021).

[16] Brown (2020); Lor and Britz (2005).

enjoyment of such works. In modern times, one of the major drive linking IPR and human development is the adoption of the World Intellectual Property Organization (WIPO) Development Agenda in 2007,[17] aiming to, among others, create a development-conscious IPR systems at the national, regional, and international levels. A glance at the twenty stated goals in the AU Agenda 2063 and the implementation report implicitly suggest that there is a significant linkage of the requisite interventions with IPR and human rights. Furthermore, the guiding principles under Article 4 of the AfCFTA IPR Protocol of 2023 emphasize on the need to formulate implementation strategies of IPR in Africa to facilitate access, support public interest, and for socio-economic development.

In another global twist, the adoption of the United Nations Sustainable Development Goals (SDGs) in 2015 has paved the way for a new research and policy platform for assessing and critiquing the current models and approaches related to the protection of proprietary technological information under the IPR and human rights regimes, viewed from the SDGs perspectives. Thus, the SDGs present a new policy and regulatory drive and benchmark that informs and reaffirm the interface of many human developmental aspects with human rights and IPR. Fittingly, the chosen theme for the 2024 World Intellectual Property Day was 'IP and the SDGs: Building our common future with innovation and creativity'.[18] The conceptions and conclusion on the interlinkage between access to information, IPR, and human rights and its linkages with sustainable economic development are varying and, in some cases, contradictory. Considering the underlying complexities, one could argue for a complete overhaul of the IPR system to give precedency on access to proprietary information as a matter of public interest driven by human rights considerations. Towards this end, there is a need for adopting and executing a holistic transformation to recalibrate intellectual property system in Africa to achieve sustainable development by, among others, constitutionalising IPR, innovation and technology transfer for a balanced regulatory strategy.[19] However, merely balancing regulatory regime for accessing technological proprietary information may not necessarily result into sustainable economic development for Africa. Other pertinent enabling factors such as local industrial absorption capacity, stable and visionary political leadership, and efficient market and supply chain systems must also be in place. Sadly, in many emerging economies including Africa, these vital complementary aspects are usually overlooked in the formulation of IPR laws and systems, resulting into their little developmental impact of such laws.

On the other hand, there is a persistent drive towards adopting a regulatory approach that prioritize protection of IPR as an incentive for further creativity to spur socio-economic development.[20] The argument in support is that such protection is likely to encourage and stimulate investments in research which would in turn

[17] WIPO (2007).

[18] WIPO (2024).

[19] Ncube (2016); Sihanya (2016); Feldman (2013).

[20] Kamil (2003).

result into development of better technical solution for the greater public benefits. Conversely, even though constitutionalising IPR and innovation could be an enticing regulatory proposition for creating a human-right-conscious IPR regime, it may still not resolve the existing regulatory dilemmas and predicaments at the continental level. After all, every African nation can opt for its own policy and statutory structure, which could result into regulatory heterogeneity and a lack of a common continent-wide approach, thus affecting access to proprietary information, which is one of the crucial and overriding components under SDGs 4, 7, and 9. Attempts to critically engage with the human rights approaches in the context of SDGs is steadily gaining momentum mainly focusing on the right to development and inclusivity in shaping national and regional development plans.[21] Notably, under the SDGs, UN member states are allowed to adopt the implementation approach of the SDGs by prioritising human rights in the creation of the necessary supportive conditions and legal framework for achieving them.[22]

4 Influencing IPR Judicial Approaches

In addition to policy and statutory prescriptions, facilitating public access to proprietary technological information, such as patented solutions or software, often requires court's intervention.[23] In cases of tension between owners and users of such information, courts of law have an important role in striking a regulatory balance between the necessity of protecting the underlying IPR and the gist of upholding public rights to accessing information protected by IPR for the greater public good. Towards such an end, the Courts should conscientiously and affirmatively apply human rights virtues and discourse in interpreting and enforcing domestic and international legal instruments on intellectual property. Such an interpretative orientation will give courts of law an expansive interpretation terrain for assessing the underlying broad socio-economic developmental perspectives arising from IPR protection. Integration of human rights precepts can drive courts of law to approach IPR -related disputes and access to proprietary information with a different mind-set guided by the technical intricacies of the law and broader human rights and developmental perspectives.[24]

Furthermore, human rights precepts have vital role in formulating a legal framework for the government's right to interfere with exclusive rights on technological proprietary information for broader public interests.[25] There are a few court judgements which buttresses this assertion. In *Patricia Asero and 2 Others v. Attorney*

[21] Winkler and Williams (2018).

[22] Saadoun (2024).

[23] Oloka-Onyango (2015), p. 197.

[24] Brown (2020), p. 58; Pogge (2010).

[25] Herr (2013).

General and Others,[26] the High Court of Kenya declared section 2 of the Anti-Counterfeit Act 2008 unconstitutional as it would limit access to affordable and essential HIV drugs and medicines, thereby undermining the right to life, human dignity, and health as guaranteed under the Constitution of Kenya.[27] In the European context, the cases of *Autronic v. Switzerland*[28] and *Khurshid Mustafa and Tarzibachi v. Sweden*[29] required the court to determine the interface between human rights protection and access to communication technology as provided under Article 10 (1) of the European Convention of Human Rights and as further expounded by the European Court of Human Rights. These rulings proffer a balanced model of how the law, when it incorporates human rights considerations, can serve as a tool for supporting innovation, dissemination, and, consequently, sustainable human development.

5 Analytical Framework

The regulatory conundrum arising from the quest for a balanced access regime to proprietary technological information under the IPR system to support development initiatives in Africa requires carrying out of an informed policy and regulatory inquiry. To identify policy and regulatory gaps, the analysis must balance two contrasting rationales: the quest for protecting IPR holders as an incentive for further creativity and the facilitation of public access to proprietary information as a human rights and developmental objective. The issue under investigation stems from a possible exclusion or lack of proper recognition of public interest considerations in regulating access to and the use of proprietary technological information for sustainable development.

Given the nature of the subject and issues under review, which questions the suitability of current IPR protection approaches whether it can support African development initiatives, the assessment applies a utilitarian theoretical construct and the rights discourse as a methodological guide. This exploratory model is appropriate because the current constitutional and statutory basis for IPR protection is potentially lopsided as it overly favours the holders of rights, often at the expense of the underlying public interest.[30] Thus, employing a human rights discourse and a utilitarian yardstick enables a balanced investigation of the needs and rights of both owners of technological information and the public, which stands to socially benefit from the use of such information without excessive inhibitive market costs.[31]

[26]Constitutional Petition No. 409 of 2009.

[27]Omolo (2021).

[28][22 May 1990] ECtHR, App. No. 12726/87.

[29][16 March 2009] ECtHR, App. No. 23883/06.

[30]Kothari (2004), p. 33.

[31]Ferrie and Hosie (2018), p. 7.

Moreover, the rights discourse is a comparatively viable methodological approach that can guide an effective and objective analysis of contemporary regional and international approaches to the enforcement of IPR, which is based on a conceptual orientation that largely treats intellectual property as mere commercial products.[32] This chapter, therefore, analyses the protection of proprietary technological information under the IPR system in Africa as influenced by both human rights and public interest rationales. The thrust is to identify common grounds for compromise concerning which African states or regional economic blocks may wish to remodel and repackage existing IPR policies and laws to achieve sustainable development goals while factoring in human rights virtues in regulating access to proprietary technological information.

6 Human Rights and IPR: Trends and Debates

Issues surrounding access to proprietary technological information have invariably attracted attention in IPR and human rights debates across various contexts. The preference for restricting access to such information stems from private rights considerations, whereas human rights, taking a liberal approach, tend to support public interest concerns.[33] Consequently, the interplay between these two concepts is partly attributable to their inherent 'magnetic' attraction and, in some cases, their repulsive effect. The attraction arises from a conceptual fusion that generally treats 'information' as a public good, which should presumably be freely accessible to the public.[34] Conversely, certain types of information, such as technical know-how, which are valuable proprietary institutional assets, require protection as an incentive for those who invested resources in developing it.[35] The regulatory tension between these two schools of thought is inadequately accommodated within the African IPR legal regimes. However, the discourse and concerns on these contradictory conceptual trends appear in various human rights literature, legal instruments, and fora.

Deciphering the right to enjoy the benefits of scientific progress as a human right and extemporising it within the IPR context, the United Nations Educational, Scientific and Cultural Organization (UNESCO) Booklet presents the outcome of an expert meeting held in Venice, Italy, on 16–17 July 2009,[36] which attempted to link the right of access to scientific progress and human rights. To emphasise the linkages, the term 'human rights' appeared 54 times in the UNESCO Booklet. The experts noted that the right to enjoy the benefits of scientific progress and its

[32] Mwakaje (2012).

[33] Shepherd (2015), pp. 715–726.

[34] Filippi and Vieira (2014), p. 110.

[35] Helfer (2003), p. 48.

[36] UNESCO (2009), p. 15.

applications could create tensions with the IPR regime.[37] Similarly, UNESCO recently voiced concern about the net economic gains of imposing a stronger IPR regime on the economies of southern African countries and its long-term impact on the progress of science and technology.[38] Such reservations against stronger IPR regimes should serve as a timely reminder of the need to revisit current policy and legislative structures to integrate human rights consideration in protecting technological proprietary information for sustainable and inclusive development in Africa.

In an attempt to create a balanced legal framework on access to proprietary information, the Addis Ababa Action Agenda of the Third International Conference on Financing for Development, adopted in 2015, strived to reformulate the current IPR regime to accommodate broad-based public interests.[39] The Agenda underscores the importance of adequate, balanced, and effective protection of IPR in both developed and developing countries in line with nationally defined priorities. Additionally, it seeks the recognition of voluntary patent pooling and other business models, which can enhance access to technologies and foster innovation.[40] Notably, the Addis Ababa Agenda is silent on the regulatory interface between access to the right to information, human rights, IPR, and sustainable development. Such a complex regulatory mix exposes an inextricably intriguing analogy linking human rights and access to and the use of scientific and technological information.[41] On the other hand, there is growing global emphasis and policy drive seeking to facilitate and ease access to proprietary knowledge and information as a necessary policy and regulatory compromise of the IPR system.[42]

Thus, there is divergence in the preferred approaches to how IPR principles, policies, and laws should be reconstructed to facilitate access to proprietary technological information for the African economic development. Admittedly, it may be a complicated mission to seek a global consensus on this subject; however, some concessions must be made to minimise the scope of protected IPR by recognising the human right to access proprietary technological information, particularly where developmental considerations or public interests are at stake.

[37] UNESCO (2009), p. 15.

[38] UNESCO (2015), p. 539.

[39] Declaration adopted at the Third International Conference on Financing for Development (Addis Ababa, Ethiopia, 13–16 July 2015) and was subsequently endorsed by the UN General Assembly (UN Resolution No. 69/313 of 27 July 2015).

[40] UN (2015).

[41] Marks (2014).

[42] Dinwoodie and Dreyfuss (2006), p. 220.

6.1 International Human Rights Legal Instruments

Provisions on human rights and IPR in international legal instruments attempt to strike a regulatory balance between the public right of access and the private ownership rights of proprietors of IPR. This trend is vindicated in the dialogues preceding the adoption of the UDHR of 1948.[43] The 'right of access' as a prerequisite guide in benchmarking human rights and property rights in the UDHR culminated with the inclusion of the guiding statement titled 'Right to Share in Progress' stipulating that every person has the right to full access and enjoying the technical and cultural achievements of civilisation.[44] This position was subsequently captured under Article 27 of the UDHR of 1948, which states:

1. Everyone has the right freely to participate in the cultural life of the community, to enjoy the arts and to share in scientific advancement and its benefits.
2. Everyone has the right to the protection of the moral and material interests resulting from any scientific, literary or artistic production of which [they are] the author.

Notably, this article is a two-faced provision. First, it captures the right to participate freely in scientific advancements, thus supporting public access to scientific innovations, inventions, and other creative works.[45] Second, it shifts the focus to the safeguarding of rights holders by prescribing a right to the protection of the moral and material interests resulting from any scientific, literary, or artistic production of which they are the authors.[46] Implicitly, the terms under Article 27 of the UDHR support intellectual property protection as they resonate with the framework on the protection of patents, copyright, and new plant varieties, which, apart from granting exclusive rights to owners of such creative works, the statutes have also made provision for the public's right to access and use such information in prescribed contexts and conditions.

Furthermore, expounding on the argument and jurisprudence on the interplay between access to proprietary technological information and human rights, the International Covenant on Economic, Social and Cultural Rights (ICESCR) of 1966[47] impose obligations to States Parties to recognise the right of everyone to enjoy the benefits of scientific progress and its applications and to benefit from the protection of the moral and material interests resulting from scientific, literary, or artistic production of which they are the author.[48] Hence, it states:

[43] Marks (2014), p. 871.

[44] UNESCO (1948), para 14.

[45] Article 27(1).

[46] Article 27(2).

[47] General Assembly Resolution 2200A (XXI) of 16 December 1966, entry into force 3 January 1976.

[48] Article 15(1)(b)(c).

1. The States Parties to the present Covenant recognise the right of everyone:
    a) To take part in cultural life.
    b) To enjoy the benefits of scientific progress and its applications.
    c) To benefit from the protection of the moral and material interests resulting from any scientific, literary or artistic production of which he is the author.
2. The steps to be taken by the State Parties to the present covenant to achieve the full realisation of this right shall include those necessary for the conservation, the development and the diffusion of science and culture.
3. The State Parties to the present Covenant undertake to respect the freedom indispensable for scientific research and creative activity.
4. The State Parties to the present Covenant recognise the benefits to be derived from the encouragement and development of international contacts and co-operation in the scientific and cultural fields.

Article 15 of the ICESCR enumerates three constituent 'rights to science': (1) the right to participate in science, (2) the right to benefit from science, and (3) the right to benefit from a person's own contribution or invention.[49] Other international and regional human rights instruments emerged decades later and became embedded in the public right to access scientific and technological discoveries.[50] A detailed analysis of the approach proffered by international human rights legal instruments suggests that the public right to access proprietary information is given more weight and prominence over owners' right to control and restrict access. For instance, this assertion is vindicated in Article 15 of the ICESCR, in which only one out of four subsections addresses owners' right to protection; the rest are either explicitly or implicitly in favour of the public right to access and use such inventions.

Consequently, the text and proffered IPR protection approach traceable from the typical international human rights legal instruments have triggered a conceptual collision with IPR treaties and conventions. Notably, the revered international legal instruments on IPR, such as the Berne Convention,[51] the Paris Convention,[52] and the Agreement on Trade-Related Aspects of Intellectual Property Rights (TRIPs Agreement),[53] have all attempted to cogently provide a balanced regulatory setting by recognising both the right to own and the right to access proprietary technological information. However, conceptual, institutional, and regulatory tensions still persist on how to calibrate the contrasting rationale on protection versus access to such information. In 2001, the UN High Commissioner for Human Rights opposed the

[49] Guidotti (2018), pp. 1–3.

[50] Article 6 of the UN Declaration on the Use of Scientific and Technological Progress in the Interest of Peace and for the Benefit of Mankind of 1975, UNESCO Universal Declaration on the Human Genome and Human Rights of 1997, and Article 15 of the Universal Declaration on Bioethics and Human Rights of 2005.

[51] Article 10 of the Berne Convention for the Protection of Literally and Artistic Works, 1886.

[52] Article 5 A(2) of the Paris Convention for the Protection of Industrial Property of 1883.

[53] Paras 5 and 6 to the Preamble and Article 30 of the TRIPs Agreement.

higher standards of IPR protection under the TRIPs Agreement. The High Commissioner's Report pointed out that the balance between public and private interests under Articles 15 of the ICESCR and 27 of the UDHR resonated with intellectual property law. Thus, pressed for a need for striking a regulatory balance between the competing interests of the owners and users of IPR.[54]

Recently, prospects for integrating human rights into the mainstream IPR protection system have been gaining momentum. In 2001, the WTO Ministerial Council unanimously adopted the Doha Declaration on the TRIPS Agreement and Public Health.[55] This Declaration emphasises the prioritisation of human rights and public interest considerations in framing and enforcing national patent laws, particularly in regulating access to essential medicines in low income countries. The Declaration is premised on the need to reorient the current patent system and address the policy space and flexibilities required for countries to determine their own approach in identifying and reconstructing the relationship between IPR, human rights, and access to medicines.[56] Such a stance reflects the ongoing global human rights advocacy, which critiques the existing patent legal regimes for ineptness and inequitably regulating issues of public health, access to educational materials, and environmental protection, to highlight a few. These are serious regulatory issues touching on sustainable development that require constructive engagement and dialogues at the national, continental, and international levels. The recent adoption of the WIPO Treaty on Intellectual Property, Genetic Resources and Associated Traditional Knowledge on 24 May 2024 testifies to the growing tensions between access rights and the protection of IPR.[57] It is expected that the WIPO Treaty, when fully implemented, it will have far-reaching regulatory implications on the IPR regimes, including patent disclosure requirements in case inventions use genetic resources or associated traditional knowledge and obligations to preserve treasured proprietary information currently in the custody of many local communities across the globe. For Africa, which is one of the continents with rich biodiversity and traditional knowledge, the WIPO Treaty presents an invaluable policy and regulatory platform and justification for review of IPR policies and laws to align with the proposed model on access and use of proprietary information at the disposal of local and traditional communities.

[54]ESCOR Sub. Comm. on the Promotion and Protection of Human Rights, 52nd Sess., Provisional Agenda Item 4 at 5, U.N. Doc. E/CN.4/Sub.2/2001/13 (2001).

[55]WT/MIN (01)/DEC/W/2, 14 November 2001. For an elaborate account of the Declaration, see Correa (2002) and Muredzi (2015).

[56]Abbott and Correa (2007), pp. 27–28; Pogge.

[57]WIPO (2024).

6.2 *Trends and Context in Africa*

In recent years, Africa has made significant strides in regulating access to information. The African Charter on Human and Peoples' Rights prescribes, in general terms, that everyone has the right to receive information.[58] The right to access information is further elaborated in various instruments, such as the Model Law on Access to Information for Africa adopted by the African Union in 2013, the Guidelines on Access to Information and Elections in Africa of 2017, and the revised Declaration of Principles on Freedom of Expression and Access to Information in Africa of 2019. However, the focus of all these initiatives is on information that is at the disposal of decision-making organs, mostly governments. In other words, in the ongoing continental initiatives, there is little focus on proprietary technological information and IPR. Still, some national statutes have expressly provided for the protection of proprietary information by presenting IPR as an exception to the general obligation of freely making information accessible to the public.[59] Admittedly, African countries are at different stages of creating an enabling legal framework for accessing proprietary technological information. Except for South Sudan,[60] other African countries have already enacted laws on key areas of IPR, with a few adopting national IPR policies with active enforcement frameworks.[61] The regional review reveals a gap between the regulation of proprietary technological information under the IPR system and the need for integrating human rights ideals to achieve an optimal and balanced approach for both rights holders and users. Notwithstanding the efforts and progress in formulating a responsive IPR regime, a pertinent pending question remains on the determination of the extent to which regulation of IPR, human rights, and developmental considerations are intertwined to achieve common development objectives. Akin to that is the review of how such regulatory interface is instrumental in achieving SDGs in Africa. A snapshot of the regional status on IPR and human rights in Africa is crucial in setting up a base for further discussion.

6.3 *Northern African Situation*

A significant regulatory variance exists among northern African countries regarding the policies and laws on access to proprietary information, human rights, and intellectual property protection. Cultural differences have influenced public attitudes

---

[58] Article 9.

[59] Section 37(1) of the Promotion of Access to Information Act, 2000 (Republic of South Africa), Section 27(2)(a) and (b) of the Access to Information Act, 2005 (Uganda), Section 6(2)(f) of Access to Information Act, 2016 (Tanzania), and Section 11 (1) of the Right to Information Act, 2019 (Ghana).

[60] Nzwili (2016).

[61] See Zyl (2023); Sikoyo et al. (2006).

towards IPR protection. Traditionally, the northern African region embraces collectivist cultures, which are in sharp contrast with the IPR conceptual orientation, which is based on individualistic rights. As a result, breaches of IPR in majority parts of northern Africa are not strictly viewed as serious offences.[62] These cultural differences are also compounded by differences in operating legal systems. Countries such as Algeria, Egypt, Libya, Morocco, and Tunisia have mixed legal systems that combine elements of civil law and Muslim law. Hence, there are overriding tendencies to treat as an anomaly any attempt to impose restrictions on access to proprietary information and the sharing of it thereof. In some countries such as Egypt and Morocco, there are defined systems for the registration of IPR, yet the enforcement processes largely remain inefficient and inadequate.[63]

In terms of membership in key international human rights and intellectual property legal instruments, most northern African countries are signatories to all key international human rights instruments such as the ICESCR and UDHR.[64] They are also signatories to conventions and treaties dealing with IPR protection, such as the Berne Convention,[65] the Paris Convention,[66] and the TRIPS Agreement.[67] Participation in and political commitment to the fulfilment of international IPR and human rights obligations offer a promising future and a useful platform for making a case for reconstructing the current IPR system to facilitate accessing proprietary technological information to achieve developmental goals. In some countries in northern Africa, national intellectual property legislation recognises proprietary rights to technological information subject to fair use or research exceptions in the recognition of the underlying public interest in accessing such information.[68]

Furthermore, the cultural setting in the northern Africa is, to some extent, in contrast with the fundamental precepts of the IPR system which are based on monopoly rights, thus, potentially limiting the effectiveness of enforcement. However, despite this potential cultural limitation, legislative development in both IPR and human rights is gaining momentum, signalling a promising legal foundation for repackaging IPR policies and laws related to access to proprietary technological information from a human rights perspective. Again, even with the existing limitations, the adoption of the AfCFTA IPR Protocol in February 2023 provides an important basis and starting point for the AU to develop a much-needed and long-overdue continental guidance for the regulatory transfusion of IPR and human rights to facilitate access to

---

[62] Stewart and Sandy (2017), pp. 51–58.

[63] Chaouch (2018), Aghrib et al. (2009).

[64] UN Treaty Body Database: https://tbinternet.ohchr.org/_layouts/15/treatybodyexternal/TBSearch.aspx?Lang=En&CountryID=3.

[65] WIPO database: https://wipolex.wipo.int/en/treaties/ShowResults?search_what=C&treaty_id=15.

[66] WIPO database: https://wipolex.wipo.int/en/treaties/ShowResults?search_what=C&treaty_id=2.

[67] WTO database: https://www.wto.org/english/thewto_e/whatis_e/tif_e/org6_e.htm.

[68] Article 10(1) and (6) of *Law No. 82 of 2002 on the Protection of Intellectual Property Rights* (Egypt) and Article 55 of Law No. 17-97 on the *Protection of Industrial Property* (Morocco).

proprietary technological information for inclusive and sustainable development in Africa.

6.4 Southern African Situation

Presently, the set-up for the protection of proprietary technological information in southern Africa varies from one country to another. The Republic of South Africa, for instance, have made significant strides in adopting laws and enforcement systems on IPR, whereas others in the region are relatively lagging behind.[69] Notably, all member states to the Southern African Development Community (SADC) are also members of the World Trade Organization (WTO) and WIPO and are signatories to several international conventions dealing with IPR and human rights. Furthermore, all SADC members, except for the Congo DRC, Angola, Madagascar, and South Africa, are members of the African Regional Intellectual Property Organization (ARIPO) and are, hence, operating within the ARIPO framework on IP matters.

There are several SADC and ARIPO initiatives supporting technology development and intellectual property, including developing intellectual property infrastructure for Anglophone African countries, mostly in southern Africa. Relevant protocols on intellectual property seeking to stimulate creativity also promote the development of science and technology.[70] In the SADC region, relevant legal instruments regulating access to proprietary technological information include the SADC Protocol on Science, Technology and Innovation of 2008 and the Draft Regional Intellectual Property Rights Framework and Guidelines, which became effective in 2018. The two instruments have been adopted to improve infrastructure for technological transfer in the region, which, by extension, entails facilitating access to proprietary technological information for socio-economic development in the region.[71] The SADC Guidelines and other provisions in the SADC Protocols set key regulatory and enforcement benchmarks in developing national intellectual property laws and policies for the achievement of national development objectives.[72] In addition, the SADC Strategic Plan for 2020–2030 explicates how IPR issues can be mainstreamed to achieve regional developmental goals.[73] However, there is no legal instrument either in SADC or ARIPO that explicitly addresses the regulatory and operational linkages of IPR and human rights regarding accessing and utilising proprietary technological information.

---

[69] Odek (2013); Ashukem (2017).

[70] ARIPO Protocols can be accessed at https://www.aripo.org/resources/protocols.

[71] Articles 4(h)(j) and 7.

[72] Articles 9 (d) and 24 of the *SADC Protocol on Trade*, 2000.

[73] See SADC Regional Indicative Strategic Development Plan (RISDP) of 2020–2030, p. 49.

From a human rights perspective, national constitutions, mostly of southern African countries, provide for the right of access to information.[74] Other countries have gone further by enacting specific legislation aimed to foster access to government-possessed information.[75] Yet there are no specific and concerted regional efforts geared towards attaining a defined legal regime on how best to handle issues on access to proprietary technological information in line with IPR and human rights ideals. Thus, the adoption of the AfCFTA IPR Protocol offers a useful platform for opening the dialogue for the formulation of on an appropriate regulatory approach for Africa, particularly on the coexistence and infusion of IPR and human rights to further facilitate access to proprietary technological information.

6.5 Western African Situation

In western Africa, many countries have reformed their policies and legal frameworks to prescribe access to information as one of the fundamental human rights. Yet the general trend, as vindicated by national legislation, has focused on general information, which is not necessarily embedded in proprietary rights. Liberia was the first country to enact a law on access to information (in 2010), followed by ten other countries, namely Benin, Burkina Faso, Ghana, Guinea, Ivory Coast, Mali, Niger, Nigeria, Sierra Leone, and Togo. The constitutions of these countries also provide for the right to receive information as one of the guaranteed rights.[76] Such national measures have made western Africa one of the regions with the largest number of countries with laws on access to information.[77] In fact, almost all countries in western Africa have intellectual property laws in place,[78] and are members of key international intellectual property conventions and institutions, such as WIPO and WTO.[79] At the regional level, however, there is a significant divide in the regulation of IPR, with some western African countries being under ARIPO[80] and many others belonging to the Organisation Africaine de la Propriété Intellectuelle (OAPI), a situation that could complicate the formulation of a unified regulatory approach to accessing proprietary technological information.

[74] Article 12 of the Constitution of Botswana and Article 62 of the Constitution of Zimbabwe; see also Mutula (2006), pp. 440–449.

[75] APAI (2013).

[76] Article 39(1) of the *Constitution of Nigeria* of 1999 as amended, Article 21(1)(f) of the *Constitution of Ghana*, Article 31 of the *Constitution of Niger*, and Article 18 of the *Constitution of Ivory Coast*.

[77] *West Africa: more transparency, accountability and access to information needed amidst the coronavirus pandemic*, https://www.article19.org/resources/west-africa-access-to-information.

[78] See the status of IPR law enactments at https://www.wipo.int/wipolex/en/main/legislation.

[79] Link to WTO members: https://www.wto.org/english/thewto_e/whatis_e/tif_e/org6_e.htm, WIPO Members states: https://www.wipo.int/members/en/.

[80] These countries are Cape Verde, the Gambia, Ghana, Liberia, and Sierra Leone (as of June 2023).

On the downside, western Africa presently lacks a defined and traceable protection model or framework for proprietary technological information that discernibly integrates the virtues of IPR and human rights into substantive and operational provisions. Nevertheless, several countries have adopted policies and regulatory measures consistent with human rights ideals, such as granting compulsory licensing to facilitate the production and supply of essential medicines for HIV/AIDS[81] and enacting laws for the provision of printed materials in a format accessible to the visually impaired within the framework of the Marrakesh Treaty of 2013.[82] A new regulatory dimension arises following the adoption of the AfCFTA IPR Protocol, which presents an opportunity for reconsideration of the current approaches to IPR protection by promoting a balance between access to while at the same vein, safeguarding of proprietary information.

6.6 *Eastern African Situation*

With the exception of Burundi, the national constitutions of all East African countries provide for the right to seek, receive, and impart information as a fundamental human right.[83] These constitutional provisions are further cemented by the enactment of national legislation on access to information. Uganda was the first East African country to enact a law on access to information in 2005, followed by Rwanda and South Sudan in 2013.[84] In 2016, Kenya[85] and Tanzania[86] followed suit by enacting laws on access to information. Paradoxically, legislation on access to information in all these countries contains a provision seeking to limit the disclosure of certain information under specified circumstances. Under the laws of Kenya and Tanzania, one of the limiting criteria relates to the disclosure of information that could infringe upon the IPR of the holder of such information or substantially prejudice the commercial interests, including IPR, of that entity or a third party from whom information was obtained.[87] Under the law of Uganda, the information officer may refuse to disclose information if, in his or her opinion, it may prejudice the *property* rights and safety of the beholder.[88] The term ‘property’ in this statutory setting also covers IPR. Similarly, the law of the Republic of South Sudan

[81] Owoeye (2014), pp. 214–219.

[82] See the status of ratification at https://www.wipo.int/wipolex/en/treaties/ShowResults?search_what=C&treaty_id=843.

[83] CIPESA (2015).

[84] CIPESA (2017).

[85] Access to Information Act No. 31 of 2016.

[86] The Access to Information Act No. 6 of 2016.

[87] Section 6(1) of the law of Kenya and section 6(2)(f) of the Law of Tanzania.

[88] Section 29(b)(i)(cc).

restricts access to information of a commercial and confidential nature.[89] These national laws on access to information offer useful insight into the regulatory connection and interplay between issues on IPR, human rights, and access to proprietary technological information development.

At the regional level, instruments establishing the East African Community (EAC) recognise the fundamentality of science and technology in fostering regional economic development.[90] Moreover, there is presently an undertaking aimed at promoting co-operation in science and technology development in the EAC through the exchange of scientific information and personnel, the promotion and publication of research and scientific findings, and the harmonisation of policies on the commercialisation of technologies and the promotion and protection of IPR.[91] In terms of commitment to protecting human rights and IPR, all the EAC partner states subscribe to international human rights conventions and are members of both the WTO and WIPO.[92]

Furthermore, there is growing legal jurisprudence regarding the interpretation of IPR provisions in line with the dictates of human rights. As already highlighted, in 2009, the High Court of Kenya delivered a landmark interventionist judgment on the interplay between IPR and human rights in a case involving the parallel importation of generic antiviral drugs for those affected by HIV/AIDS. The court noted that even though issues on IPR focused on pharmaceutical products, the operational effect of intellectual property protection inhibiting the availability of such drugs to affected individuals touches on the fundamental right to life guaranteed under the Constitution of Kenya. The court emphatically stated that human rights considerations should be prioritised and placed above the private rights of the owners of IPR in such pharmaceutical products.[93] Other court cases have used the human rights yardstick to address issues on exceptions to copyright protection in matters of public interests.[94] Arguably, the legal and institutional foundation is in place in most eastern African countries for the infusion of human rights and IPR in regulating access to proprietary technological information.

[89] Right of Access to Information Act, No. 65 of 2013, sections 25–33.

[90] See Article 80 of the Treaty Establishing the East African Community (EAC).

[91] See Article 103 of the Treaty Establishing the East African Community.

[92] WTO (2002).

[93] See Patricia's case.

[94] *Communications Commission of Kenya & 5 Others v Royal Media Services Limited & 5 Others* [2014] eKLR. For an extensive discussion on the jurisprudence of this case, see Nzomo (2016), p. 53.

7 Protection of Information as IPR

The legal system of IPR deals with the protection of intangible property most of which exist in the form of expressions or written information, which are retrievable electronically or physically. Technical or proprietary information can benefit from the IPR protection system using various statutory mechanisms and models, depending on the nature of the relevant information and the operating legal framework.[95] For instance, inventive technological information is protectable under the patent system,[96] whereas technical information which qualifies as literary work under computer programs and is protectable under copyright.[97] Trade secrets are another legal mechanism for the protection of proprietary information. The rationale for protecting such information is based on the need to encourage creativity under a reward system for inventors and authors by granting exclusive rights for a limited period of time. Such exclusive rights give owners a business or economic opportunity to recoup the investments and other resources expended in developing such useful ideas.

Ultimately, the underlying objective of IPR protection is to prevent others from deceitfully profiting from the creative endeavours of others with impunity. A generally upheld view is that the public stands to benefit from such protection by ensuring a continuous thread of innovation and creation of better solutions to the problems facing the society through the built-in incentive framework. Hence, in that respect, a connection between IPR, human rights, and development is drawn. Conceptually, the scope of protection under the IPR system is not absolute because there are statutory exceptions that prescribe scenarios allowing the public to freely access and use such proprietary technological information to strike a regulatory balance between the interests of the holders and users of IPR.[98] Arguably, the justification for the inclusion of IPR exceptions in the statutes is strongly rooted in human rights considerations as stipulated under Article 27 of the UDHR. It is essential for policy and law-makers to appreciate the operational connection of IPR protection and human rights in the ongoing efforts and national initiatives for the implementation of the SDGs.

8 Interface Between IPR and Human Rights

Apparently, the statutory exceptions to the general protection of IPR hint at the inextricable linkage between IPR and human rights. All key international human rights legal instruments have either expressly and impliedly recognised IPR aspects.

---

[95] Lor and Britz (2005).

[96] Article 1(1) of the TRIPs Agreement.

[97] See Article 10 of the TRIPs Agreement.

[98] Oozeer (2014), pp. 719–722.

In fact, as previously alluded, some provisions in the UDHR of 1948, the International Covenant on Civil and Political Rights (ICCPR) of 1966, and the ICESCR of 1966 have a direct bearing on the protection of IPR. The two key facets under which the subject of IPR connects with human rights are (1) the basic framework for recognising property rights as an inherent human right and (2) the public interest dimensions that necessitate considering a balanced approach to IPR protection to facilitate access.[99] These two parameters are appreciable in the structure of the international instruments on human rights and IPR as well.

8.1 *Proprietary Rights as Human Rights*

Proprietary or property rights constitute one of the fundamental human rights under the human rights framework.[100] The UDHR specifies the proprietary rights arising from scientific, literary, or artistic productions. Those three components relate to IPR works, which are protected as patents, copyrights, or trademarks. In this regard, Article 27(2) of the UDHR states: 'Everyone has the right to the protection of the moral and material interests resulting from any scientific, literary or artistic production of which he is the author.' This provision constitutes a plausible convergence point between IPR and human rights; therefore, it should serve as a basis for formulating national and regional laws on IPR guided by human rights principles. With reference to 'moral and material interests', UDHR provisions support the current structural basis of the copyright system for the protection of moral and economic rights. The ICESCR recognises the right of an author to 'benefit from the protection of the moral and material interests resulting from any scientific, literary or artistic production'.[101] The recognition of the author's rights under the UDHR is complemented by the proclamation of his general right to own property and the prohibition on the arbitrary deprivation of his property.[102] The implication of prohibiting the arbitrary taking of property suggests that while states have a right to regulate property rights, including IPR, they must do so in accordance with due process of law. In terms of SDGs, the legal assurance of the right to own and the protection of property is a pertinent observation and has a pivotal bearing on the fight against poverty. In the same vein, the protection of private property against unlawful deprivation extends to all forms of property, including intangible ones, like intellectual property. Thus, human rights considerations are vital in strengthening and balancing the IPR protection regime in order to factor in human welfare and development.

---

[99] Forsyth (2016).

[100] Article 27(2) of the UDHR.

[101] Article 15(1)(c).

[102] Article 17(1)(2).

Apparently, the national constitutions of many countries in Africa have established the right to own property as a fundamental human right.[103] Implicitly, a solid foundation for the protection of IPR, fused with a human rights perspective, already exists and should arguably be used to inform the necessary review of IPR policies and laws to attain various developmental objectives.

8.2 *Right of Public Access—A Balancing Act*

Over the years, national statutory frameworks have adopted a counter-balancing approach under which the IPR protection is treated as an offset of the public right to accessing and utilisation in certain specified instances as a measure adopted in response to growing public disillusion of excessive outreach of IPR protection.[104] As stated earlier, the UDHR provides for the right to enjoy the creative works of others by positing that everyone has 'the right to freely participate in the cultural life of the community, *to enjoy* the arts and to share in scientific advancement and its benefits'.[105] Implicitly, the implementation of this provision entails the formulation of balanced policies and laws for the protection of proprietary technological information, focusing on facilitating public access in cases where there is overriding public interest and pressing developmental needs. In this regard, the IPR legal framework ought to conscientiously accommodate the public right of access, subject to reasonable statutory restrictions. These contrasting objectives have created a never-ending debate on the appropriate scope of regulatory concessions on the right to access proprietary information under IPR law.

Driven by human rights considerations, IPR policies and laws have been diversely structured to achieve two important regulatory objectives: (1) to accommodate the protection of proprietary information as a private right to incentivize owners and (2), in appropriate cases, to facilitate access to such information for the broader public interest. These two contrasting objectives resonate with issues touching on IPR and human rights. Yet the unresolved paradox remains on the unclarified parameters regarding which of the two rights should take precedence over the other in the formulation of national IPR policies and laws.[106] The debate on the *coexistence* and *intersection* of human rights and intellectual property is likely to continue for many years, given the inherent theoretical and doctrinal divide regarding the fundamental tenets of their underlying systems. Arguably, the tension between these two competing frameworks can result in four distinct consequences: (1) an increased motivation to develop soft law human rights norms, (2) the treatment of consumers

---

[103] Article 24 of the Constitution of the United Republic of Tanzania, Article 40 of the Constitution of Kenya, Article 43 of the Constitution of Nigeria, and Article 16 of the Constitution of Namibia.

[104] Mwakaje (2012), p. 85.

[105] Article 27(1).

[106] Darch (2013).

of intellectual property products as holders of guaranteed right to access proprietary information, (3) the provision of a guidance regarding 'maximum standards' of intellectual property protection as a means to curb the potential overreaching effect of IPR, and (4) a new way of developing human rights norms in established intellectual property lawmaking venues, such as WIPO and the WTO.[107] These four dimensions are vital in reformulating IPR laws in Africa to create a balanced legal regime on access to proprietary technological information to achieve developmental goals.

9 Policy and Regulatory Issues

Within the IPR protection spectrum, there is a growing policy and regulatory space that can help many African countries to achieve the IPR objectives benchmarked on human rights and development by facilitating access to proprietary technological information. These policy and regulatory options are traceable to international and local legal instruments for protecting IPR. The Berne Convention provides for the fair use of and public access to proprietary information protected under copyright.[108] The TRIPs Agreement specifically provides for compulsory patent licensing to address problems of public magnitude as well as the free use of patent information for research and educational purposes.[109] In addition, a number of global initiatives under the WTO,[110] WIPO, UNESCO, and World Health Organization (WHO)[111] aim to facilitate broader access to proprietary information as part of public policy objectives. It is thus argued that within these international legal and institutional structures, African countries can find a necessary framework to adopt model legal instruments for reorienting the existing IPR policies and laws for achieving public policy objectives by facilitating access to proprietary technological information in line with human rights tenets and the SDGs.

9.1 Access Rights vs Public Interest

One of the major policy paradoxes in regulating the ownership and use of proprietary technological information is formulating an appropriate and balanced framework that can facilitate public access while providing requisite protection as incentives to

[107] Helfer (2003), p. 57.

[108] Appendix to the *Berne Convention for the Protection of Literary and Artistic Works*, which provides a grace period for developing countries for certain concessions on copyright protection.

[109] Article 5.

[110] The Doha Declaration on Public Health and Access to Essential Medicines, 2001.

[111] WHO (2011).

owners of such information. In this regard, human rights principles and instruments present a useful guiding benchmark since it captures and seeks to harmoniously accommodate the two contrasting objectives.[112] As previously argued, IPR laws and policies must recognise the inherently contrasting interests between the users and owners of proprietary technological information. Most significantly, the interest of each group should be an integral part of the fundamental public policy objective with equal weight in framing policies and laws. Once this dimension is taken on board, a consensus can be reached without much public and regulatory tension.

The extent of concession may also depend on the specific type of proprietary information and its corresponding public use. To illustrate the case, the immense public policy drive has forced developed countries to concede and allow patent information on pharmaceutical inventions to be freely accessible for use by local industries in least-developed countries to facilitate mass production and enhance public access to essential medicines. Recent examples can be drawn from pandemics and other diseases, such as HIV/AIDs,[113] Covid-19,[114] and others mostly endemic to low-income countries.[115] African countries such as Mozambique, Zambia, and Zimbabwe have already applied compulsory licensing provisions in dealing with HIV/AIDS.[116]

9.2 *Utilisation of Patent Flexibilities*

Flexibilities in IPR systems refer to the policy and regulatory space afforded to governments in executing their intellectual property obligations based on the needs and conditions obtaining in their respective jurisdictions.[117] The objective of these flexibilities is to allow countries to structure their IP policies and laws to safeguard their national interests and achieve the much-needed socio-economic development. Admittedly, the effective use of IPR flexibilities can create a platform for integrating human rights ideals into the existing IPR regimes in Africa regarding the access and use of proprietary technological information.[118] Also, the effective use of IPR flexibilities helps create the public acceptance of IPR laws, particularly in cases where the waiver of IPR is secured to abate a monumental public threat or problem. Infusing human rights principles in IPR can ensure the availability of the requisite balance between the right of access and the right to use proprietary technological

[112] Adeleke (2013), p. 89.

[113] WTO (2002).

[114] Recent development at the WTO: https://www.wto.org/english/tratop_e/trips_e/trips_and_covid19_e.htm.

[115] Dovlo (2020), p. 53.

[116] WHO (2014), p. 4.

[117] Article 6 and the Preamble to the TRIPs Agreement.

[118] Adusei (2011), pp. 1–20.

information. Thus, the negotiation of the annexes to the AfCFTA IPR Protocol should consider the available IPR flexibilities to create an IPR regime in Africa that is conscious of broad-based public interests and the developmental goals as reflected under the SDGs.

9.3 IPR Problem as a Human Right

Even though the right to science and culture features in various human rights instruments, such as the UDHR and the ICESCR, treating IPR as a purely human right concept creates its own conceptual and operational drawbacks. Conceptually, human rights are predicated on fundamental tenets, which treat them as inherent and inalienable rights. In contrast, IPR does not have either of those two elements because (1) they are statute-created rights and (2) they are protected for a limited time and may be revoked to revert to the public domain under specified statutory conditions. Yet there are several angles from which the conceptual setting and application of intellectual property mirror human rights ethos.

Copyright, for instance, requires national policies and laws to respect and protect the moral and material interests of authors resulting from artistic or literary productions, which also constitute a human rights theme.[119] In addition, the automatic protection of copyright echoes the concept of inherency of rights under human rights.[120] Invariably, the protection of human rights is not often absolute because of the inherent public interest inhibitions. Similarly, the rights of IPR holders can be waived on public interest grounds, such as fair use,[121] compulsory licensing, and other exceptions under patents.[122]

Therefore, a proper restructuring of IPR policies and associated legislation along the lines of human rights considerations in Africa requires a conversation on critical and informed appreciation of the nature and context in which the two conceptual orientations operate.[123] The adoption of the AfCFTA IPR Protocol, which will be followed by an extensive negotiation of the annexes to the Protocol, with the principal aim of addressing specific substantive issues on IPR, offers a useful platform for Africa to repackage the current IPR protection approaches by integrating human rights virtues into the IPR protection boundaries, thus bolstering access to proprietary technological information for development purposes.[124]

---

[119] See UN General Assembly, *Report of the Special Rapporteur in the field of cultural rights, copyright policy and the right to science and culture*, A/HRC/28/57, p. 7.

[120] Article 5(2) of the Berne Convention for the Protection of Artistic and Literally Works.

[121] *Ibid.* Article 10.

[122] Article 12(3)(b)(c) of the AfCFTA IPR Protocol and Articles 30 and 31 of the TRIPs Agreement.

[123] Golder (2021), pp. 32–35.

[124] Ncube (2022), p. 108.

10 Conclusion

The protection of proprietary technological information in line with human rights and IPR could continue to present a controversial policy and regulatory dialogue. African countries need to carefully and clearly delineate the benchmarks in shaping the jurisprudence on intellectual property and human rights, having the broader public interest and national development concerns in mind. The interwovenness of the nature of IPR and human rights necessitates a wholesome review of national IPR policies and laws to address the pressing continental needs pertaining to affordable public access to educational materials,[125] essential medicines,[126] and other useful technologies for environmental protection. As such, there is an overriding need for a well-thought and balanced approach to accommodating the competing interests of the holders and users of IPR. Admittedly, striking an optimal regulatory balance can be an audacious attempt because of the inherent rivalrous interests of the two sides of the equation.[127] Yet, under upcomming negotiations on the annexes to the AfCFTA IPR Protocol, there is tenable hope. Overall, this chapter has articulated Africa's need to develop model guidelines on how the intersection of IPR and human rights can be effectively integrated to facilitate orderly access to proprietary technological information as an integral part of the goal to achieve the SDGs. In this regard, African countries can build on the foundation laid down thus far within the IPR flexibilities and human rights instruments. Ultimately, the proposed approach can serve as a basis for further policy and regulatory review aimed at reconstructing the current IPR regime by clothing it with a human rights outlook to achieve developmental objectives.

References

Abbott FM, Correa CM (2007) World Trade Organization Accession Agreements: intellectual property issues. Global Economic Issues Publication, Geneva, Quaker United Nations Office

Adeleke F (2013) Constitutional domestication of the right of access to information in Africa: retrospect and prospects. In: Diallo F, Calland R (eds) Access to information in Africa: law, culture, and practice. Brill, Netherlands

Adusei P (2011) Exploiting patent regulatory "flexibilities" to promote access to antiretroviral medicines in Sub-Saharan Africa. J World Intellect Prop 14(1):1–20

Aghrib S, El-Moujaddidi N, El Ouazzani A (2009) ACA2K Country Report - Morocco (African Copyright and Access to Knowledge Project). https://idl-bnc-idrc.dspacedirect.org/bitstream/handle/10625/39725/128561.pdf?sequence=1

APAI (2013) Access to information in Africa: examining progress since APAI Declaration

Arup C, Plahe J (2023) Patents and other conditions of access to vaccines. J World Intellect Prop 26: 41–62. https://doi.org/10.1111/jwip.1225

[125] Mwakaje (2021), pp. 215–238.

[126] Morris (2022).

[127] Shyllon (2018).

Ashukem JCN (2017) A comparative analysis of the right to access to environmental information in South Africa and Uganda. South Afr J Hum Rights 33(3):452–471

Brown AEL (2020) Access to essential technologies: the role of the interface between intellectual property, competition and human rights. Int Rev Law Comput Technol 24(1):51–61. https://doi.org/10.1080/13600860903570178

Chaouch K (2018) Digital copyright issues in Moroccan Scientific Research and Higher Education: the need for up-to-date legislation, WTO-WIPO Colloquium of Teachers of Intellectual Property 2018. https://www.wto.org/english/tratop_e/trips_e/colloquium_papers_e/2018_african/chapter_15_2018_african_edition_e.pdf

Chiumbu SH (2006) Communications and global intellectual property rights: ICTs and development in Africa. Crit Arts 20(1):83–95. https://doi.org/10.1080/02560040608557778

CIPESA (2015) The state of right to information in East Africa. CIPESA ICT Policy Briefing Series No. 05/15. https://cipesa.org/?wpfb_dl=198

CIPESA (2017) Position paper: comparative analysis of access to information legislation in East Africa. https://cipesa.org/?wpfb_dl=245

Correa CM (2002) Implications of the Doha Declaration on the TRIPs Agreement and Public Health. World Health Organization (WHO) Publications, Geneva

Darch C (2013) The problem of access to information in African jurisdictions: constitutionalism, citizenship. In: Diallo F, Calland R (eds) Access to information in Africa: law, culture, and practice. Brill, Netherlands

Dinwoodie GB, Dreyfuss RC (2006) Patenting science: protecting the domain of accessible knowledge. In: Guibault L, Hugenholtz PB (eds) The future of the public domain: identifying the commons in information law. Kluwer Law International, The Netherlands

Dovlo D (2020) People and their health systems: the right to universal health coverage and the SDGs in Africa. In: Kaltenborn et al (eds) Sustainable development goals and human rights. Interdisciplinary Studies in Human Rights, vol 5. Springer Nature, Switzerland AG

Elkin-Koren N, Netanel NW (eds) (2002) The commodification of information. Kluwer Law International, The Hague

Feldman R (2013) Intellectual property wrongs. Stanford J Law Bus Finance 18:250

Ferrie J, Hosie A (2018) Methodological challenges in developing an evidence base and realising rights. Int J Hum Rights 22(1):5–21

Filippi P, Vieira MS (2014) The commodification of information commons: the case of cloud computing. Columbia Sci Technol Law Rev 16:102–143

Forsyth M (2016) Making the case for a pluralistic approach to intellectual property regulation in developing countries. Queen Mary J Intellect Prop 6(1):3–26

Golder B (2021) The morals of the market: human rights and the rise of neoliberalism. Contemp Polit Theory 20:32–35

Gopal RJR et al (2011) Information mining - reflections on recent advancements and the road ahead in data, text, and media mining. Decis Support Syst 51(4):727–731

Guidotti TL (2018) Scientific freedom and human rights. Arch Environ Occup Health 73(4):1–3. https://doi.org/10.1080/19338244.2017.1364522

Haugen HM (2010) Access versus incentives: analyzing intellectual property policies in four UN specialized agencies by emphasizing the role of the world intellectual property organization and human rights. J World Intellect Prop 13(6):697–728

Helfer LR (2003) Human rights and intellectual property: conflict or coexistence? Minn Intellect Prop Rev 5:47–61

Herr RE (2013) Can human rights law support access to communication technology? A case study under Article 10 of the right to receive information. Inf CommunTechnol Law 22(1):1–13

Kaltenborn et al (2020) Sustainable development goals and human rights. Interdisciplinary Studies in Human Rights, vol 5. Springer Nature, Switzerland AG

Kamil I (2003) Intellectual property- a power tool for economic growth. Geneva, WIPO Publication No. 888

Klug H (2012) Access to medicines and the transformation of the South African State: exploring the interactions of legal and policy changes in health, intellectual property, trade, and competition law in the context of South Africa's HIV/ AIDS pandemic. LSI 37:297

Kothari CR (2004) Research methodology: methods and techniques. New Age International (P) Limited, New Delhi
Lor PJ, Britz J (2005) Knowledge production from an African perspective: international information flows and intellectual property. Int Inf Libr Rev 37(2):61–76
Makulilo AB (2021) Between “free use” and denial of access: a critical analysis of the copyright licensing scheme for scholarly materials in higher education in Tanzania. Afr Rev 48(1): 196–214
Marks SP (2014) Human rights and the challenges of science and technology. Science and engineering ethics. Springer
Martin WJ (1988) The information society - idea or entity? ASLIB Proc 40:11–12
Morris PS (2022) Patents, human rights, and access to medicines. Hum Rights Law Rev 22(4). https://doi.org/10.1093/hrlr/ngac029
Muredzi P (2015) Intellectual property, public health, biotechnological inventions and food security. Masters in Intellectual Property (MIP) Book, Mutare, Africa University
Mutula SM (2006) Freedom of information in the SADC region: implications for development and human rights. Libr Rev 55(7):440–449
Mwakaje SJ (2012) Regulatory framework of intellectual property products: the case of university research and patents law in Tanzania. PhD Thesis, University of Dar es Salaam, Tanzania
Mwakaje SJ (2018) Fair use under copyright law: theoretical basis and enforcement approaches in selected East Africa States. East Afr Law Rev 45(2):1–34
Mwakaje SJ (2020) Access to educational publications and the copyright law in Tanzania: revisiting the underlying opposing interests. J Educ Humanit Sci 9(1):72–91
Mwakaje SJ (2021) Accession by Tanzania to the Marrakesh Treaty on access to publications for visually impaired persons: policy and legal implications. Afr Rev 48(1):215–238
Ncube CB (2016) Decolonising intellectual property law in pursuit of Africa’s development. WIPO J 8(1):34–40
Ncube CB (2022) Intellectual property and the African Continental Free Trade Area: lessons and recommendations for the IP Protocol. J Int Trade Law Policy 21(2):105–121. https://doi.org/10.1108/JITLP-09-2021/-0051
Nzomo VB (2016) In the public interest: how Kenya quietly shifted from fair dealing to fair use. WIPO-WTO Colloquium Papers, pp 49–57. https://www.wto.org/english/tratop_e/trips_e/colloquium_publication_e.htm
Nzwili F (2016) As South Sudan joins East African Community, some experts worry over its IP laws. IP Watch. https://www.ip-watch.org/2016/03/08/as-south-sudan-joins-east-african-community-some-experts-worry-over-its-ip-laws/
Odek JO (2013) Situational analysis of legal and policy framework for intellectual property rights in EAC, SADC and COMESA
Oloka-Onyango J (2015) Using courts of law to tackle poverty and social exclusion: the case of post-2010 Kenya. Law Democr Dev 19:193–210. https://www.saflii.org/za/journals/LDD/2015/12.pdf
Omolo J (2021) Rethinking Patricia Asero Ochieng and Two Others v. The Attorney General and Another. J Intellect Prop Inf Technol Law 1(1):115–130
Oozeer A (2014) Information technology and intellectual property law. Commonwealth Law Bull 40(4):719–722
Owoeye OA (2014) Compulsory patent licensing and local drug manufacturing capacity in Africa. Bull World Health Organ 92(3):214–219
Pogge T, Rimmer M, Rubenstein K (2010) Incentives for global public health: patent law and access to essential medicines. Cambridge University Press, Cambridge
Saadoun S (2024) A human rights economy is key to sustainable development - ‘pact for the future’ opportunity for meaningful reforms. https://www.hrw.org/news/2024/01/17/human-rights-economy-key-sustainable-development
Shepherd E (2015) Freedom of information, right to access information, open data: who is at the table? Round Table 104(6):715–726
Shyllon O (ed) (2018) The model law on access to information for Africa and other regional instruments: soft law and human rights in Africa. Pretoria University Law Press, Pretoria

Sigurdson J (1993) Global companies as generators and controllers of knowledge: the new challenge for developing countries. In: Brundenius C, Goransson B (eds) New technologies and global restructuring: the Third World at a crossroads. Taylor Graham, London
Sihanya B (2016) Intellectual property and innovation law in Kenya and Africa: transferring technology for sustainable development. Sihanya Mentoring & Innovative Lawyering, Nairobi
Sikoyo GM, Nyukuri E, Wakhungu JW (2006) Intellectual property protection in Africa: status of laws, research and policy analysis in Ghana, Kenya, Nigeria, South Africa and Uganda, Nairobi. African Centre for Technology Studies (ACTS)
Stewart KN, Sandy HM (2017) North Africa: implications for information creation and access. Int Inf Libr Rev 49(1):51–58
Sundaram J (2018) Pharmaceutical patent protection and world trade law: the unresolved problem of access to medicines. Routledge, Taylor and Francis Group
UN General Assembly, Report of the Special Rapporteur in the field of cultural rights, Copyright policy and the right to science and culture, A/HRC/28/57
UNDP (2014) Using competition law to promote access to medical technologies: a guidebook for low- and middle-income countries. United Nations Development Programme. www.undp.org/publications/using-competition-law-promote-access-medicine-0
UNESCO (1948) Human Rights: Comments and interpretations - Grounds of an International Declaration of Human Rights. UNESCO/PHS/3/rev
UNESCO (2009) The right to enjoy the benefits of scientific progress and its applications. UNESCO, Paris
UNESCO (2015) UNESCO Science Report: Towards 2030. Place de Fonteno, p 539
Vadi V (2008) Sapere Aude! Access to knowledge as a human right and a key instrument of development. Int J Commun Law Policy 12:345–368
Webster F (2002) What information society? In: Alberts DS, Papp DS (eds) The information age: an anthology of its impacts and consequences. National Defence University, Washington D.C.
WHO (2011) Global strategy and plan of action on public health, innovation and intellectual property. World Health Organization, Paris. https://apps.who.int/gb/ebwha/pdf_files/EB148/B148_10-en.pdf
WHO (2014) Access to affordable medicines for HIV/AIDS and hepatitis: the intellectual property rights context. WHO Publication, New Delhi
Winkler I, Williams C (eds) (2018) The sustainable development goals and human rights: a critical early review. Routledge Taylor and Francis Group
WIPO (2007) Development Agenda for WIPO. https://www.wipo.int/ip-development/en/agenda/
WIPO (2024) Sustainable Development Goals and Intellectual Property. https://www.wipo.int/sdgs/en/
WTO (2002) The Doha Declaration on TRIPs Agreement and Public Health. WT/MIN (01)/DEC/2
Zeng F et al (2020) The role of information systems in the sustainable development of enterprises: a systematic literature network analysis. Sustainability 12(8):3337. https://doi.org/10.3390/su12083337
Zyl C (2023) Intellectual property protection in Sub-Saharan Africa: progress and challenges. https://www.dennemeyer.com/ip-blog/news/intellectual-property-protection-in-sub-saharan-africa-progress-and-challenges/

Saudin Jacob Mwakaje Associate Professor, University of Dar es Salaam School of Law; Partner and Advocate at NexLaw Advocates.

A Bundle of Belongings Isn't the Only Thing a Refugee Brings to His/Her New Country

A Rights-Based Response to COVID-19 in South Africa

Vimbai Chibango

1 Introduction

The chapter focuses on assessing how the South African systems implemented or failed to realise the rights of refugees and asylum seekers during the course of the pandemic. Refugees and asylum seekers, like any other immigrants, also contribute to the economic development of their host country, hence the need for them to be supported in their economic endeavours. The title of this chapter—*A Bundle of Belongings Isn't the Only Thing a Refugee Brings to His New Country*—is a quote from a renowned author and scholar, Albert Einstein, who was a German-born theoretical physicist and Nobel Laureate. Forced from his home, Einstein sought refuge in the United States and settled in Princeton, NJ. As there were no programmes or aid agencies to ensure the safety of fellow refugees, Einstein took matters into his own hands. He and his wife made visa applications for other German Jews and personally vouched for refugees fleeing the Nazi rule.[1] The implication of this famous quote from Einstein is that refugees should not be considered a burden in their country of arrival because they possess important skills and expertise, and if given an opportunity, they can make massive contributions towards the economic growth of their new country. It is in the interest of this chapter to share reflections on how South Africa has dealt with the plight of refugees and asylum seekers in terms of social relief initiatives during the COVID-19 pandemic.

This chapter is divided into various sections. I will define the terms that are central to migration and how migration is viewed from a human rights perspective. Then an overview of the contribution of refugees to economic development is provided. The

[1] For a full explanation, see Einstein (2017).

V. Chibango (✉)
Durban University of Technology, Durban, South Africa

I. Kajiru et al. (eds.), *Economic Development and Human Rights in Contemporary Sub-Saharan Africa*, Ius Gentium: Comparative Perspectives on Law and Justice 122, https://doi.org/10.1007/978-3-031-81400-6_6

next section is an analysis of South Africa's policy and practices in its response to the challenges of vulnerable migrants in line with its COVID-19 relief services. The vulnerabilities encountered by refugees and asylum seekers in the face of COVID-19 are also discussed. The chapter also highlights the contributions made by refugees to the welfare of their communities in the midst of the pandemic. The chapter further provides examples of how other countries have dealt with the plight of refugees during the pandemic and concludes by giving a few recommendations on how South Africa can try and accommodate the needs of refugees in the midst of such a catastrophe.

2 Migration Terms

There are two major types of migration: internal and international. Internal migration is the movement of people across provinces and cities within a country, while international migration is the movement of people from their country of origin across borders to their destination country. However, the International Organization for Migration (IOM) also states that there is no universally agreed definition of what a migrant is, but its definition of a migrant does concur with the common understanding of migration. The IOM defines a migrant as

> An umbrella term, not defined under international law, reflecting the common lay understanding of a person who moves away from his or her place of usual residence, whether within a country or across an international border, temporarily or permanently, and for a variety of reasons. The term includes a number of well-defined legal categories of people, such as migrant workers; persons whose particular types of movements are legally-defined, such as smuggled migrants; as well as those whose status or means of movement are not specifically defined under international law, such as international students.[2]

The focus of this chapter is international migration, where migrants cross national boundaries due to various push factors. Although refugee migrants are central to this chapter, it is essential to provide an overview of international migration in terms of its current types.

Previous studies organise migration into different categories. The most common is labour migration, which is also known as economic migration, forced or asylum migration, international retirement migration, chain migration, environmental migration and return migration.[3,4] The interest of this chapter is forced or asylum migration as it is the category within which refugees belong. Forced migration comprises refugees and asylum seekers, who leave their country to seek protection in other countries due to conflicts, civil wars and political unrest in their home country.[5]

---

[2] See International Organisation for Migration (2020), n.p.

[3] Bell et al. (2010), pp. 1–49.

[4] See Jennissen (2004).

[5] Wickramasinghe and Wimalaratana (2016), pp. 13–32.

The United Nations High Commissioner for Refugees (UNHCR) defines a refugee as 'people who have fled war, violence, conflict or persecution and have crossed an international border to find safety in another country'.[6] Another definition that is even clearer is given by the Refugee Convention and Protocol of 1951, which states that a refugee is one who

> ...Owing to well-founded fear of being persecuted for reasons of race, religion, nationality, membership of a particular social group or political opinion, is outside the country of his nationality and is unable or, owing to such fear, is unwilling to avail himself of the protection of that country; or who, not having a nationality and being outside the country of his former habitual residence as a result of such events, is unable or, owing to such fear, is unwilling to return to it.[7]

The above definition is important as it provides guidance on who is to be considered a refugee and who is eligible for protection according to the United Nations' mandate. It is also important to note that for the purpose of this study, the term 'refugees' will apply not only to individuals who have obtained a refugee status but also to those in the process of requesting a refugee status, also known as asylum seekers. The IOM defines an asylum seeker as

> An individual who is seeking international protection. In countries with individualized procedures, an asylum seeker is someone whose claim has not yet been finally decided on by the country in which he or she has submitted it. Not every asylum seeker will ultimately be recognized as a refugee, but every recognized refugee is initially an asylum seeker.[8]

An asylum seeker is therefore entitled to an asylum seeker permit, which is provided in accordance with section 22 of the Refugees Act.[9] This allows them a legal right to live in South Africa, but this does not give them the right to work or study until their refugee status is granted.[10] For the purpose of this study, refugees and asylum seekers will be considered inclusively in the review of how South Africa has handled the plight of these groups of migrants because their historical narratives and contexts are usually similar, with the exception that one group has a refugee status while the other has not.

Unlike other international migrant workers, who, due to the poor economic status of their country, migrate to look for better jobs and livelihoods in other countries,[11] refugees are often at high risk because they are exposed to myriads of risks and vulnerabilities as they pass through states, provinces and borders to their country of destination. Studies have recorded some challenges, which include human

---

[6]UNCHR (2010).

[7]See UNCHR (2010).

[8]See International Organisation for Migration (2020).

[9]See Dalton-Greyling and Auckland Park Campus (2008).

[10]See again Dalton-Greyling and Auckland Park Campus (2008).

[11]Individuals who often leave their country due to economic reasons, such as employment, are also known as migrant workers or economic refugees.

trafficking[12] and the lack of protection against crimes.[13] Also, the definition from the Convention and Protocol of 1951[14] clearly shows that refugees may not be able to return to their home country for fear of persecution or violence.

3 Legislation on Refugees and Asylum Seekers

South Africa, like many other countries, is a signatory to international conventions and treaties protecting the rights of non-nationals.[15] These include the 1951 United Nations Refugee Convention in Relation to the Status of Refugees, the 1969 Organisation of African Unity (OAU) Convention governing the specific aspects of refugee problems in Africa and other human rights instruments.[16] These conventions are in line with the Refugees Act No. 130 of 1998, which provides information like the definition of a refugee, the processes governing an asylum application as well as the rights and obligations of a refugee.[17] In acceding to these conventions, South Africa assumed the obligations, within its borders, to receive and treat refugees according to the standards and principles that are stipulated under international law.[18]

In Chapter 5 of the Refugee Act No. 130 of 1998, South Africa provides certain principles and obligations for the protection and general rights of refugees. Under this legislation, refugees have rights to, for example, employment, formal recognition of their status, and full legal protection for as long as they are within the Republic. They are also eligible to apply for an immigration permit upon certification by the Standing Committee, which allows them to remain as a refugee indefinitely after 5 years of continuous residence in the Republic. Additionally, they have the right to obtain an identity document (see section 30) and to access basic health and basic primary education, like any other residents of the Republic.[19]

In ensuring the safety, livelihoods and needs of refugees, especially in the time of the COVID-19 pandemic and other calamities, these provisions provide guidance to South Africa in protecting the rights of refugees.

[12] For details, see Wilson (2011).

[13] For a detailed report on the challenges faced by refugees in South Africa, see Smith and Rugunanan (2011), pp. 705–718.

[14] UNCHR (2010).

[15] Smith and Rugunanan (2011), pp. 705–718.

[16] See Khan and Rayne (2020).

[17] See again Khan and Rayne (2020).

[18] See South African Refugee Act No. 130 of 1998.

[19] See again South African Refugee Act No. 130 of 1998.

4 Refugees and Economic Development

South Africa is a host to many refugees, migrants and asylum seekers predominantly from the Southern African Development Community (SADC). In 2020, approximately 266,700 refugees and asylum seekers lived in South Africa: 30% of these were from Somalia, 29% from the Democratic Republic of the Congo and 20% from Ethiopia, with the remainder mostly from Zimbabwe and other countries.[20] Several economic, social and physical push factors contributed to the decision of individuals, families and communities to seek refuge in another country. The Office of the United Nations High Commissioner for Refugees (UNHCR) states that by 2019, approximately 79.5 million refugees were forced from their countries due to war, internal conflicts, drought or poor economies,[21] and the same reasons are true for refugees who come to South Africa.

One of the areas that has not been well studied is the contribution of refugees and other migrants towards economic development in their country of arrival. Some of the findings from existing studies show that

> ... Immigrants are, in fact, net contributors, not parasites.... Consequently, they [immigrants] draw comparatively less on social welfare and other social services. Many pay tax and, through their entrepreneurship, make a positive injection into local economic development.[22]

Although the above quote refers to immigrants in general, it also talks about refugees since they form part of the definition of immigrants. The quote implies that not only do immigrants come to the host country to be recipients of services, but they also possess certain skills, which they can utilise, when given the opportunity, to contribute to their new country. Maharaj refers to most South African immigrants as economic refugees because they reasonably have good education, as well as vocational experiences and skills, and their main reason for leaving their home country is the lack of employment opportunities.[23] It can therefore be argued that refugees are more likely to be injecting more revenue into the economy through their entrepreneurial activities and education while taking less from social services (see F. Meintjies).

A recent study conducted on the largest migrant-receiving countries shows a general shift from viewing migrants as burdensome to being instrumental in the development of the host countries. About ten countries were surveyed, and results showed that most of them, including the United Kingdom, the United States, Germany, Australia and Canada, view migrants as a strength rather than a burden.[24] The same study, however, found that in Greece, Hungary, South Africa, Russia and

---

[20] For further details, see Ponde (2020).

[21] See Akademie (2021).

[22] See Meintjies (1998).

[23] For further details, see Maharaj (2002), pp. 47–57.

[24] Gonzalez-Barrera and Connor (2019).

Israel, migrants are seen as a burden to their countries. Thus, it can be noted that the manner in which the public views migrants has an impact on the way they treat them. These negative perceptions towards migrants and refugees help explain the xenophobic attacks, as well as other hostile treatment, against this group. Hostility and xenophobic attacks against refugees and other migrants negatively impact their human rights as well as economic development. Some of the undesirable outcomes resulting from xenophobic attacks are the loss of human life, injuries, the lack of protection and the displacement of families as they flee from these attacks. Some of the xenophobic or hostile practices include the denial of primary health, education and other basic needs. Such practices negatively impact refugees not only from a human rights perspective but also economically since the victims would not be able to function in a manner that allows them to raise income for their families and contribute to economic development overall.

The contribution of refugees and asylum seekers to development in their host country is affected by many factors that are at play during the process of their integration into the communities. In South Africa, one of the most difficult challenges is to get stable and formal employment. Research has shown that the South African government has been struggling to manage the unprecedented flow of refugees and asylum seekers in terms of assisting them to settle.[25] The failure of the government to process important documents for refugees can have negative repercussions on their attainment of services and opportunities for work, education, shelter and other basic needs. Therefore, delay in processing the documents impacts their contribution to economic development and also deprives them of access to basic needs, which, in essence, are basic human rights.

5 South Africa's Response to COVID-19

The coronavirus caused severe devastation in South Africa and across the globe and continued to spread at a very alarming rate. In South Africa, the first COVID-19 case was confirmed on 5 March 2020. The South African COVID-19 portal shows that as at July 2021, over 2.2 million people tested positive for the virus; close to 66,385 died; just above five million were vaccinated; and approximately two million recovered from COVID-19.[26]

In order to control the rapid spread of infections, as well as help the health system find ways to contain the infection rates, the South African government announced and imposed a nationwide lockdown on 26 March 2020. The same approach was also taken by other countries across the globe. There were very stringent measures, such as the closing of businesses, the banning of non-essential travel across international and inter-provincial borders as well as the banning of the sale of alcohol and

[25] See Smit and Rugunanan (2014), pp. 4–26.

[26] For further details, see South African COVID-19 (2021).

cigarettes.[27] As time went by, the South African government, in consultation with the National Coronavirus Command Council (NCCC), provided guidance on the different levels of lockdown as well as the restrictions that were to be adhered to in order to limit and contain the spread of the virus. Although these measures were essential in controlling the spread of COVID-19 and in ensuring that the health of the nation was secured, the adverse economic consequences of these measures were significant as economic activities came to a standstill.

One of the major interventions by the South African government was the allocation of social relief services, which provided support to vulnerable individuals and families that were severely affected by the impacts of the virus. The Special COVID-19 Social Relief of Distress grant, a fixed monthly total of ZAR 350.00, was provided to applicants who met the criteria upon the successful submission of an online application.[28] This was primarily meant for individuals who were unemployed and were not receiving any other form of social grant or Unemployment Insurance Fund (UIF) payment. Additional financial measures also included an increase in the total amount paid for the Child Support Grant, as well as an increase in other grants.[29] Another criterion for individuals to qualify for any of the grants was that they had to be South African citizens, permanent residents or refugees registered with the Department of Home Affairs.

In addition to the measures described above, business persons were also provided with financial support to facilitate their operations during the pandemic. Various support funds that were provided included the Debt Relief Finance Scheme, the Business Growth Resilience Facility, the Agricultural Disaster Support Fund, loans, the Tourism Relief Fund and the Spaza Support Scheme.[30] However, companies had to be registered and be tax compliant to qualify for the tax and government support.[31]

Non-financial support, such as food assistance, was provided by the South African Social Security Agency (SASSA) through vouchers and cash transfers to the communities in need. Furthermore, the Department of Social Development worked jointly with the Solidarity Fund, non-governmental organisations as well as community-based organisations to allocate food parcels across the country.

While the South African government made these efforts to ensure that vulnerable communities were served, these services were not fully realised among the refugees' communities. A document reporting this shortcoming presented a recommendation for the South African government stating that

> The South African government has been ordered to include asylum seekers and special permit holders from Lesotho, Angola and Zimbabwe as recipients of the R350 COVID-19 Social Relief of Distress grant. The court declared a regulation, made by Social Development Minister… as unconstitutional. The administration of the grant seems to have turned into a

[27] See Channing et al. (2020).

[28] See the South African Government (2020).

[29] South African Government (2020).

[30] See the South African Government (2020).

[31] South African Government (2020).

> nightmare for the government as the South African Social Security Agency released a statement admitting that they were aware of large-scale unhappiness about grant applications being refused.[32]

However, the lack of proper documentation to qualify for either social grants or support for business continued to prevent huge numbers of refugees and asylum seekers from benefiting from these interventions. In explaining the reasons accounting for the lack of documentation among these migrant communities, previous studies noted that issues that had to do with a lack of personnel capacity and efficient logistics in dealing with the processing of the huge influx of asylum seekers and refugees resulted in a backlog in the processing and issuance of documents.[33] This delay in the processing of documents was also evident in 2015, when South Africa had over a million asylum applications that were pending at any stage of the asylum application processes.[34] The delays in the processing of asylum permits subsequently affected the issuance of refugee statuses for the applicants. Given this background challenge that refugees encountered, it was impossible for them to access any of the financial support services and social relief funds provided by the government during the COVID-19 outbreak.

At the time of the pandemic, South Africa had already begun the rollout of the COVID-19 vaccine. However, conflicting messages left undocumented migrants with unanswered questions. On the one hand, the President of the Republic, Cyril Ramaphosa, stated that the government intends 'to make the vaccine available to all adults living in South Africa, regardless of their citizenship or residence status'.[35] On the other hand, the Minister of Health, Zweli Mkhize, clearly pointed out that due to the fact that they are incapacitated, the government would not be able to provide the vaccine to undocumented foreign migrants and could only provide the vaccine to registered South African citizens.[36] The President's statement of non-discrimination on the ground of nationality is in line with the principles governing the treatment of refugees, as stated in Chapter 5 of the Refugee Act No. 130 of 1998, which explains that a refugee is entitled to the same basic health services and basic primary education that the inhabitants of the Republic receive. This is a progressive decision that ensures that every person in the Republic gets vaccinated since this is a serious public and global health issue. Following this decision, it is expected that even undocumented migrants will get vaccinated; however, the commitment made by the President to vaccinate undocumented migrants has raised concerns as some South African citizens have displayed feelings of contempt following this move.[37] While some South Africans do not approve of the vaccination of undocumented migrants, the virus does not choose who to infect. From a human rights perspective,

[32] Ellis (2020).

[33] See Sikanyiso (2020).

[34] Sikanyiso (2020).

[35] See Mavhinga (2021).

[36] Mavhinga (2021).

[37] For a full report, see Nkgadima (2021).

the denial or reluctance to provide COVID-19 vaccine to migrants at the same pace as other inhabitants of the Republic can be viewed in itself as a direct violation of human rights. Hence, the vaccination of all, including of undocumented migrants, is part of the solution to prevent the further spread of the virus.

6 The Impact of COVID-19 on Refugees

Like many other individuals and groups in South Africa and globally, refugees and asylum seekers have been adversely affected by the COVID-19 pandemic. However, due to the already existing vulnerabilities of this community, the consequences have been dire for them. Some of these include food insecurity, poor sanitation and a lack of basic needs.

6.1 Food Insecurity

At the macro-level, the COVID-19 crisis adversely affected the supply of food in a variety of ways, including the closure of markets, shortages in labour as well as the slowing down of operations due to lockdowns and other COVID-19 workplace restrictions.[38] Countries that rely primarily on the import of food as a means to ensure food security were the most affected by this crisis due to the closure of borders and lockdowns and the restriction on the movement of goods and services across international borders. In many countries, COVID-19 also prevented international donors, philanthropic organisations and non-governmental organisations from providing humanitarian assistance due to social distancing restrictions and the closure of borders.[39]

Like many other South Africans, refugees and asylum seekers also suffered job loss as a result of lockdown containment measures. Various researchers note that this was one of the immediate challenges experienced by refugees, especially those within informal sectors and those in low-income households.[40,41] In their study among refugee communities in South Africa, Mutambara, Crankshaw and Freedman cited a participant who described how food insecurity affected them and their children:

> I was very shocked, very shocked. I was thinking how am I going to survive with my children? I don't have money in any account, I don't have food, my children were eating only porridge. I would just cook porridge and eat with my children. From the morning until

[38]Food and Agricultural Organisation of the United Nations (2020).

[39]See Dempster et al. (2020).

[40]Mutambara et al. (2022), pp. 704–721.

[41]See Stiegler and Bouchard (2020), pp. 695–698.

in the evening when I get some beans, I make the beans and then cook with some pap (thickened porridge made from mealie meal) for my children. Sometimes we don't even have beans, my sister it was very bad.[42]

The provision of food parcels to communities that had food shortages was one of the initiatives of the South African government. However, it was observed that foreign immigrants formed the largest number of people who sought food assistance.[43] Like any other requirement for COVID-19 Social Relief of Distress grants or services, recipients needed to have a South African identity document, a special permit or a refugee permit. Given that the majority of asylum seekers did not have sufficient documentation, they were unfortunately excluded from receiving food parcels. South African-based organisation Human Rights Watch and the South African Human Rights Commission both noted that in 2020, they received similar reports stating that the COVID-19 food aid programmes and other services of the South African government did not account for refugees and asylum seekers, who live on the economic fringes of society.[44]

6.2 Economic Exclusion

Before the advent of the COVID-19 pandemic, refugees faced a myriad of *de jure*[45] and *de facto*[46] hindrances as far as economic inclusion was concerned. They faced challenges that were significantly different from those experienced by the residents of their host country.[47] Economic inclusion is one of the aspects of refugee integration that is also acknowledged in the 1951 Refugee Convention. Scholars define economic inclusion as

> … The achievement of decent work and income commensurate with one's skills. To create the conditions necessary for economic inclusion, a wide range of barriers that refugees typically face—including legal administrative, practical, discriminatory, and social barriers—must be removed and/or lowered. These include the inability to obtain proper identification including work permits or business licenses, restricted freedom of movement, difficulty accessing financial services including social safety nets, a lack of job opportunities, unsafe working conditions, poor access to childcare, and more. Some of these barriers apply to other vulnerable populations as well, but the challenges are typically most acute for refugees.[48]

[42] Mutambara et al. (2022), pp. 704–721.

[43] See an article by the Unemployment Insurance Fund (2020).

[44] See the full article by Human Rights Watch (2020).

[45] A situation where refugees are not given the same rights in law as the citizens.

[46] Applies to a situation in which the law stipulates that refugees can work. However, certain barriers prevent them from exercising such rights.

[47] Dempster et al. (2020).

[48] See Dempster et al. (2020), pp. 3–4.

Due to the fact that most refugees fail to get appropriate documentation that can facilitate their employability, they fail to get decent work in line with their skills and qualifications. As a result, refugees engage in informal employment or low-paid jobs, which have no or very little security; thus, they are vulnerable to abuse and exploitation. A study conducted among refugees in Cape Town found that more than a third of the refugees are employed in the informal sector, while those in the formal sector are likely to be in the mining, construction, agriculture and hospitality industries.[49]

Although the South African government provides economic COVID-19 relief funds as one of the means to mitigate the effects of the virus among small business owners, as well as UIF support for the unemployed, this safety net has not reached most migrant workers, including those with refugee status. Refugees and other foreign permit holders who are legally employed and are tax compliant complained about not receiving UIF payments while their fellow South African employees were able to receive such.[50] As for special permit holders, it was learnt that the reason they failed to get UIF payment was that the system that processes payment does not read passport numbers but only reads South African identity numbers.[51] Asylum seekers have also struggled to receive their salaries through the Temporary Employer-Employee Relief Scheme (TERS), which was designed to provide income to workers who have to stay away from work due to COVID-19 containment restrictions. TERS is a fund administered by the Department of Employment and Labour through the UIF.[52] The justification for the non-payment of TERS is the application of the 'no work, no pay' principle to their situations.[53] This has exacerbated the pre-existing vulnerability of migrant communities as they cannot fend for their families.

6.3 *Housing and Sanitation*

Proper housing and sanitation are important determinants of health. But usually, most of the refugees and asylum seekers reside in overcrowded spaces, such as camps, where sanitation is highly compromised. Additionally, some refugees are homeless and live on the streets and in places surrounding urban spaces. Due to the limited space they share, diseases that affect the respiratory system, such as coronavirus, are easily transmissible. Hence, refugee camps are at a high risk as far as the spread of COVID-19 is concerned. Similar spaces, such as informal settlements, have a high risk of transmission, and it is in such dwellings that some of the refugees

[49] Ferraro and Weideman (2020).

[50] Mukumbang et al. (2020), pp. 1–7.

[51] South African Government (2020).

[52] For details, see Kavuro (2020).

[53] South African Government (2020).

reside due to their inability to afford rent in decent residential suburbs. These circumstances make it difficult to practice social distancing, which is one of the major COVID-19 restrictions.

Sanitation is a public health issue in refugee camps and more so in the context of COVID-19. A study conducted in KwaZulu-Natal among relief aid workers found that due to the lack of financial resources to sustain their families during the pandemic, refugees have to choose between buying sanitisers and getting basic commodities.[54] They prefer to use the little money they have to buy food rather than sanitary items.[55] These are very difficult choices to make as sanitisers, masks and other items for sanitisation are essential for protection against COVID-19 infection. In addition, refugees usually live in shelters where access to running water for the regular washing of hands to prevent the further spread of COVID-19 is not readily available.[56] These conditions thus put the refugee communities as well as the general community at risk of increased COVID-19 infections. Previous research found that most governments do not seem to prioritise the security of refugees. Without sustainable resources in place, the health and security of refugees can be jeopardised. Similar findings can be said of the experiences at the Moria refugee camp in Greece, where the government failed to provide sustainable sanitation and adequate housing to refugees' communities during the COVID-19 pandemic.[57] The implications of these findings are that beyond COVID-19 and other emergencies that can impact refugees' security, the government needs to come up with sustainable and proactive mechanisms to improve sanitation and accommodation within refugees' communities. This will ensure security to the health and sanitation of these vulnerable groups in the unfortunate event of unforeseeable disasters and pandemics.

6.4 *Impacts of COVID-19 on Women*

COVID-19 causes various challenges in all spheres of life. These crises are not gender-neutral, and women bear the brunt of COVID-19's social and economic effects. In an assessment of the impact of COVID-19 on women, the United Nations highlights major areas in which women are most affected. Firstly, the economic impacts are deeply felt among women and girls as they are less paid and have less secure jobs than their male counterparts.[58] Secondly, their reproductive health needs are not attended to due to their need to reallocate resources for food and other

[54] Cloete et al. (2020), pp. 30–31.

[55] See Cloete et al. (2020), pp. 30–31.

[56] For more details, see Kluge et al. (2020), pp. 1237–1239.

[57] For more details, see Bohnet and Rüegger (2021), pp. 353–368.

[58] United Nations Policy Brief (2020).

household supplies.[59] Thirdly, the burden of unpaid work has increased for women as they need to take care of their families, including those infected with COVID-19, as well as mind their children because either schools are closed or the children do not attend school every day.[60] Another burden that some women face is gender-based violence fuelled by the COVID-19 crisis, especially that lockdown restrictions also limit their movements to seek help.[61] These unprecedented challenges are rather extreme for refugee women because the pre-existing hardships and inequalities they encounter at various levels include those from their country of origin as well as those they experience in their host country.[62]

A recent study conducted in KwaZulu-Natal in South Africa unpacked a myriad of challenges faced by refugee women as a result of COVID-19. One of the major hardships is economic insecurity as most of the women are employed in precarious jobs, such as vending, child minding, car guarding and in salons, among others.[63] It can be said that the leading reason why refugee women end up in such insecure jobs is their lack of proper legal documentation, which deprives them of getting employed in jobs that are commensurate with their skills and qualifications. Economic insecurity also impacts their many other responsibilities as there is a shortage of money to pay rent and provide food for their families.[64] The challenge of economic exclusion that is experienced by refugees is a call for governments to come up with policies that ensure sustainability and inclusion for all, including refugees. The United Nations 2013 Agenda for Sustainable Development Goal 8 promotes equal employment opportunities, decent work for all and social protection for all.[65] In as much as governments encounter challenges in providing timely documentation to refugees, which would allow them to secure decent work, this same challenge denies refugees the opportunity to fully participate in the economic realm. The implications of these findings are that the government could implement holistic and sustainable approaches to refugee management. Research has shown that in the absence of proper documentation, opportunities for refugees and their access to basic services are compromised.

[59] United Nations Policy Brief (2020).

[60] See a full report by the United Nations Policy Brief (2020).

[61] United Nations Policy Brief (2020).

[62] Mutambara et al. (2022), pp. 704–721

[63] Read again Mutambara et al. (2022), pp. 704–721.

[64] Mutambara et al. (2022), pp. 704–721.

[65] Goal 8 of the United Nations is aimed at promoting sustained, inclusive and sustainable economic growth; full and productive employment; and decent work for all. Read the UN 2030 Agenda on Sustainable Development Goals.

7 Lessons Learnt from Other Refugee-Hosting Countries

The coronavirus disease is a global pandemic that has adversely affected the economies of all states. Countries that are host to refugees and asylum seekers have made various efforts to ease the burdens faced by this group. The common rationale for adopting this approach is that in most countries, refugees and asylum seekers constitute one of the most vulnerable communities.[66] In the context of COVID-19 and other challenges, the impacts of COVID-19 on the well-being and livelihoods of refugees and asylum seekers are therefore huge.

Portugal

In response to the COVID-19 crisis, Portugal has temporarily granted all migrants and asylum seekers full citizenship rights so that they are able to access healthcare services without any hindrances.[67] This is very progressive as many other countries have not adopted policies that allow refugees and other migrants to benefit from critical services.[68]

Malaysia

The Malaysian government has formulated and implemented COVID-19 testing and treatment policies that are inclusive of undocumented foreign migrants. The policies enable all foreign nationals, including refugees and asylum seekers, to be screened and receive treatment for coronavirus, whether they are documented or not, and they are not detained or arrested for lack of documentation.[69] Due to the fear of arrest and detention on the ground of lack of adequate documentation, undocumented foreign migrants often avoid seeking healthcare services. Hence, the Malaysian policies on the screening and treatment of foreign migrants are helpful in ensuring the identification of COVID-19 cases as well as the treatment of refugee communities.

Spain

Spain is one of the countries in the European Union that has been severely affected by the COVID-19 pandemic. By the end of June 2021, the country had recorded a total of just over 4.1 million COVID-19 cases and approximately 81,000 deaths.[70] In response to these challenges of increasing cases and deaths, the Spanish government put in place special measures to help contain the virus among the refugees' and asylum seekers' communities. Firstly, the government temporarily suspended the requirement for refugees and asylum seekers to possess valid documents. This facilitated their continuous access to aid covering their basic needs. Secondly, telephonic interviews were conducted with refugees and asylum seekers who applied for aid, with simultaneous interpretation provided, to assess the applicants' degree of vulnerability and prioritise access to the system by those most in

[66] See Gordon (2021), pp. 1–6.

[67] Zanker and Moyo (2020), pp. 100–112.

[68] Read the full article on how COVID-19 was exploited to harden migration policies (Reidy 2020).

[69] See the United Nations High Commissioner for Refugees (2020).

[70] See the full report on Spain by the Worldometer (2021).

need. Lastly, asylum seekers who had not been able to submit their official asylum applications could request access to and benefit from the system during the pandemic.[71] These measures have been instrumental in ensuring that refugees and asylum seekers benefit from the support given to vulnerable groups during the pandemic.

Belgium

As the influx of refugees continues, the Belgian government has decided to provide safety to vulnerable migrants by offering them individual accommodation. They have relocated families from refugee camps and shelters to individual residences or facilities and ensured that families can stay together.[72] In addition, the new arrivals are medically screened with a COVID-19-specific medical questionnaire and temperature measurements before integrating into the community.[73] The move to provide individual accommodation is practical and has reduced infection, which is common in crowded spaces.

Turkey

Like Belgium, the Turkish government conducts pre-admission health screening and regular follow-ups by healthcare practitioners from the Provincial Directorate.[74] Migrants who have just arrived are quarantined for a maximum of 14 days before being allocated a place to stay.[75] In addition, accommodation centres for refugees are regularly disinfected, and the inhabitants are provided with sanitary kits and personal protective equipment.[76]

One of the common practices among these countries, as well as others that have made efforts to ensure that refugees and asylum seekers are not excluded, is translating COVID-19 messages into various languages understood by these diverse migrant communities. This has ensured that they are not discriminated against or deprived of accessing healthcare services and other basic needs.[77]

Other than the economic contributions that refugees have made to South Africa, some of them have taken initiatives to provide basic needs to communities and individuals severely affected by the COVID-19 pandemic, as a way of giving back to the country. For example, a group of refugees of Somalian origin launched a compassion campaign during the March 2020 lockdown. They started by distributing items such as masks, hand sanitisers and food parcels to residents living in informal settlements around the cities of Pretoria and Johannesburg and then

---

[71] For details on how Spain introduced special COVID-19 integration measures, see European Commission (2020).

[72] United Nations High Commissioner for Refugees (2020).

[73] United Nations High Commissioner for Refugees (2020).

[74] See United Nations High Commissioner for Refugees (2020).

[75] For practical recommendations and good practices to address protection concerns in the context of COVID-19, see United Nations High Commissioner for Refugees (2020).

[76] United Nations High Commissioner for Refugees (2020).

[77] United Nations High Commissioner for Refugees (2020).

extended their efforts to other parts of the country.[78] These individual actions are important contributions made by private persons during the crisis. Sustainable innovations from interdisciplinary stakeholders, such as humanitarian organisations and the government, would however, have a more positive impact on the well-being of refugees during the pandemic.

Refugees in other countries have also shown various acts of kindness towards the communities within which they live during the lockdown. In the midst of the pandemic, refugees who trained as medical doctors and are being hosted in Iran and Ecuador have stepped up to visit communities and provide tips on how people can protect themselves from COVID-19.[79] In addition, refugees who have qualifications in community health assist in identifying suspected COVID-19 cases and subsequently refer them to health facilities.[80] In Kenya and Mexico, refugees are making soap, face masks and washing machines to support frontline workers.[81]

Refugees' efforts demonstrate their role in contributing to economic development. Firstly, refugees are willing to contribute to the well-being of their host countries; they are not mere recipients of goods and services. Secondly, the variety of outputs portrayed in these few examples demonstrates that refugees possess important skills that, when given the opportunity, they can use to contribute significantly to the socio-economic development of their host countries. It can be argued that countries that host refugees are faced with potential economic recession, increasing xenophobia, and high levels of unemployment, which may lead to increased scepticism about the economic inclusion of refugees.[82] However, research shows that economic inclusion is in the best interest of not only the refugees but also their host country, as well as its neighbouring countries.[83] This view is in line with Eistein's perspective on refugees—that given the necessary support, they can extensively contribute to the economic development of their host country.

8 Recommendations

The COVID-19 pandemic has had an adverse socio-economic impact on South Africa, and this has been felt deeply by vulnerable communities. The refugee communities are among those that struggle to fend for their families even in the absence of a pandemic like COVID-19, which has further exacerbated their socio-

---

[78] For the full article, see Ponde (2020).

[79] For details on how refugees helped in the COVID-19 battle, see United Nations High Commission for Refugees (2020).

[80] United Nations High Commission for Refugees (2020).

[81] Read again United Nations High Commission for Refugees (2020).

[82] Read more from the Policy Paper by Dempster et al. (2020), pp. 1–44.

[83] Read a more detailed analysis from Dempster et al. (2020), pp. 1–44.

economic challenges. The following recommendations may be useful for South Africa to consider in its bid to contain the further spread of the virus.

8.1 Increase Human Capacity and Skills at the Department of Home Affairs

Since there is a backlog in the processing of refugees and undocumented migrants, this will facilitate the efficient processing of asylum and refugee permits. This will ensure that refugees get the necessary documents and can seek employment that is in line with their skills and qualifications. The positive outcomes associated with the possession of proper documentation are vast, including the ability to support their families, improved housing, enhanced health and sanitation, and better standards of living, among others.

8.2 Opt for an Inclusive Policy in Times of Crises

The coronavirus infects and affects everyone regardless of nationality. It is a highly contagious virus that spreads easily from one person to another. Hence, it is necessary to follow precautions such as wearing masks, maintaining social distancing and practising sanitation to prevent its spread. Refugees and asylum seekers are some of the most vulnerable groups in the country, owing to the pre-existing challenges associated with their status, and this fact needs to be taken into consideration when designing and providing safety nets for the country's citizens. It is thus important for the government to ensure that it includes refugees and asylum seekers in its plans, especially those concerning the provision of basic needs, like food, sanitation and other COVID-19-related relief services.

8.3 Stakeholder Engagement

The South African government can collaborate with organisations that already provide services to refugees and asylum seekers in an effort to find the best ways to serve these vulnerable communities. Such organisations are likely to have information on the families and communities that need help and can advise the government on how best to provide assistance. Given that the number of undocumented migrants is huge and that the government might not have access to their records, the organisations that serve these communities can play a key role in identifying gaps and assisting the government in reaching out to the needy.

8.4 Fostering Sustainable Approaches

The chapter has demonstrated that the support given to refugees during the pandemic has been short-lived. It is therefore crucial for refugee host countries to come up with sustainable approaches to addressing the challenges faced by refugees. Research has shown that solutions given to meet the needs of the refugees are meant to assist those who stay for a short time in a certain place and time, while on the other hand refugees can stay for a long time in the same space until they can be granted for example, permanent accommodation and documentation.[84] Aligning efforts to facilitate the transition of refugees with the sustainable development goals can be one of the leading approaches that will ensure successful integration of refugees in social and economic development.

9 Conclusion

The chapter has highlighted the experiences encountered by refugees and asylum seekers during the COVID-19 pandemic. It has also outlined the measures taken by the South African government to provide social and business relief services to individuals and companies that qualify for assistance. However, the findings gathered from various sources demonstrate that there are loopholes in the manner in which the government deals with refugees and asylum seekers as far as COVID-19 intervention measures are concerned, as many of them are being excluded. It is understandable that, like all other countries, the South African government was not prepared for this calamity; hence, such loopholes are bound to occur. Nevertheless, the government can take advantage of this pandemic to fix and correct these shortcomings by forming and implementing all-inclusive and sustainable policies that seek to protect the human rights of refugees and asylum seekers during life-threatening crises. The examples learnt from other countries that host refugees can provide a framework for assisting refugees and asylum seekers during these challenging circumstances, as well as in the future.

References

Akademie DW (2021) Refugees and Migration in Africa Project, 2021. https://www.dw.com/en/refugees-and-migration-in-africa-project/a-48817149. Accessed 7 May 2021

[84] Read Seifert et al. (2023), pp. 1554–1586 and more. The main drawn is that 'a key reason for this poor outcome is that host country governments plan refugee camps as short-term shelters, but refugees stay in these camps for more than a decade on average due to ongoing conflicts in their home country'.

Bell S, Alves S, de Oliveira ES, Zuin A (2010) Migration and land use change in Europe: a review. Living Rev Landsc Res 4(2):1–49

Bohnet H, Rüegger S (2021) Refugees and Covid-19: beyond health risks to insecurity. Swiss Polit Sci Rev 27(2):353–368

Channing et al. (2020) COVID-19 lockdowns, income distribution, and food security: an analysis for South Africa, 26. Global Food Security (2020), 100410

Cloete A, Davids A, Reddy P (2020) Leaving no one behind during Covid-19: relief workers' concern for migrants, refugees and asylum seekers. Hum Soc Res Council Rev 18(3):30–31

Dempster H, Ginn T, Graham J, Ble MG, Jayasinghe D, Shorey B (2020) Locked down and left behind: the impact of COVID-19 on refugees' economic inclusion. Center for Global Development, Refugees International, and International Rescue Committee, 8

Einstein A (2017) Albert Einstein's legacy as a refugee. International Rescue Committee. https://www.rescue.org/article/albert-einsteins-legacy-refugee. Accessed 14 May 2021

Ellis E (2020) Special permit holders and asylum seekers in SA must get COVID-19 grant, court orders, Daily Maverick, 19 June 2020. https://www.dailymaverick.co.za/article/2020-06-19-refugees-and-asylum-seekers-in-samust-get-COVID-19-grant-court-orders/. Accessed 25 Jun 2021

Ferraro F, Weideman M (2020) Labour-related experience of migrants and refugees in South Africa. Scalabrini Institute for Human Mobility in Africa, Cape Town

Gonzalez-Barrera A, Connor P (2019) Around the world, more say immigrants are a strength than a burden: public divided on immigrants' willingness to adopt host country's customs. https://www.pewresearch.org/global/2019/03/14/around-the-world-more-say-immigrants-are-a-strength-than-aburden/. Accessed 21 Jul 2021

Gordon SL (2021) Addressing the marginalisation of refugees and asylum seekers in South Africa, Human Sciences Research Council, Policy Brief, February 2022. http://hdl.handle.net/20.500.11910/15967

Jennissen RPW (2004) Macro-economic determinants of international migration in Europe. Rozenberg Publishers, Amsterdam

Kavuro C (2020) South Africa excludes refugees and asylum seekers from COVID-19 aid, Mail and Guardian, 18 May 2020. https://mg.co.za/coronavirus-essentials/2020-05-29-south-africa-refugees-coronavrus-exclude-law/. Accessed 24 Jun 2021

Khan F, Rayne N (2020) Country Fiche South Africa, University of Cape Town, 2020. https://www.asileproject.eu/wp-content/uploads/2021/03/Country-Fiche_South-Africa_Final_Pub.pdf. Accessed 28 May 2021

Kluge HHP, Jakab Z, Bartovic J, d'Anna V, Severoni S (2020) Refugee and migrant health in the COVID-19 response. Lancet 395(10232):1237–1239. https://doi.org/10.1016/S0140-6736(20)30791-1

Maharaj B (2002) Economic refugees in post-apartheid South Africa–Assets or liabilities? Implications for progressive migration policies. GeoJournal 56:47–57. https://doi.org/10.1023/A:1021756902951

Mavhinga D (2021) Ensuring equitable COVID-19 vaccine distribution in South Africa - inclusive, nondiscriminatory approach needed to curb pandemic, Human Rights Watch, 3 February 2021. https://www.hrw.org/news/2021/02/03/ensuring-equitable-COVID-19-vaccine-distribution-south-africa. Accessed 20 Jul 2021

Meintjies F (1998) Immigrants are people like us. Sunday Times Business Times, 20 Sep 1998, 20

Mukumbang FC, Ambe AN, Adebiyi BO (2020) Unspoken inequality: how COVID-19 has exacerbated existing vulnerabilities of asylum-seekers, refugees, and undocumented migrants in South Africa. Int J Equity Health 19(1):141. https://doi.org/10.1186/s12939-020-01259-4

Mutambara VM, Crankshaw TL, Freedman J (2022) Assessing the impacts of COVID-19 on women refugees in South Africa. J Refug Stud 35(1):704–721. https://doi.org/10.1093/jrs/feab044

Nkgadima R (2021) Refugees and asylum seekers in SA will receive COVID-19 vaccine jab. Independent Online, 2 February 2021, https://www.iol.co.za/news/politics/refugees-and-asylum-seekers-in-sa-will-receive-COVID-19-vaccine-jab-f0250d20-adcd-47a1-b739-469425a23dba. Accessed 20 Jul 2021

Ponde K (2020) Refugees in South Africa share acts of kindness with their hosts, 2020. https://www.unhcr.org/afr/news/stories/2020/10/5f7ec0574/refugees-south-africa-share-acts-kindness-hosts.html. Accessed 23 June 2021

Reidy E (2020) How COVID-19 is being exploited to harden migration policies. The New Humanitarian, 17 April, 2020, https://www.thenewhumanitarian.org/analysis/2020/04/17/coronavirus-global-migration-policiesexploited. Accessed 13 Jul 2020

Seifert L, Kunz N, Gold S (2023) Sustainable innovations for humanitarian operations in refugee camps. Int J Oper Prod Manag 43(10):1554–1586

Sikanyiso M (2020) How South Africa is denying refugees their rights: what needs to change. The Conversation, 13 May 2020. https://www.polity.org.za/article/how-south-africa-is-denying-refugees-their-rightswhat-needs-to-change-2020-05-13. Accessed 16 Jul 2021

Smith R, Rugunanan P (2011) From precarious lives to precarious work: the dilemma facing refugees in Gauteng, South Africa 45. South African Review of Sociology 2(2014):4–26

Smit R, Rugunanan P (2014) From precarious lives to precarious work: the dilemma facing refugees in Gauteng, South Africa. South Afr Rev Sociol 45(2):4–26. https://doi.org/10.1080/21528586.2014.917876

Stiegler N, Bouchard JP (2020) South Africa: challenges and successes of the COVID-19 lockdown. Annales Médico-psychologiques, revue psychiatrique 178(7):695–698. https://doi.org/10.1016/j.amp.2020.05.006

Wickramasinghe A, Wimalaratana W (2016) International migration and migration theories. Soc Aff 1(5):13–32

Wilson AP (2011) Trafficking risks for refugees. In: Third Annual Interdisciplinary Conference on Human Trafficking. University of Nebraska, Lincoln

Zanker FL, Moyo K (2020) The corona virus and migration governance in South Africa: business as usual? Afr Spectr 55(1):100–112. https://doi.org/10.1177/0002039720925826

Vimbai Chibango Lecturer of development studies at Durban University of Technology. She may be contacted at vmchibango@gmail.com. Her main research areas are gender, HIV, and Sexual and Reproductive Health.

Promoting the Economic Rights of Persons with Disabilities

The Law and Challenges in Mainland Tanzania

Ines Kajiru, Scholastica Mality, and Baraka Mkami

1 Introduction

Human rights and economic development are two fundamental components that intersect and are crucial to achieving a just and equitable society.[1] Recognising economic rights as a fundamental human right is essential and is protected by international law.[2] In Tanzania, where more than 3.3 million people have disabilities, the journey towards economic development is intrinsically linked to the protection and improvement of the economic rights of all citizens, including those with disabilities.[3]

People with disabilities (PWDs), however, face unique and often insurmountable challenges in accessing and enjoying their economic rights, particularly in developing countries where resources and services are limited. These challenges include limited access to education and vocational training, discrimination in the workplace, lack of accessible transportation, and inadequate social protection measures.[4] Poverty rates among PWDs remain alarmingly high, particularly in rural areas, where access to resources and services is limited. This is a significant concern, given the interconnectivity of economic and social rights.[5] Access to work, social security, housing, food, water, healthcare, and education are all essential components of

[1] See Marslev and Sano (2016), p. 8.

[2] See United Nations (2024).

[3] See National Bureau of Statistics, Disability Monograph, January (2016), p. 1.

[4] See Uromi and Mazagwa (2014), p. 159.

[5] See International Disability Alliance (2022), pp. 7–35.

I. Kajiru (✉) · S. Mality · B. Mkami
School of Law, University of Dodoma, Dodoma, Tanzania
e-mail: ines.kajiru@udom.ac.tz

I. Kajiru et al. (eds.), *Economic Development and Human Rights in Contemporary Sub-Saharan Africa*, Ius Gentium: Comparative Perspectives on Law and Justice 122, https://doi.org/10.1007/978-3-031-81400-6_7

economic rights, and they are all interconnected.[6] Without access to these resources, PWDs may face significant barriers to achieving economic independence and the ability to participate fully in society.

To address these issues, Tanzania has put in place a robust legal framework to protect and improve the economic rights of its citizens. The country has ratified several international legal instruments, including the International Covenant on Economic, Social, and Cultural Rights, 1966 (ICESCR) and the Convention on the Rights of Persons with Disabilities, 2006 (CRPD). These instruments are domesticated in the Law of the Child Act, Cap 13 R.E 2019 (Cap 13), and the Persons with Disability Act, 2010 (PWDs Act). The Employment and Labour Relations Act, Cap 366 R.E 2019 (Cap 366), provides a comprehensive legal framework for the protection of the economic rights of PWDs. This demonstrates the country's commitment to ensuring the economic rights of all its citizens, including those with disabilities.

This chapter provides a comprehensive analysis of the legal framework in place to safeguard the economic rights of PWDs in Tanzania. It explores the extent to which national and international laws have been implemented and the progress made in ensuring that PWDs have the accessibility and freedom to fully enjoy their human and economic rights. The chapter aims to contribute to the ongoing global conversation surrounding economic rights and their relationship with human rights and economic development. By reducing poverty among PWDs and their families, Tanzania is taking a significant step towards achieving a just and equitable society.

2 Human Rights, Economic Development, and the Inclusion of Persons with Disabilities

Realising economic rights is crucial for attaining human rights and sustainable development.[7] Economic rights involve the entitlements and freedoms that every individual and community should possess to lead a life of dignity, including the right to work and social security.[8] These rights are essential for the exercise of people's civil and political rights as they ensure access to basic needs such as food, clothing, housing, healthcare, education, and social security.[9]

The historical development of economic rights can be traced back to religious traditions that emphasise the care and protection of the poor, destitute, and disabled.[10] For example, in Islam, the concept of Zakat, an obligatory charity given by Muslims to the poor and needy, highlights the importance of economic rights for

[6] See Poverty and Human Rights (2023) and Talawar (2022), p. 2.

[7] See Economic Social and Cultural Rights (2023).

[8] See Arts 6.1, 6.2, and 7 of the ICESCR and Arts 9 and 10 ICSCR on social security.

[9] See Talawar (2022), p. 3.

[10] See Center for Social Concern (2023).

marginalised individuals and communities.[11] This emphasis was later echoed by philosophers such as Paine, Marx, and Kant, who wrote about these rights.[12] From a legal perspective, the International Labour Organization (ILO) recognised economic rights in the early twentieth century by developing minimum employment criteria, non-discrimination policies, and insurance programmes for illness, accidents, invalidity, and old age.[13] The United Nations Charter, 1945 (UN Charter), was introduced due to these developments. It advances economic rights by calling all members to raise their living standards and promote full employment, growth, and development on all fronts.[14]

In 1966, two important international treaties were introduced: the International Covenant on Economic, Social and Cultural Rights (ICESCR) and the International Covenant on Civil and Political Rights (ICCPR). These two covenants recognised different categories of rights, with economic rights falling under the second generation and not enforceable by law. These rights were categorised by ideological differences, with civil and political rights associated with Western capitalist values and economic, social, and cultural rights related to socialism.[15] It is worth noting that despite their categorisation, these rights are all interconnected, equally important, and essential for promoting human dignity. The two covenants were meant to be a single treaty, but countries could ratify either.[16] However, economic rights are often overlooked in favour of civil and political rights in many countries.[17] It is essential to protect and promote economic rights alongside civil and political rights.

Despite these developments, the realisation of economic rights remains a challenge, particularly for persons with disabilities (PWDs). *Disability* is a complex and evolving concept that is shaped by environmental and attitudinal factors.[18] The World Health Organization (WHO) definition of disability refers to physical or mental impairments limiting a person's ability to participate in daily activities.[19] Schalk believes disability is linked to a 'socially constructed system that categorises, values, and ranks bodies and minds as normative or marginal'.[20]

Visiting legal instruments, the CRPD provides that 'persons with disabilities include those who have long-term physical, mental, intellectual or sensory impairments which, in interaction with various barriers, may hinder their full and effective

[11] See Kakar et al. (2022), pp. 86–91.

[12] See Talawar (2022), p. 4.

[13] See Part XIII of the Versailles Treaty, 1919, in particular Arts 387 and 392, which established the International Labour Office, and Art 427 of the Versailles Treaty.

[14] See Art 55 of the UN Charter, 1945.

[15] See Smismans (2005), p. 6. See also Veit-Wilson (2007), pp. 57–83.

[16] See Poverty and Human Rights (2023).

[17] See Hertel (2006), p. 215.

[18] See WHO (1976), pp. 143–73.

[19] See United Nations (2023b).

[20] See Schalk (2018).

participation in society on an equal basis with others'.[21] In the PWD Act, disability is defined as 'a limitation or loss of opportunities to take part in the normal life of the community on an equal level with others due to physical, mental or social factors'.[22] The Tanzania National Policy on Disability, 2004 (NPD), defines disability as the loss or limitation of opportunities to participate in the community's everyday life on an equal level with others due to physical, mental, or social factors. It also defines a person with a disability as an individual whose prospects of obtaining and retaining employment are significantly reduced due to known physical, mental, or social factors.[23] In all the definitions, disabilities cover the medical and social models, as stated and argued by the UN and Schalk. However, this definition fails to account for the social constraints imposed on PWDs by discriminatory practices, which restrict their full economic, political, and social involvement.[24]

To address this issue, the social and medical models of disability have become the accepted norm. The social model emphasises disability as a social concept that attributes exclusion to the physical and social environment rather than the individual.[25] The dispersion of the social model of impairment replaces the centrality of disability in the medical model, recognising that while some human characteristics may cause impairment, they do not define the person.[26] A person who uses a wheelchair may face challenges in accessing buildings or transportation.[27] Still, these challenges can be addressed through policy and infrastructure changes, indicating that they are not inherent to the person.

Efforts should focus on creating an environment where people with disabilities can earn from their capabilities independently, thus promoting economic development and respecting their human rights. In this context, the concept of sustainable development, as defined by the Brundtland Commission report, is relevant as it emphasises the need to meet present needs without compromising the ability of future generations to meet their own needs.[28] Sustainable development goes beyond addressing environmental health and economic growth alone and also encompasses social justice issues such as poverty, racism, inequity, democracy, and peace.[29] Sustainable human development (SHD) stresses that economic growth should not be the sole basis for development.[30] It is centred on the belief that development is realised when people are given the chance to own their full development, encompassing all dimensions of human life. This approach highlights the importance

[21] See Art. 1 CRPD.

[22] See Sect. 2 PWDs Act.

[23] See Tanzania Ministry of Labour, Youth Development and Sports (2004), p. 1.

[24] See Kajiru and Nyimbi (2020), p. 76.

[25] See Hendriks (2002), pp. 199–203.

[26] See Stone-MacDonald and Butera (2014), pp. 2–3.

[27] See Gervas (2019).

[28] See World Committee on Environment and Development (1987), p. 43.

[29] See Landorf et al. (2008), p. 223.

[30] See Landorf et al. (2008), p. 224.

of building people's capacity to express and participate in deciding what affects their lives.[31] In this context, efforts should focus on creating an environment where people with disabilities can earn from their capabilities independently, thus promoting economic development and respecting their human rights. By prioritising poverty reduction, productive employment, social integration, and environmental regeneration, SHD can foster sustainable economic growth and promote human rights for people with disabilities.[32]

Including PWDs in economic development is a matter of social justice and is a transformative opportunity for sustainable human development. By addressing the social and environmental constraints that limit their full participation in economic, political, and social activities, inclusive policies can unlock the untapped potential of PWDs, benefiting individuals and society as a whole, as discussed above. The involvement of PWDs in economic development is not for individual rights but for building a more inclusive and prosperous society.[33] Studies have consistently shown that companies that employ PWDs experience job satisfaction, productivity, and retention rates.[34] This emphasises that including PWDs in economic development can significantly contribute to reducing poverty and inequality as PWDs are often disproportionately affected by these issues.

Therefore, economic rights are fundamental to sustainable human development. Including PWDs in economic development requires addressing the social and environmental constraints that limit their participation in economic, political, and social activities. Policies that promote inclusive employment practices, accessible infrastructure, and social protection programmes can ensure that PWDs have equal access to economic rights and opportunities. By recognising disability as a social concept rather than an individual attribute, we can develop policies that address the social and environmental constraints that limit the full participation of PWDs in economic, political, and social activities. This is because including PWDs in economic development benefits society as a whole, including higher job satisfaction, productivity, and reduced poverty and inequality.

3 Legal and Institutional Framework Governing PWDs' Human and Economic Rights

This part presents a discussion on the legal and institutional framework that governs human rights and economic development for persons with disabilities. There is no doubt that significant steps have been taken globally, regionally, and nationally—particularly in Tanzania—to promote and protect the human rights of persons with

[31] See Plewes (1996), p. 216.

[32] See UNDP (1994), 4.

[33] See Long and Guo (2023), p. 3.

[34] See Fantinelli (2022).

disabilities (PWDs). To achieve this, a number of International Covenants and Regional Treaties have been established, and national laws have been enacted and amended. Below is a critical examination of the said instruments and their potential to adhere to the human rights of PWDs while promoting their economic development in Tanzania.

3.1 International Instruments on Economic Rights of Persons with Disabilities

3.1.1 The Universal Declaration of Human Rights, 1948

The economic development of persons with disabilities (PWDs) in Tanzania is a crucial issue that needs to be addressed urgently. Despite being a member state of the Universal Declaration of Human Rights, 1948 (UDHR), Tanzania is still struggling to provide and protect the economic rights of PWDs. These economic and social rights are recognised under the UDHR through Articles 22–28. The UDHR provides for the security and protection of a person's economic rights and the right to own property, either on an individual basis or in association with others.[35] The Declaration also emphasises that no one shall be arbitrarily deprived of his property.[36] As a Member State, Tanzania is obligated to provide and protect the economic rights of its people. Despite the Declaration, which guarantees the right to enjoy economic rights equally, and Tanzania's several efforts as far as the development of PWDs is concerned, poverty exists among the PWDs. This study is of the view that a sound mechanism is needed to help PWDs earn independently and achieve sustainable income rather than rely on the charity and goodwill of the government or others.

3.1.2 The International Covenant on Economic, Social and Cultural Rights, 1966

Tanzania is a state party to the International Covenant on Economic, Social and Cultural Rights (ICESCR), ratified on 11 June 1976.[37] The ICESCR obligates the states parties to ensure the equal rights of its citizens to enjoy all the economic rights set in the Covenant.[38] Thus, everyone, including PWDs, should enjoy economic rights. Tanzania should implement mechanisms to support PWDs and ensure their enjoyment of this right.

[35] See Art. 17.1 of the UDHR.

[36] See Art. 17.2 of the UDHR.

[37] See United Nations (2023a).

[38] See Art. 3 of the ICESCR.

There are several ways in which a person can enjoy economic rights. To acquire personal and national income, every able person should have the opportunity to work. The ICESCR recognises and protects the right to work by emphasising that everyone is entitled to earn a living through work. This work should be freely chosen and accepted, and a state party should ensure that its citizens have the proper means, skills, and environment to facilitate this. Laws, policies, and programmes should be in place so everyone, including those with disabilities, can work.[39] Tanzania is required to ensure access to employment by avoiding measures that discriminate against marginalised groups, like PWDs, and implementing sustainable national plans of action.[40]

The ICESCR not only protects the right to work to earn a living but also ensures that the work is just and the working conditions are conducive and fair. People should earn equally for their work without being discriminated against for any reason. The ICESCR provides that 'rest, leisure and reasonable limitation of working hours and periodic holidays with pay, as well as remuneration for public holidays'.[41] The issue is whether this is equally guaranteed to PWDs in Tanzania. As much as Tanzania is making efforts to fulfil this requirement, the working conditions, however, still do not meet the above obligations towards PWDs. For instance, public transportation remains unfriendly to PWDs' needs, buildings sometimes lack elevators, and roads are often without signs for PWDs. All of these hinder PWDs from working efficiently, performing accordingly, and earning as much as those without disabilities.

Article 9 of the ICESCR protects 'the right of everyone to social security, including social insurance'. One may term this right as a purely social right, which is true. However, social security is also an economic right because it has a financial effect. To access social security in Tanzania, individuals must have a formal or informal means of income because social security institutions will support members only if they contribute, which means PWDs without the capacity to contribute cannot enjoy the benefits of social security.[42] According to the CESCR, 'the right to social security includes the right to access and maintain benefits without discrimination to help secure protection from lack of work-related income, unaffordable access to healthcare, and insufficient family support (in the case of children and adult dependents)'.[43]

The right to an adequate standard of living includes adequate food, clothing, housing, and the continuous improvement of living conditions. States must 'take

[39] See Art. 6 of the ICESCR.

[40] See CESCR, General Comment No. 18, Article 6 of the International Covenant on Economic, Social and Cultural Rights, UN Doc. E/C.12/GC/18, 6 February 2006, para. 31.

[41] See Art. 7 of ICESCR.

[42] See Sect. 5A, 6, and 12 of the National Social Security Fund Act [CAP. 50. RE 2018] and Sect. 18 of the Public Service Social Security Fund Act No. 2 of 2018.

[43] *See* CESCR, General Comment No. 19, The Right to Social Security (Art. 9), UN Doc. E/C.12/GC/19, 4 February 2008, para. 2.

appropriate steps to ensure the realisation of this right'.[44] They must take action to guarantee individuals' access to the minimum conditions necessary for a life of dignity, rather than merely ensuring survival, to realise an adequate standard of living.[45] As a state party to the Covenant, Tanzania must meet the minimum core obligations entailed by the right to an adequate living standard. For example, it must ensure the general availability of essential food, primary health care, basic shelter, and basic education.[46]

In all of its efforts to promote the economic development of PWDs, Tanzania must guarantee non-discrimination, as required by Article 2 of the ICESCR. This includes avoiding measures that discriminate against marginalised groups like PWDs and implementing sustainable national plans of action to ensure equal access to economic rights.[47] This can be achieved by providing equal opportunities, fair working conditions, social security, and an adequate standard of living.

3.1.3 International Covenant on Civil and Political Rights, 1966

Tanzania ratified the International Covenant on Civil and Political Rights (ICCPR) in June 1976.[48] The Covenant obliged Tanzania to ensure that its citizens have the right to freely pursue their economic development.[49] In doing so, the country should ensure that there is no discrimination in the enjoyment and protection of the right based on race, colour, sex, language, religion, political or other opinions, national or social origin, property, birth, or other status.[50] To uphold these rights, the government of Tanzania should implement mechanisms that facilitate enjoyment by PWDs of the same economic opportunities and protection as those exercised by people without disabilities. This means that the government must provide individualised support to PWDs to ensure that they can access and participate in the economic sector without any hindrances.

However, despite Tanzania's commitment to these human rights principles, many PWDs still face major barriers to economic opportunities, including lack of accessibility, discrimination, and stigma.[51] Therefore, the government must continue to take proactive measures to ensure that PWDs are not left behind in the country's economic development. By prioritising the economic inclusion of PWDs, Tanzania

[44] See Art. 11 of the ICESCR.

[45] See CESCR, General Comment No. 4, The Right to Adequate Housing, UN Doc. E/1992/23, 1 January 1992, para. 7.

[46] See CESCR, General Comment No. 3, The Nature of States Parties Obligations, para. 10.

[47] See CESCR, General Comment No. 20, Non-discrimination in Economic, Social and Cultural Rights, UN Doc. E/C.12/GC/20, 2 July 2009, para. 7.

[48] See United Nations (2023a).

[49] See Art. 1 of the ICCPR.

[50] See Art. 22 of the ICCPR.

[51] See MOCLA (2013), p. 43.

will be able to uphold its human rights obligations while also benefitting from the diverse perspectives and talents that PWDs bring to the table.

3.1.4 The Convention on the Rights of Persons with Disabilities, 2006

The CRPD is a legally binding treaty that aims to protect the rights of people living with disabilities (PWDs) across the globe. The main purpose of the Convention is to protect, promote, and ensure the full and equal enjoyment of PWDs of all human rights and fundamental freedoms and to foster respect for their inherent dignity.[52] This Convention has played a significant role in establishing the rights of PWDs. It has played a crucial role in transforming the global perception of PWDs from viewing them as incapableindividuals, objects of charity, medical burdens, or sources of family poverty,[53] and people who require social protection at all times, towards viewing PWDs as full members of society with equal human rights.[54]

Moreover, the CRPD was enacted to fill the gaps in other human rights instruments regarding PWDs. These gaps are evident as PWDs continue to face barriers in their efforts to participate as equal members of society, as recognised under other human rights instruments. The member states are required to promote and fully realise all human rights and fundamental freedoms of all PWDs without discrimination.[55] Regarding economic rights, states parties must take measures using the maximum available resources to progressively achieve the full realisation of these rights without prejudice to other obligations immediately applicable under the Convention.[56] Article 32 requires states to ensure that development cooperation is inclusive and accessible to persons with disabilities. It also creates the possibility of mainstreaming disability rights throughout the public administration and the different levels of power, but to avoid isolated and, at times, inconsistent measures, coordination is necessary.[57]

Also, to ensure state monitoring and the implementation of the Convention, the CRPD mandates the formation of disability focal points within systems or organisations in particular states.[58] According to Possi, ‘a disability focal point within a government can be either a statutory organ (autonomous or not) or an administrative unit within a government ministry. Within a government ministry, there may also be a combination of the statutory organ and an administrative entity’.[59]

---

[52] See Art. 1 CRPD.

[53] See Plessis and Van Reenen (2011), p. xxiii.

[54] See United Nations (2023c).

[55] See Art. 4.1 of the CRPD.

[56] See Art 4.2 of the CRPD.

[57] See Art. 33(1) CRPD.

[58] See Art. 33 of CRPD.

[59] See Possi (2016), p. 194.

In Tanzania, the government has made significant strides in ensuring that PWDs are included in development programmes and initiatives. However, much still needs to be done to promote their economic rights. The CRPD provides more assistance and protection than tools for their economic independence, leaving a gap that needs to be filled. To address this gap, it is crucial to mainstream disability rights throughout the public administration and different levels of power in Tanzania.

Therefore, while the CRPD has played a significant role in establishing the rights of PWDs, it is the Tanzanian government's task to promote their economic development and ensure that they are included in development programmes and initiatives. The government must take the necessary measures to fill the gap in the CRPD and promote the economic rights of PWDs to achieve inclusive and sustainable economic development.

3.1.5 Optional Protocol to the Convention on the Rights of Persons with Disabilities, 2006

Tanzania ratified the Optional Protocol to the Convention on the Rights of Persons with Disabilities (OP-CRPD) in 2009, indicating its commitment to protecting the rights of persons with disabilities.[60] The Protocol allows the Committee on the Rights of Persons with Disabilities to receive and consider communications from individuals or groups claiming to be victims of violations of the Convention by the state party.[61] This is a significant step towards ensuring that the rights of persons with disabilities are protected in Tanzania as the Protocol provides an avenue for recourse for those who have been victimised. However, it is important to note that all domestic remedies must be exhausted before lodging a complaint with the Committee.[62] This requirement ensures that individuals and groups have first attempted to seek redress within the Tanzanian legal system before seeking recourse at the international level.

Tanzania's ratification of the Optional Protocol to the CRPD is a positive step towards protecting the rights of persons with disabilities. However, there is still work to be done to ensure that they are fully included in society and have access to opportunities for economic development.

[60] See https://indicators.ohchr.org/.

[61] See Art. 1 of the OP-CRPD.

[62] See Art. 2 of the OP-CRPD.

3.2 Regional Instruments on Economic Rights of Persons with Disabilities

When it comes to promoting economic development and safeguarding the rights of persons with disabilities (PWDs) in Tanzania, adherence to international and regional agreements is crucial. As a member state of the African Union (AU), Southern African Development Community (SADC), and East African Community (EAC), Tanzania is obligated to ensure that PWDs have equal access to economic opportunities and that their rights are protected. In this sub-chapter, we will examine the regional instruments that Tanzania has ratified as well as their impact on national laws, with a particular focus on the African Charter on Human and Peoples' Rights and the Protocol to the African Charter on Human and Peoples' Rights on the Rights of Persons with Disabilities in Africa.

3.2.1 African Charter on Human and Peoples' Rights, 1981 (the African Charter)

Tanzania is a signatory to the African Charter on Human and Peoples' Rights (ACHPR), which provides for non-discrimination while enjoying any right enshrined in the Charter.[63] The Charter recognises the economic rights of individuals and groups, including persons with disabilities (PWDs), such as property rights, the right to work, the right to dispose of their wealth and natural resources freely, and the right to economic development.[64]

Despite these rights enshrined in the Charter, PWDs in Tanzania face significant economic challenges. Discrimination remains prevalent, and many PWDs are not fully included in economic development initiatives.[65] This denies PWDs their inherent rights and undermines Tanzania's economic development.

Therefore, Tanzania has a legal and moral obligation to take measures necessary to ensure that PWDs are guaranteed their economic rights. This includes equal employment opportunities, entrepreneurship, and access to financial services. Additionally, the government must ensure that PWDs are included in all economic development planning and implementation aspects. By fulfilling its obligations under the Charter, Tanzania can promote inclusive economic growth and development while empowering PWDs to reach their full potential. It is time to recognise the importance of PWDs' economic rights and take concrete steps towards their realisation in Tanzania.

[63] See Human Rights Library (2023), Arts. 2 and 19 of the ACHPR.

[64] See Arts. 14, 15, 19, 21, and 22 of the ACHPR.

[65] See Art. 18 of the ACHPR.

3.2.2 The Protocol to the African Charter on Human and Peoples' Rights on the Rights of Persons with Disabilities in Africa (Disability Protocol), 2018

The Protocol to the African Charter on Human and Peoples' Rights on the Rights of Persons with Disabilities in Africa (Disability Protocol) is a comprehensive and crucial instrument aimed at promoting, protecting, and ensuring the full and equal enjoyment of all human and people's rights by all persons with disabilities (PWDs) in Africa. Adopted by the heads of state and government members of the African Union (AU) in January 2018, the Protocol supplements the provisions of Article 66 of the African Charter and Article 18(4) of the same Charter, which provides for the right to special protection measures for PWDs in keeping with their needs.

The Protocol has yet to be ratified by at least 15 member states, and Tanzania is one of the countries that has not ratified it. However, the Protocol recognises that PWDs have duties like those without disabilities, enabling them to use their capabilities and earn for themselves. This can reduce poverty and promote independence, leading to economic development.

The Protocol provides several rights to PWDs, including the right to equality, the right to work, and an adequate standard of living. The right to equality, as outlined in Article 6, states that every PWD is equal before the law and should fully and equally enjoy all human rights. The right to work, outlined in Article 19(1)(2)(a), states that PWDs have the right to decent work with just and favourable conditions and prohibits all forms of discrimination. This article also promotes opportunities for PWDs to initiate self-employment.

Furthermore, the Protocol recognises the right to an adequate standard of living, which can be viewed as a social right. However, this will never be realised in Africa without economic implications.[66] The Protocol, therefore, provides a framework that can enable PWDs to participate in economic activities, earn a decent living, and reduce poverty levels.

Therefore, the Disability Protocol is a crucial instrument that can significantly impact the lives of PWDs in Tanzania and Africa. Its implementation will shift attitudes and approaches towards PWDs, promote their integration into development programmes, and enable them to reach their full potential. Tanzania should, therefore, ratify and domesticate the Protocol to ensure that PWDs enjoy their human and people's rights fully and equally.

[66] See Art. 20 of the Disability Protocol.

3.3 National Laws Governing Economic Rights of Persons with Disabilities

This sub-chapter focuses on the domestic laws that support and promote the economic rights of persons with disabilities (PWDs) in Tanzania. It aims to analyse the legal instruments regulating economic rights concerning PWDs. These instruments have been critical in domesticating international agencies' provisions, such as the Persons with Disabilities Act, the Local Government Act, and the Employment and Labour Relations Act, which have been instrumental in promoting economic development and protecting the rights of PWDs in Tanzania. The economic rights of persons with disabilities (PWDs) in Tanzania have been a critical area of concern as they face significant challenges in accessing employment, education, and other essential economic opportunities. To address these challenges, the government has put in place several legal instruments to promote and protect the economic rights of PWDs.

The Constitution of the United Republic of Tanzania (CURT), 1977, recognises the economic rights of every individual, including PWDs. However, these rights are not enforceable in a court of law, as provided under Article 7(2) of CURT. This limitation creates a gap in the protection and promotion of the economic rights of PWDs', which could perpetuate poverty and unemployment among this vulnerable group.

To address these issues, Tanzania enacted the Persons with Disabilities Act of 2010, which aims to protect and promote the rights of PWDs, including their economic rights. The Act provides a comprehensive definition of disability and ensures that PWDs are included in all spheres of life, including political, social, and employment opportunities.[67] It also guarantees social security, the right to work, and a good standard of living, making it an offence to deny PWDs participation in economic activities.[68]

Moreover, the Act mandates employers to provide working tools and ensure safe and healthy working conditions for all employees with disabilities, a significant step towards promoting equal access to employment opportunities.[69] However, the Act does not explicitly provide for the right to own property, which could limit the economic growth and development of PWDs.

To further support the economic development of PWDs, the Local Government Act Cap. 290 [R.E.2019] requires local government authorities to allocate to PWDs 2% of their revenues as interest-free loans.[70] While this effort is commendable, the

---

[67] See Kajiru and Nyimbi (2020), p. 74.

[68] See Sect. 62(i) on offence and Sect. 4 on the standard of living; Sects. 5.1(g), 30.1, 31.2, 32, 34.1 (a–c), and 50 cover work-related issues, and for social security, see Sect. 54.2 of the Disabilities Act.

[69] See Sect. 34.1 of the Disabilities Act.

[70] See Sect. 37A(1)–(3) of the Local Government Act.

procedures for accessing the loans are unclear, which could hinder the intended economic growth and development of PWDs.

The Employment and Labour Relations Act (ELRA) Cap. 366 [R.E. 2019] of Tanzania was implemented to protect fundamental labour rights, promote equal employment opportunities, and establish basic employment standards. This Act provides a legal framework for effective and fair employment relations, including minimum work conditions and dispute resolution.[71] Sections 7 and 8 of ELRA require employers to eliminate discrimination in any employment policy or practice, including those based on physical appearance and the ability to perform work due to impairment. Discrimination against persons with disabilities is unconstitutional and against the law. ELRA prohibits direct and indirect discrimination on several grounds, including disability.[72]

However, despite the provisions in ELRA, unemployment rates for PWDs in Tanzania remain higher than those for non-disabled individuals.[73] This discrepancy highlights the need for employers to create a work environment that is inclusive and accommodating of PWDs. It is essential to recognise that PWDs can compete and perform the same work as non-disabled individuals. Employers must provide reasonable accommodations to enable PWDs to perform their duties, promoting economic development and supporting the human rights of PWDs in Tanzania.

ELRA provides a crucial foundation for protecting labour rights in Tanzania. However, more must be done to ensure that employers create an inclusive work environment that promotes equal opportunities and eliminates discrimination against PWDs. By doing so, Tanzania can promote economic development and support the human rights of all its citizens.

It is sufficient to say that Tanzania has made significant efforts to promote and protect the economic rights of persons with disabilities through various domestic laws and policies. However, there is still a long way to go in ensuring the effective implementation and enforcement of these laws to create a truly inclusive and accessible society. It is essential to address the gaps in the existing legal framework and to adopt a more comprehensive approach that considers the unique needs and challenges faced by persons with disabilities in accessing economic opportunities and resources. This requires a multi-stakeholder approach involving the government, civil society, and the private sector to work together towards promoting disability-inclusive economic growth and development.

---

[71] See Sect. 3(b) of ELRA.

[72] See Kudo (2010), 5–25.

[73] Ibid.

4 Promotion of Economic Rights of PWDs in Tanzania

The promotion of economic rights for persons with disabilities (PWDs) is crucial for ensuring their full and equal participation in society. In Tanzania, the government has taken steps to protect the economic rights of PWDs through legislation and policy frameworks. This part explores the current situation of PWDs in Tanzania in terms of their economic rights, including the legal framework, policy initiatives, and data on PWDs in the country. Non-discrimination and equality are essential principles underpinning the right-based approach. It examines how policies impact the realisation of rights among different groups and eliminate all forms of discrimination, prioritising those who face more significant barriers in realising their rights, like PWDs.[74]

4.1 PWDs and Economic Rights Situation in Tanzania

Before 1981, Tanzania lacked a legal framework on rights and services for persons with disabilities, which had significant implications for the enjoyment of their human rights and hindered their full participation in economic development. Without clear policies in place, there was inadequate provision of services to persons with disabilities, depriving them of essential support and opportunities for economic empowerment.

The international community's declaration of 1981 as the International Year of Disabled Persons played a crucial role in raising awareness of the rights of individuals with disabilities.[75] It brought attention to the Tanzanian government's need to address the shortcomings with regard to service provision. This recognition of the importance of human rights led to the preparation of a Cabinet paper in 1981, which signalled a commitment to addressing the challenges faced by persons with disabilities and ensuring their inclusion in society.[76]

The Cabinet paper comprised two parts. The first part acknowledged the detrimental impact of the absence of clear policies on service provision, recognising the violation of human rights experienced by persons with disabilities due to the lack of access to adequate services and support. The second part of the Cabinet paper outlined the responsibilities of various stakeholders, including government institutions, families, relatives, local governments, and non-governmental organisations, in providing care and support to persons with disabilities.[77] By delineating these responsibilities, the government aimed to protect and promote the human rights of persons with disabilities.

---

[74] See ENNHRI (2023).

[75] See No. 19 of 1981.

[76] See Tanzania Ministry of Labour, Youth Development and Sports (2004), p. 1.

[77] Tanzania Ministry of Labour, Youth Development and Sports (2004), p. 1.

In conjunction with the Cabinet paper, the 1981 Census, which identified 457,569 persons with disabilities, shed light on the magnitude of the issue. This data highlighted the need for inclusive policies and measures that would enable persons with disabilities to fully participate in economic development.[78] Recognising and respecting the human rights of persons with disabilities is crucial for fostering an inclusive and equitable society, where all individuals have equal opportunities to contribute to and benefit from economic progress.

In response to these developments, the Disabled Persons (Employment) Act was enacted in 1982, seeking to promote economic opportunities for persons with disabilities.[79] By implementing measures such as quarter schemes, reservation of posts, and the creation of suitable working environments, the government aimed to address the economic disparities faced by persons with disabilities.[80] This legislative action was grounded on the understanding that economic development cannot be achieved without the full inclusion and participation of all members of society, including persons with disabilities.

Additionally, the Disabled Persons Care and Maintenance Act,[81] enacted in the same year, emphasised the shared responsibility among different entities, including families, relatives, local governments, the central government, and non-governmental organisations, to provide care and support for persons with disabilities.[82] This recognition of collective responsibility aligns with the principles of human rights, emphasising the importance of solidarity and societal support in realising the rights of all individuals, regardless of their abilities.

The subsequent adoption of the National Policy on Disability in 2004[83] and the ratification of international conventions, such as the Convention on the Rights of Persons with Disabilities, further reinforced the commitment to human rights and economic development for persons with disabilities.[84] These policy measures recognised the barriers faced by persons with disabilities in accessing employment opportunities and called for the enactment of laws to protect their rights and promote their independence.[85] By aligning national policies with international standards, Tanzania demonstrated its commitment to creating an enabling environment that fosters the economic inclusion and development of persons with disabilities.

In this context, organizations of persons with disabilities (OPDs) emerged as key stakeholders in advocating for the rights of persons with disabilities. These organisations, including civil society organisations (CSOs) and the Tanzania Federation of Disabled Peoples' Organizations (SHIVYAWATA), played a crucial role in raising

---

[78] Possi (1996), p. 158.

[79] See Act No. 2 of 1982.

[80] See Sects. 4, 13-7 of Act No. 2, 1982.

[81] See Act No. 3 of 1982.

[82] See Sects. 14-9 of Act No. 3, 1982.

[83] See Joseph (2022), p. 5.

[84] See National Bureau of Statistics (2016), p. 1.

[85] See Ministry of Labour, Youth Development and Sports, p. 4.

awareness about disability rights, conducting accessibility audits, and improving service provision. Their efforts were instrumental in promoting the human rights of persons with disabilities and fostering an environment conducive to economic development for all.

The availability and accuracy of data on persons with disabilities (PWDs) in Tanzania are crucial for addressing the intersection of human rights and economic development. According to national surveys, there are variations in the prevalence rates of disability due to inconsistencies in defining disability across different surveys. For example, the 2017/18 Tanzania Household Budget Survey (HBS) notes a 6.8% prevalence of disability, while the Population and Housing Census (PHC) survey reports it to be 9.3%. This inconsistency hampers the formulation of targeted policies and interventions needed to empower PWDs and promote their economic inclusion. To address this issue, it is essential to establish a standardised and comprehensive approach to data collection, ensuring that accurate information is available to guide human-rights-based strategies for economic development.

The literacy rates among PWDs in Tanzania, particularly among females, indicate the need for improved access to education and transportation. According to the 2012 Census report, out of 3,450,986 persons with disabilities aged 5 years and above, 64.6% were literate. The literacy rate among males with disabilities was 69.6%, while for females, it was 60.1%.[86] These figures highlight the importance of prioritising an inclusive education system that accommodates the diverse needs of PWDs.[87] Bridging the literacy gap and enhancing educational opportunities can empower individuals with disabilities, enabling them to participate fully in economic activities and exercise their human rights.

When examining the economic activity status of PWDs in Tanzania, it is evident that a significant proportion of them are engaged in agriculture and related industries. However, barriers such as limited access to credit and social protection programmes hinder their economic progress. The 2012 Census data shows that two-thirds (70.2%) of PWDs aged 15 and above were employed, with farming, livestock keeping, and fishing being the primary occupations.[88] For instance, in one incident in Ukerewe, it was observed that a PWD was denied a loan from the bank simply because of his condition.[89] To overcome these barriers, it is crucial to establish inclusive financial systems and social safety nets tailored to the specific needs of PWDs.[90] This would ensure that they have equal opportunities to access resources and participate in the formal economy, thereby promoting their economic development.

The disproportionate prevalence of male-headed households among PWDs in Tanzania reflects a gender imbalance in household leadership and decision-making.

[86] See National Bureau of Statistics (2016), p. 17.

[87] See Joseph (2022), p. 2.

[88] See National Bureau of Statistics (2016), p. 26.

[89] See Uromi and Mazagwa (2014), p. 159.

[90] See Mwendwa et al. (2009), p. 665.

According to the data, 68.3% of households headed by persons with disabilities were headed by males.[91] This gender disparity highlights the existing gender-based discrimination and inequalities that hinder the realisation of human rights for PWDs, particularly women. To promote inclusive economic development, it is crucial to address these gender disparities by empowering women with disabilities, enhancing their access to resources, and challenging social norms that perpetuate gender inequality.

The data also reveals that a significant proportion of PWDs in Tanzania, particularly children and older adults, struggle to fend for themselves and lack access to essential services in rural areas. Comprehensive social support systems are urgently needed to cater to the specific needs of PWDs across all age groups, ensuring their access to healthcare, rehabilitation services, and social assistance. This calls for comprehensive support so that Tanzania can uplift PWDs from poverty and enable them to contribute to the country's economic development actively.

To facilitate the realisation of human rights and economic development for persons with disabilities, it is essential to recognise the symbiotic relationship between the two. Upholding human rights ensures that persons with disabilities are treated with dignity, have equal access to opportunities, and are included in decision-making processes. This goes hand in hand with the availability and accuracy of data on PWDs in Tanzania, which is essential for formulating evidence-based policies that promote their human rights and economic development. Simultaneously, economic development that is inclusive and sustainable provides avenues for empowerment, job creation, and poverty reduction among persons with disabilities. With these interconnected factors being considered in policies and practices, Tanzania can realise the full potential of persons with disabilities, contributing to both their well-being and the overall economic prosperity of the nation.

4.2 *Efforts and the Extent of Progress in the Implementation of PWDs' Economic Rights and the Reduction of Poverty Among PWDs in Tanzania*

The Government of Tanzania has made commendable efforts to address the economic rights of persons with disabilities (PWDs) and reduce their poverty. While recognising that the realisation of economic rights cannot happen overnight, states must work towards this goal progressively.[92] Poverty itself constitutes a denial of human rights.[93] However, it is crucial to critically examine the effectiveness of Tanzania's efforts and identify areas that require further attention.

---

[91] See National Bureau of Statistics (2016), p. 33.

[92] *See* CESCR, General Comment No. 3, The Nature of States Parties Obligations, UN Doc. E/1991/23(SUPP), 1 January 1991, para. 9.

[93] See CESCR (2001), para 1.

Tanzania's commitment to realising the rights of PWDs is evident through the establishment of the National Policy on Disability (NPD) in 2004. This comprehensive policy aims to create an enabling environment for PWDs to engage in productive work, access services, and improve their overall well-being.[94] It is important to evaluate the implementation and impact of the NPD to ensure that the policy translates into tangible improvements in the lives of PWDs. This assessment should involve a thorough examination of resource allocation, monitoring and evaluation mechanisms, and the extent to which the policy's objectives are being met.

To accelerate inclusive economic growth and poverty reduction, Tanzania's National Five-Year Development Plan (FYDP III) emphasises equitable participation through education.[95] The plan ensures fee-free education for PWDs in public schools and prioritises their inclusion, particularly at the secondary level.[96] A critical analysis of the quality of education provided to PWDs is necessary to ensure that schools are adequately equipped and staffed to cater to their diverse needs. Additionally, attention should be given to support systems for PWDs who require specialised education or assistive devices. Evaluating the inclusivity of the educational system will help ensure that PWDs receive the quality education that prepares them for meaningful economic participation.

In addition to policy initiatives, the government has taken steps to increase the visibility and representation of PWDs in governance.[97] Affirmative action and seating reservation measures have been implemented to enhance the participation of PWDs in decision-making processes. However, it is important to realise the effectiveness of these measures and assess whether they lead to meaningful participation and the exercise of decision-making power for PWDs. Special attention should be given to the representation of marginalised groups, such as women and youth with disabilities, to ensure their voices are adequately represented in shaping policies that affect their lives.

In a situation where these issues are addressed, Tanzania can further advance the realisation of economic rights and promote inclusive economic development for PWDs. This requires a continued commitment to progressive realisation, implementation of inclusive policies, provision of accessible services, and meaningful participation of PWDs in decision-making processes.[98] The regular monitoring, evaluation, and engagement of all relevant stakeholders are essential to identifying challenges and refining strategies to promote the economic inclusion and human rights of PWDs.

Further, in ensuring that PWDs achieve economic independence, the government of Tanzania, through the FYDP III, has implemented strategies to promote the

---

[94] See Tanzania Ministry of Labour, Youth Development and Sports (2004), p. 10.

[95] See FYDP III, p. 5.

[96] See FYDP III, p. 21.

[97] See Sect 51(3)(viii) of the Disabilities Act.

[98] *See* CESCR, General Comment No. 3, The Nature of States Parties Obligations, UN Doc. E/1991/23(SUPP), 1 January 1991, para. 9.

diversification of investment portfolios in strategically important value-added production and employment-generating activities. These strategies include the promotion of not-for-profit social enterprises in sectors such as food processing, handcrafting, and agriculture, with a focus on social and environmental impact.[99] Recognising the importance of innovation in small and medium enterprises, the government aims to establish legal and operational business systems that address the specific needs of PWDs and start-ups.[100]

To address the diverse needs of PWDs, the Persons with Disabilities Act assigns responsibilities to key ministries and establishes the National Advisory Council for Persons with Disabilities (NAC) as a forum for advising the government on disability-related matters.[101] The Ministry of Health and Social Welfare is responsible for ensuring effective welfare services.[102] While the Ministry of Labour and Employment enforces minimum employment quotas for PWDs.[103] The Ministry of Education and Vocational Training oversees educational services for PWDs at all levels, including special schools and inclusive educational settings,[104] and the Ministry of Works ensures the accessibility of buildings and transportation infrastructure.[105] The Regional Administration and Local Government, under the Prime Minister's Office, play a crucial role in service delivery at the regional, district, and ward levels.[106] Additionally, the President's Office, Public Service Management, is responsible for facilitating PWDs' employment in the public sector and ensuring the availability of adequate public facilities.[107] The Ministry of Community Development, Gender, and Children addresses issues related to women and children with disabilities.[108]

While the government's efforts to support the economic rights of PWDs in Tanzania are commendable, it is important to recognise the interrelatedness of human rights, including economic and social rights. In the African context and specifically in Tanzania, the discussion of economic rights cannot be detached from social rights due to the country's level of development. Therefore, a comprehensive approach is necessary to address the holistic well-being of PWDs and to ensure that economic rights are realised in conjunction with social rights.

Poverty and its relationship with politics and governance play a crucial role in shaping policy choices and economic development. When governance is ineffective,

---

[99] See FYDP III, p. 47.

[100] See FDYP III, p. 52.

[101] See Possi (2016), pp. 201–203.

[102] See Sect. 43 of the Disabilities Act.

[103] See Sect. 46 of the Disabilities Act.

[104] See Sect. 42.2 of the Disabilities Act.

[105] See Sect. 44 of the Disabilities Act.

[106] See Sect. 45 of Disabilities Act.

[107] See Sect. 45 of the Disabilities Act.

[108] See Sect. 42 of the Disabilities Act.

it can lead to poor policy decisions that perpetuate poverty.[109] In such cases, individuals have limited voice and power, which can hinder economic growth, even in resource-rich countries. Defining and identifying poverty is critical to addressing poverty-related concerns. Economists often refer to the poverty line, which signifies a certain income level below which individuals are considered to be living in poverty.[110] However, alternative perspectives, such as the basic needs approach, focus on income inadequacy and the deprivation of capabilities, particularly affecting PWDs.[111] Poor individuals frequently face environmental and structural risks that compromise their health and accessibility to nutritious food, clean water, suitable housing, and medical care.[112] These risks can further exacerbate poverty among PWDs.

The CRPD has played a transformative role in perceiving disability as a specific human rights issue, necessitating policy and legal approaches that eliminate barriers across various aspects of life for PWDs. The goal is to ensure that PWDs can exercise their economic, social, political, civil, and cultural rights on an equal footing with those without disabilities.[113] Articles 4, 5, and 32 of the CRPD emphasise the principles relevant to inclusive development and poverty reduction. In Tanzania, the National Strategy for Growth and Reduction of Poverty (MKUKUTA II) acknowledges disability as a factor contributing to poverty. Strategies are being implemented to foster sustainable, productive activities; decent employment opportunities; and poverty reduction among PWDs.[114] The government has established mechanisms within the financial sector to support the creation of employment opportunities, including credit schemes, start-up capital, empowerment funds, and special entrepreneurship and mentorship programmes.[115] Formalising and regularising businesses and properties for PWDs are also part of the government's efforts.[116]

Recognising the multidimensional nature of poverty, it is essential to consider the role of monetary income for PWDs. Micro-finance, micro-credit, saving schemes, apprenticeships, and insurance schemes are crucial in supporting PWDs.[117] Many PWDs are engaged in the informal sector, with a significant proportion being self-employed.[118] Providing adequate support and capital is vital for the sustainability of their businesses.[119] The FYDP III and the NPD emphasise access to micro-finance and savings schemes. Structured dialogic platforms, such as the Tanzania National

[109] See Adejumobi (2006), p. 3.
[110] See Groce et al. (2011), p. 1496.
[111] See Groce et al. (2011), p. 1497.
[112] See Groce et al. (2011), p. 1498.
[113] See Mwendwa et al. (2009), p. 663.
[114] See Ministry of Finance and Economic Affairs (2010), pp. 36 and 56.
[115] See Ministry of Finance and Economic Affairs (2010), pp. 56–57.
[116] See Ministry of Finance and Economic Affairs (2010), p. 58.
[117] See Beisland and Mersland (2010).
[118] See ILO (2009).
[119] See Groce et al. (2011), p. 1505.

Business Council (TNBC), have been established to address business challenges and promote social and economic development through consensus building. A comprehensive framework that includes new private sector operators and PWDs at the sector level is also important.[120] The government has designated a focal point responsible for realising the rights of people with disabilities, based on the Disability Act 2010, which is aligned with the CRPD.

The current policy and legal framework for persons with disabilities, particularly the Persons with Disability Act 2010, represents a significant improvement and enjoys wide support from disabled peoples' organisations (DPOs) and the disability movement.[121] Addressing barriers to employable skills is crucial, particularly for PWDs. In addition to supporting private enterprise growth, interventions such as skill development programmes and low-interest-rate loans should be reviewed and strengthened.[122] The Local Government Act plays a role in providing support to PWDs,[123] and a predictable budget allocation is in place to finance these initiatives.[124]

In summing up this part, it is clear that Tanzania's commitment to realising the economic rights of persons with disabilities and reducing poverty among them is commendable. Efforts such as diversifying investments, promoting social enterprises, ensuring access to education and employment, and improving infrastructure accessibility demonstrate a dedication to inclusive economic development. However, it is crucial to adopt a comprehensive approach that addresses the interconnectedness of economic and social rights for persons with disabilities. By critically evaluating and improving policies, investing in skill development, and strengthening support systems, Tanzania can continue advancing human rights and sustainable economic development for persons with disabilities.

5 Challenges in Promoting the Economic Rights of PWDs in Tanzania

Tanzania has undoubtedly made efforts to promote the economic rights of persons with disabilities (PWDs). However, numerous challenges hinder the full realisation of these rights, with implications for human rights and economic development.

One significant challenge stems from the historical perception of caring for PWDs as an act of charity rather than recognising it as a legal right. This prevailing culture of charity extends even to civil society institutions and disability organisations, inhibiting a comprehensive understanding of the social model of disability and

[120] See FDYP III, p. 49.

[121] See FYDP III, p. 23.

[122] See FYDP III, pp. 56–57.

[123] See Sect. 37A of CAP. 290 R.E.2019.

[124] See FYDP III, p. 257.

impeding the effective enforcement of the UN Convention. Shifting this mindset and fostering a human-rights-based approach within the disability sector is crucial for advancing the economic rights of PWDs.

Another obstacle is the varying degrees of legal protection for economic, social, and cultural rights (ESCR) across international and regional human rights instruments. While Tanzania has ratified both the International Covenant on Civil and Political Rights (ICCPR) and the International Covenant on Economic, Social, and Cultural Rights (ICESCR), the latter is not domesticated.[125] As a result, economic rights in Tanzania are not justiciable, meaning they cannot be effectively enforced through legal channels, limiting their practical impact.

Economic rights in Tanzania are primarily clustered under the Fundamental Objectives and Directive Principles of State Policy (FODPSP).[126] Unfortunately, these principles lack enforceability, rendering economic rights elusive for PWDs.[127] Rights must be legally enforceable to have real value within liberal democracies, and the absence of enforceability undermines the protection and realisation of economic rights in Tanzania. [128]

Despite the progress made through the Constitution of the United Republic of Tanzania, Article 14, and sections 7(b) and 31(2) of the Persons with Disabilities Act of 2010, which aim to prevent discrimination and promote employment opportunities for PWDs, ableism and stereotypes persist in Tanzanian society. Many employers continue to discriminate against workers with disabilities at every stage of employment, undermining their economic inclusion. The requirement for employers to ensure that three per cent of their workforce consists of PWDs often remains only on paper, particularly in the formal sector.

Coordination among multiple government ministries, agencies, and departments creates further challenges. The involvement of different organs such as the Ministry of Education, Science, Technology and Vocational Training; the Special Need Unit of the Ministry of Education, Science, and Technology; and the Ministry of Health, Community Development, Gender, Elderly and Children in disability programmes leads to confusion and underperformance. Streamlining and improving coordination mechanisms can enhance the effectiveness of policies and strategies aimed at advancing the economic rights of PWDs. [129]

While the government has made some progress in ensuring physical accessibility, such as investing in infrastructure and public transport, challenges persist. Guidelines on accessibility tools and renovation procedures, as mandated by the 2010 Act, have not been adequately distributed to relevant stakeholders. Furthermore, accessibility audits have not been completed, impeding the full realisation of physical

[125] See Economic, Social and Cultural Rights (2023).

[126] See Art 7.2 CURT.

[127] See Litinski (2019).

[128] See Dean (2002), p. 186.

[129] See UNICEF (2021), p. 127.

accessibility for PWDs. These challenges hinder developmental efforts to reduce poverty among PWDs despite the existence of good laws, policies, and strategies.

Addressing these challenges requires prioritising the economic rights of PWDs and a comprehensive approach that tackles attitudinal barriers, strengthens legal frameworks, enhances coordination among government entities, and ensures the effective implementation of accessibility measures to promote human rights.

6 Conclusion and Recommendations

Not only is the promotion of economic rights for persons with disabilities (PWDs) a matter of human rights, but it also plays a vital role in fostering economic development. In Tanzania, where a significant number of people have disabilities, addressing the unique challenges faced by PWDs in accessing and enjoying their economic rights is crucial for achieving a just and equitable society. The interconnectedness of human rights and economic development is undeniable, and economic rights such as the right to work, social security, education, and healthcare are fundamental components of human rights, ensuring individuals' dignity and well-being.

Tanzania has taken significant steps towards protecting and improving the economic rights of PWDs by ratifying international legal instruments and enacting domestic legislation. However, the effective implementation and enforcement of these laws are crucial to realising the full potential of these rights. Addressing the barriers and discrimination faced by PWDs in education, employment, transportation, and social protection is essential for their economic inclusion and active participation in society.

To ensure equal access to opportunities and resources, Tanzania must promote inclusive employment practices, invest in accessible infrastructure, and prioritise poverty reduction and social integration. Inclusive employment practices not only empower PWDs but also benefit employers by enhancing diversity, innovation, and productivity in the workforce. Accessible infrastructure and transportation systems enable PWDs to access employment opportunities, essential services, and markets, thereby fostering economic growth and social inclusion.

Therefore, there is a need to strengthen the implementation of laws and policies protecting the economic rights of PWDs, including establishing monitoring mechanisms, providing training, and allocating resources for implementation. Improving access to quality education and vocational training for PWDs, including reasonable accommodations and support services, empowers them to acquire skills, enhances their employability, and fosters economic development. Encouraging employers to adopt inclusive employment practices, such as reasonable accommodations and non-discrimination policies, can promote awareness among employers about the benefits of hiring PWDs, including increased productivity and diverse perspectives.

Investing in the development of accessible infrastructure and transportation systems, ensuring equal access for PWDs, enhances their mobility, facilitates their participation in economic activities, and promotes economic growth. Empowering PWDs and involving them in decision-making processes related to economic rights and development is crucial. It ensures their meaningful participation, representation, and inclusion in relevant forums and organisations.

Conducting awareness campaigns to challenge societal attitudes and stereotypes towards PWDs is essential to promote a culture of inclusivity, respect, and equal opportunities, fostering human rights and economic development. Finally, fostering collaboration among government agencies, civil society organisations, and the private sector to address the economic rights of PWDs can collectively mobilise resources, expertise, and networks for effective and sustainable initiatives.

References

Adejumobi S (2006) Governance and poverty reduction in Africa: a critique of poverty reduction strategy papers. Economic Community of West African Studies: Abuja

Beisland A, Mersland R (2010) The use of microfinance services among economically active disabled people: evidence from Uganda. J Int Dev, 2010, at http://onlinelibrary.wiley.com/doi/10.1002/jid.1720/full

Center for Social Concern (2023) The preferential option for the poor and vulnerable. https://socialconcerns.nd.edu/content/4-preferential-option-poor-and-vulnerable

CESCR (2001) General Statement, Substantive Issues Arising in the Implementation of the International Covenant on Economic, Social and Cultural Rights: Poverty and the International Covenant on Economic, Social and Cultural Rights. E/C.12/2001/10, 10 May 2001

Dean H (2002) Welfare rights and social policy. Prentice Hall. https://doi.org/10.4324/9781315847726

Economic Social and Cultural Rights (2023). https://ijrcenter.org/thematic-research-guides/economic-social-and-cultural-rights-2/

ENNHRI (2023) Human Rights-Based Approach. https://www.un.org/en/global-issues/human-rights

Fantinelli S et al (2022) Self-perceived employability of workers with disability: a case study in an educational farm. Front Psychol 13:871616. https://doi.org/10.3389/fpsyg.2022.871616

Gervas Z (2019) Obstacles in public transport: what solution for people with physical disabilities? Updated 27 December 2021, https://www.inclusivecitymaker.com/obstacles-public-transport-physical-disability/

Plessis G, Van Reenen T (eds) (2011) Aspects of disability law in Africa. Pretoria University Law Press, Pretoria

Groce N et al (2011) Disability and poverty: the need for a more nuanced understanding of implications for development policy and practice. Third World Quarterly. Disabil Global South 32(8):1493–1513

Hendriks A (2002) Different definitions — same problems — one way out? In: Breslin M, Yee S (eds) Disability rights law and policy. International and national perspectives. Transnational Publishers, Ardsley, NY, pp 195–122

Hertel S (2006) Why bother? Measuring economic rights. Res Agenda Int Stud Persp 7(3):215–230

Human Rights Library (2023) Ratification of international human rights treaties- Tanzania. https://www.hrlibrary.umn.edu/instree/z1afchar.htm

ILO (2009) Bureau of library and information services, Resource guide on disability. ILO, Geneva

International Disability Alliance (2022) IDA's Compilation of CRPD Committee's Concluding Observations, Article 27 CRPD (Work and employment). 1-48. https://www.internationaldisabilityalliance.org/sites/default/files/article_27_crpd.pdf

Joseph M (2022) The effectiveness of the laws on persons with physical disabilities at work in Tanzania. J Legal Stud Res 8(1):1–12

Kajiru I, Nyimbi I (2020) The right to work and equality in the workplace for persons with disabilities in Tanzania. EALR 47(2):72–105

Kakar S, Zaenal M, Jalil F (2022) Islamic social welfare and the role of Zakat and Islamic Charity in the family resilience: the theoretical review. In: Proceedings, 6th Indonesian Conference of Zakat (ICONZ), 30 November – 1 December 2022, Semarang, Indonesia, ISSN: 2655-6251. 83–98

Kudo T (2010) Japan's employment rate of persons with disabilities and outcome of employment Quota system. Japan Labor Rev 7(2):5–25

Landorf H et al (2008) Education for sustainable human development towards a definition. Theory Res Edu 6(2):221–236

Litinski R (2019) Economic rights: are they justiciable, and should they be? https://www.americanbar.org/groups/crsj/publications/human_rights_magazine_home/economic-justice/economic-rights%2D%2Dare-they-justiciable%2D%2Dand-should-they-be-/

Long T, Guo J (2023) Moving beyond inclusion to belonging. Int J Environ Res Public Health 20(6907):1–10. https://doi.org/10.3390/ijerph20206907

Marslev K, Sano H (2016) The economy of human rights exploring potential linkages between human rights and economic development. The Danish Institute for Human Rights. Human Rights Research Paper, No 2/2016. 1–32

Ministry of Constitutional and Legal Affairs (MOCLA) (2013) United Republic of Tanzania National Human Rights Action Plan 2013-2017

Ministry of Finance and Economic Affairs (2010) National strategy for growth and reduction of poverty II

Mwendwa T et al (2009) Mainstreaming the rights of persons with disabilities in national development frameworks. J Int Dev 21:662–672

National Bureau of Statistics (2016) Disability Monograph. January 2016

Plewes B, Sreenivasan G, Draimin T (1996) Sustainable human development as a global framework. Int J New Dev Debate 51(2):211–234

Possi A (2016) Implementing Article 33 of the Convention on the Rights of Persons with Disabilities: Tanzanian Approach. Afr Disabil Rights Yearb 4:190–212

Possi M (1996) Gender and education of people with disabilities in Tanzania. DAFITJ (New Series) 3(2):155–168

Poverty and Human Rights (2023). https://maytree.com/what-we-focus-on/poverty-human-rights/backgrounder-economic-social-rights/

Schalk S (2018) Bodyminds reimagined: disability, race, and gender in Black Women's speculative fiction. https://www.dukeupress.edu/bodyminds-reimagined

Smismans S (2005) How to be fundamental with soft procedure? The open method of coordination and fundamental social rights. Urge Research Unit on European Governance

Stone-MacDonald A, Butera G (2014) Cultural beliefs and attitudes about disability in East Africa. Rev Disabil Stud Int J 8(1):1–19

Talawar N (2022) Economic Rights. https://blog.ipleaders.in/economic-rights/

Tanzania Ministry of Labour, Youth Development and Sports (2004) National Policy on Disability. https://www.kazi.go.tz/uploads/documents/en1599783389National%20Policy%20on%20Disability%202004.pdf

UNDP (1994) Human development report. Oxford University Press, New York

UNICEF (2021) Situation analysis of children and young people with disabilities in Mainland Tanzania and Zanzibar. UNICEF

United Nations (2023a) UN Treaty Body Database. https://tbinternet.ohchr.org

United Nations (2023b) Peace, dignity and equality on a healthy planet. https://www.un.org/disabilities/documents/convention/convention.

United Nations (2023c) Department of Economic and Social Affairs Disability: Convention on the Rights of Persons with Disabilities (CRPD). Available at <https://www.un.org/development/desa/disabilities/convention-on-the-rightsof-persons-with-disabilities.html>

United Nations (2024) The Foundation of International Human Rights Law, https://www.un.org/en/about-us/udhr/foundation-of-international-human-rights-law

Uromi S, Mazagwa M (2014) Challenges facing people with disabilities and possible solutions in Tanzania. J Edu Policy Entrep Res (JEPER) 1(2):158–165

Veit-Wilson J (2007) Some social policy implications of a right to social security. In: Van Langendonck J (ed) The right to social security. Intersentia, Antwerpen – Oxford, pp 57–83

WHO (1976) International classification of impairments, disabilities, and handicaps. Published by resolution WHA29.35 of the Twenty-ninth World Health Assembly, 1976. https://apps.who.int/iris/bitstream/handle/10665/41003/9241541261_eng.pdf;jsessionid=1D0A983177B65D670DD9D4CF26E2EA39?sequence=1

World Committee on Environment and Development (1987) Our common future. Oxford University Press, New York

Ines Kajiru PhD in Law from Kwazulu-Natal, South Africa and LL.B and LL.M from Mzumbe University, Tanzania; Dean at the University of Dodoma School of Law.

Scholastica Mality LL.B and LL.M from the Ruaha Catholic University—Tanzania and PGDLP from the Law School of Tanzania, PhD in Law candidate at the University of Dar es Salaam; an Assistant Lecturer at the University of Dodoma School of Law. Email: scscholastica.mality@udom.ac.tz

Baraka Mkami LL.B, LL.M, PGDLP, and PhD (Law), Lecturer at the University of Dodoma School of Law and advocate of the High Court of Tanzania and Notary Public and Commissioner for Oaths. He can be accessed through baraka.mkami@udom.ac.tz.

Reflections on Governance Architecture, Human Rights and Economic Development in Twenty-First-Century Nigeria

Trends and Current Challenges

Stanley Osezua Ehiane, Bontle Masilo, and Ayoola Abuloye

1 Introduction

In contemporary times, countries all over the world adhere to the view that respect for human rights within their societies is compulsory. This is true for all systems of government; even authoritative regimes claim to adhere to human rights in arriving at and implementing government policies. Both at universal and regional levels, countries have, in one way or another, manifested their support for the Universal Declaration of Human Rights (UDHR).[1] Human rights issues have continued to generate interest and controversy around the world. This is because the organized world community has placed considerable emphasis, now more than before, on human rights violations, especially in the developing world. The history of human rights spans thousands of years, drawing upon religious, cultural, philosophical, and

[1] Obidimma (2020), pp. 11–29.

S. O. Ehiane (✉)
Department of Political Science and Administrative Studies, University of Botswana, Gaborone, Botswana

Department of Development Studies, School of Social Sciences, University of South Africa (UNISA), Pretoria, South Africa
e-mail: ehianes@ub.ac.bw

B. Masilo
Department of Political Science and Administrative Studies, University of Botswana, Gaborone, Botswana
e-mail: masilo@ub.ac.bw

A. Abuloye
Faculty of Law, Obafemi Awolowo University, Ile Ife, Nigeria
e-mail: aabuloye@oauife.edu.ng

I. Kajiru et al. (eds.), *Economic Development and Human Rights in Contemporary Sub-Saharan Africa*, Ius Gentium: Comparative Perspectives on Law and Justice 122, https://doi.org/10.1007/978-3-031-81400-6_8

legal developments throughout recorded history.[2] Most countries in the world have already entrenched human rights concepts in their constitutions, and emerging independent countries in Africa, of course, is not left behind. Human rights are guaranteed in the constitutions of various countries in the world. There are legal and institutional mechanisms in place to protect the human rights guaranteed in their constitutions. The idea of human rights is that certain rights are inherently attached to individuals. These rights are regarded as sacrosanct and should not be taken away except in circumstances considered reasonable and allowed by law.[3] For example, in a country like Nigeria, where capital punishment is still being practised, the right to life could be derogated in the execution of a court sentence in a criminal offence where an individual has been found guilty. The right to personal liberty could also be curtailed to prevent the unlawful entry of any person into the country or the lawful removal of any individual from the country.[4]

The struggle for democratic governance and human rights is not a new phenomenon in post-colonial Africa. Indeed, democratic governance and human rights were some of the most significant reasons for the anti-colonial struggle in Africa.[5] The emerging independent African states of the 1960s declared their unflinching dedication to democracy, good governance, and respect for human rights. This would have been effortlessly plausible because most of the independence constitutions of many African countries came with a flowery package of rights for their citizens, apparently fashioned after the constitutional provisions of Western countries, particularly the American Bill of Rights.

Human rights are among the essentials of democracy and good governance. They help human beings live a fulfilled life. And where they are denied, life becomes meaningless and hopeless. All contemporary states endeavour to ensure that human rights are guaranteed in all their practices, and they are expected to uphold them in every facet of their national life.[6] Human rights violations also occur when actions by state or non-state actors ignore or deny basic human rights, including the civil, political, cultural, social, and economic rights of the people.[7] The foundation of democracy in any country is seen in the observance of the rule of law. Consequently, issues regarding the enforcement of fundamental rights have continued to be prominently featured in Nigerian courts due to the increasing consciousness in the sanctity and need to protect these rights. Fundamental rights are rights that have constitutional backing and that, upon an actual breach or threat of breach, are enforceable in court. Due to the constitutional nature of these rights, they are placed on a higher pedestal than ordinary civil matters, where a claim for damages resulting from a

[2]Nwufor (2010), pp. 203–216.

[3]Umuzurike (1995), p. 141.

[4]See section 35 (1) of the Constitution of the Federal Republic of Nigeria 1999 (as amended).

[5]Addaney (2018), pp. 181–197.

[6]Ogoloma and Sampson (2015), p. 1.

[7]Ogoloma and Sampson (2015).

proven injury has to be specifically made and proved.[8] The Constitution mandates: 'this constitution is supreme, and its provisions shall have binding force on all authorities and persons throughout the Federal Republic of Nigeria'.[9]

The notion of a governance 'architecture' is adopted here as a heuristic lens capable of accommodating a rationalist concern for structure and its potential effects on the (principally instrumental) behaviour of governance actors, as well as a relationship-based analysis of 'global governors' and the interactional effects of political units within authorizing structures.[10] The emerging post-colonial Africa declared its unflinching dedication to democracy, good governance, and respect for human rights. Despite this comprehensive regional governance architecture and human rights system, a glance at events in twenty-first-century Africa shows that the continent still faces issues of poor governance, retarded and unbalanced development, as well as disregard for human rights. The prevailing situation in Africa is a lucid demonstration of how the undermining of human rights has produced the antithesis of democracy and good governance and vice versa. This chapter notes that the human rights situation in Nigeria is most certainly in a state of considerable flux. This chapter focuses on the problems of human rights violations and their impact on good governance and economic development in Nigeria.

2 Conceptual Clarifications

2.1 Governance

The concept of 'governance' is not new. It has been around in both political and academic discourses for a long time, referring in a generic sense to the task of running a government or any other appropriate entity, for example a nation. In essence, the concept of governance is not new and is probably as old as human civilization. It broadly means the process of decision-making and the process by which decisions are implemented or not. The concept of governance relates to the quality of the relationship between the government and the citizens, whom it serves and protects.[11]

The concept of governance is traditionally linked to ruling and control, specifically the manner of exercise of power. Governance refers to the exercise of economic, political, and administrative authority to manage a country's affairs at all levels.[12] Governance is described by the World Bank as the way the state exercises

[8]Kalu et al. (2020); see also section 1(3) of the Constitution, which provides that any other law that is inconsistent with the provisions of the Constitution is void.

[9]See section 1(1) of the Constitution of the Federal Republic of Nigeria 1999 (as amended).

[10]Pegram (2015), pp. 618–639.

[11]Afegbua and Adejuwon (2012), pp. 141–157.

[12]Afegbua and Adejuwon (2012), pp. 141–157.

and acquires authority.[13] Sahni noted that the concept of governance is not new and probably as old as human civilization.[14] It broadly means the process of decision-making and the process by which decisions are implemented or not implemented. Governance is emerging as an interactive process, aimed at balancing social forces and reconciling social interests and enabling the members of society to organize themselves in the realization of their goals.[15] Governance can be said to refer to the way power is exercised in the management of a country's economic and social resources for development (World Bank 2021).[16] Akinola[17] regards governance as an approach or perspective that focuses on the state and institutions crafted by the people, the relationship between them, and how rules are made in a society that is accepted as legitimate by individuals and groups within that society. To Ndehfru,[18] governance is the fundamental process by which the lives and dreams of the people are jointly pursued, through deliberate and systematic strategies and policies, for the attainment of their maximum potential. The government has the responsibility to ensure equality and promote fundamental human rights. Heyman[19] refers to the logic behind the historical Bill of Rights and insists that those who drafted it were not concerned that the government might do too little but were apprehensive that it might engage in so much responsibility. Therefore, governance is involved in the process of achieving all these lofty goals of liberty and societal good.

Governance means the exercise of political power to manage the affairs of the state. Governance, therefore, has undoubtedly emerged as one of the crucial issues in many countries. The exercise of political authority is central to governance. It is therefore important to recognize that the rationale for government decision-making is more often political and economic than anything else.[20] Governance is legitimate in a positive sense when the government is installed by the people through institutional arrangements that are put in place by them, and when the performance of the ruler is adjudged good and accepted by the people and the people have no power to remove the ruler in case of a very grievous offence, such a government is legitimate and democratic.[21] Governance is the deliberate and conscious management of regime structures to enhance the public realm. Governance for development ought to be accountable, participatory, responsive, effective, and efficient for promoting the rule of law, safeguarding the interests of citizens, and marching towards holistic development. Thus, governance transcends the collective meaning of related concepts like the state, the government, and the regime. It integrates several elements

[13]Nwufor (2010), pp. 203–216.
[14]Sahni (2004).
[15]Adejuwon (2012), p. 25.
[16]Obadan (1998).
[17]Akinola (2000).
[18]Ndehfru (2017), p. 1.
[19]Heyman (2004), p. 117.
[2021] Ajulor and Adejuwon (2010), pp. 7–31.
[21]Afegbua and Adejuwon (2012), pp. 141–157.

and principles of 'good governance'.[22] Anyanwu[23] identified three dimensions of governance: political, technical, and institutional. The political dimension involves the establishment of objectives and the exercise of leadership. The technical dimension refers to the constraints imposed by natural resources, levels of education, manpower skills, and installed industrial capacity. The institutional or managerial dimension refers to the ability to get things done.

2.2 Human Rights

The term human rights does not lend itself to a precise definition. Indeed, there has not been an acceptable definition of 'human rights' among jurists, scholars, and commentators. It is a concept that can best be described rather than defined.[24] Human rights have been variously described as the rights of a man or his fundamental freedoms. They are claimed and asserted to be those that should be, or sometimes stated to be those that are, legally recognized and protected and that secure for everyone the fullest and freest development of personality and spiritual, moral, and other independence.[25] Human rights are inherent in all human beings all over the world and are not gifts to be withdrawn, withheld, or granted at someone's whim or will. In this sense, they are said to be inalienable or imprescriptible.[26] Human rights represent the legal expression of life. Therefore, without human life, there can be no human rights. Human rights are the result of an age-long struggle against oppression and exploitation.[27] Human rights are 'rights derived from the inherent dignity of the human person'. They are universal rights of enabling qualities of human beings or individuals of the human race, attaching to the human being wherever he appears without regard to time, place, colour, sex, race, parentage, or environment. Thus, they are rights that naturally accrue to every person in his/her existence as a human being, rights that by their nature have become fundamental to existence. The term 'human rights' is used to denote a broad spectrum of rights ranging from the right to life to the right to cultural identity. They involve all elementary preconditions for a dignified human existence. Human rights are basic rights that people possess simply because they are human beings, regardless of their nationality, ethnicity, gender, language, race, or other status. They are the basic standards without which people cannot live in dignity. They are rights held by all persons equally and eternally. Human rights are universal, interdependent, inalienable, and indivisible and are based on equality, human dignity, non-discrimination,

[22] Afegbua and Adejuwon (2012), pp. 141–157.
[23] Anyanwu (1998).
[24] Ojo (2006), pp. 15–29.
[25] Obaseki (1992).
[26] Ogbu (1999).
[27] Igwe (2002), p. 1.

and responsibility.[28] Human rights are set out in the Universal Declaration of Human Rights of 1948 and are codified and further spelt out in a series of international and regional conventions—the International Covenant on Civil and Political Rights (ICCPR), the International Covenant on Economic Social and Cultural Rights (ICESCR), the Convention Against Torture (CAT), the Convention on the Elimination of All Forms of Discrimination Against Women (CEDAW), the European Convention (EU Convention), and the African Charter on Human and Peoples Rights (ACHPR), among others. These instruments lay down the minimum standards to ensure human dignity, drawing on the values found in different religions and philosophies.[29] Human rights refer to 'the basic rights and freedoms to which all humans are entitled'. Examples of rights and freedoms that are often considered human rights are civil and political rights, such as the right to life and liberty, freedom of expression, equality before the law, and social, cultural, and economic rights, including the right to participate in culture, the right to work, and the right to education.[30] Human rights are, in general term, 'rights' which all human beings, by virtue of their humanity, possess, and they include the right to life, personal liberty, a fair hearing, the dignity of a human person, and freedoms of thought, conscience, and religion. These 'rights' provide common standards of behaviour among humans and are natural, inviolable, rational, and unalterable as the deprivations of such rights would constitute grave offences to the citizens' sense of justice.[31]

2.3 *Economic Development*

Economic development is the sustained improvement in citizens' standard of living, transitioning from a low-income to a high-income economy.[32] A rapid economic development in a given state is majorly hinged on certain forces, such as labour, capital, technology, natural resources, land, education, and skills. These forces account for material success, to fulfil the wider objective of equitable distribution of income, employment and poverty alleviation.[33] It is a process that involves a chain of interrelated changes in demand and supply, leading to a rise in the economy of a nation. However, despite the availability of these forces, a state may be retrogressive and may not experience sustained development because of some factors, such as political instability and the lack of human development.

Economic development entails sustainable development. Sustainable development encompasses present and future economic growth. It stipulates a quality of life

[28] Federal Ministry of Women Affairs and Social Development (2007).

[29] United Nations (2007).

[30] Nwufor (2010), pp. 203–216.

[31] Onwuazombe (2017), pp. 115–160.

[32] Panth (2020).

[33] Soliyev (2021).

for people and future generations by making the right economic choices and policies. It prioritizes poverty reduction, productive employment, social integration, and environmental regeneration.[34] Natural resources are a very important tool in achieving sustainable economic development. However, the desired development may not be achieved if natural resources are not harnessed and utilized properly. For instance, nations like Japan and Singapore do not have abundant natural resources like some African countries, such as Nigeria. Nonetheless, these nations have been able to manage the little resources they have and have also explored other areas, such as technology, human development, and entrepreneurship, in achieving sustainable economic development.

3 Governance, Human Rights, and Development

The struggle for democratic governance and human rights is not a new phenomenon in post-colonial Africa. Indeed, democratic governance and human rights were some of the most significant reasons for the anti-colonial struggle in Africa and provided powerful mobilizing rhetoric for Africa's post-World War II anti-colonial movement.[35] Human rights and good governance are the salient elements of a well-functioning state and society. They are also mutually reinforced.[36] They also provide a set of performance standards against which these actors can be held accountable. Moreover, human rights principles inform the content of good governance efforts; they may inform the development of legislative frameworks, policies, programmes, budgetary allocations, and other measures. However, without good governance, human rights cannot be respected and protected sustainably. The implementation of human rights relies on a conducive and enabling environment. This includes appropriate legal frameworks and institutions as well as political, managerial, and administrative processes responsible for responding to the rights and needs of the population. One of the foremost instruments recognized by the United Nations as suitable for the implementation of the Sustainable Development Goals (SDGs) globally, and by extension Nigeria, is the institutionalization of human rights through good governance because it determines the extent to which the rights of adults and children—civil, cultural, economic, political, and social rights— can be realized. The UN Commission for Human Rights recognizes the primacy of institutions of governance as critical instruments for guaranteeing the right to health, adequate housing, cheap and affordable food, quality education, fair justice, and personal security.

The observance of human rights is closely connected to other good governance intervention sectors, including democratization, the role of civil society, and the rule

[34] Soliyev (2021).

[35] Prempeh (2009), pp. 469–473.

[36] Obidimma (n.d.), pp. 11–29.

of law. Human rights principles provide a set of values to guide the work of governments and other political and social actors. They provide a set of performance standards against which these actors can be held accountable. Good governance promotes human rights in several ways. It encourages public participation in government, inclusion in lawmaking and policymaking, and accountability of elected and appointed officials. It enables civil society to become actively involved in policymaking and leads to the wide representation of societal interests in decision-making. In this manner, disadvantaged groups, including women and minorities, are empowered to defend their rights. The result may be laws and policies that better respect cultural diversity, contribute to the resolution of social conflicts and tensions, and address the challenges of inequality and poverty.[37]

Within the context of human rights, good governance is critical and is one of the preconditions for the realization of human rights. Indeed, without good governance, human rights cannot be respected and protected sustainably, for the implementation of human rights relies on a conducive and enabling environment. This includes appropriate legal frameworks and institutions as well as political, managerial, and administrative processes responsible for responding to the rights and needs of the people. The relationship between human rights and good governance need not be seen as solely conflicting, with human rights serving merely as a legal corrective to good governance policies. There is no doubt that nurturing good governance is essential to ensuring respect for human rights. The crisis of governance not only undermines the quality of governance and the 'dividends' of democracy presumably expected by all and sundry but also negatively impacts the practice of human rights in Nigeria. The grossly inept leadership and the governance crisis that has plagued Nigeria have facilitated the violations of the basic rights of the Nigerian people.

4 Human Rights Provisions and Economic Development in Nigeria

The human rights concept has become part and parcel of the Nigerian Constitution. Its inclusion in the Nigerian Constitution has its explanation in the history of the political process that necessitated it. So much was this historical commitment that the Nigerian Constitution from 1979 has clear provisions for it; beyond this, the international system, with its supranational powers, also has a way of ensuring that basic treaties in the international communities are adhered to by member states. Thus, Nigeria, being a member of the international community and a signatory to international protocols on human rights, derived its human rights constitutional provisions from two primary sources: the United Nations Universal Declaration of Human Rights of 1948 and the African Charter on Human and Peoples Rights.[38]

---

[37] United Nations (2007).

[38] Animashaun (2013), pp. 59–64.

Since its independence in 1960, successive Constitutions of Nigeria have continued to include provisions on human rights protections. This commitment to human rights has been attributed to the historical emergence of the Nigerian nation.[39] The entrenchment of human rights provisions in our Constitutions was aimed at creating a society where there is political freedom, the social and economic well-being of the people. However, despite the guarantee of fundamental rights and liberties in the Nigerian Constitutions since 1960, the country has had the misfortune of military interruptions. This had profound and far-reaching effects on the promotion and protection of democratic values and fundamental freedoms among Nigerians.[40]

The 1999 Constitution is replete with provisions on human rights. Chapter IV of the 1999 Constitution, from sections 33 to 46, contains some basic human rights referred to as fundamental rights. The rights provided for in this chapter are similar to the civil-political rights or the first-generation rights contained in Articles 3–21 of the Universal Declaration of Human Rights and Articles 3–27 of the 1966 International Covenant on Civil and Political Rights (ICCPR). These rights, as contained in the 1999 Constitution, are the right to life, right to dignity of human persons, right to personal liberty, right to fair hearing, right to private and family life, right to freedom of conscience and religion, right to freedom of expression, right to freedom of association, right to freedom of movement, right to freedom from discrimination, right to compensation for compulsory acquisition, and right to seek redress in court.[41] The 1999 Constitution, outside the fundamental rights stipulated in Chapter IV, also provides for other human rights in its Chapter II. The rights contained in that chapter belong to those categorized as economic, social, and cultural rights, as enshrined in Articles 22 to 28 of the UDHR and ICESCR, or second-generation rights as well as third-generation rights. These are referred to as the Fundamental Objectives and Directives Principles of State Policy in sections 13 to 24. However, as lofty as the fundamental objectives are, they are not justiciable. These rights are not enforceable in the courts of law. Section 6(6)(c) provides that the powers of the judiciary in interpreting the law shall not apply to Chapter 2. The courts have also upheld this non-justiciability provision in a plethora of decided cases.[42] However, in comparison with South Africa, which is also an African country, there is no distinction between fundamental rights and economic, social, and cultural rights.[43] Article 7(2) of the South African Constitution emphasized that the state must respect, protect, and fulfil the rights contained in the Constitution. In India, however, where there is a non-justiciability provision on economic, social, and

[39] Nwafor (2009), pp. 1–11.

[40] National Human Rights Commission (2018).

[41] National Human Rights Commission (2018).

[42] See *Okogie v A.G Lagos State* (1981) 1 NCLR 218, which decision had been re-echoed in several cases, like *Uzuokwu v Izeonu* (1991) 2 NWLR PT 200, p. 708, and *A.G Ondo State v A.G Federation* (2002) FWLR, p. 111, 1972.

[43] See *Soobramoney v Minister of Health KwaZulu Natal* 1998 (1) SA 765 (C); Expert Chairperson of the Constitutional Assembly: In Re Certification of the Constitution of the Republic of South Africa, 1996, 1996 (4) SA 744.

cultural rights, similar to Nigeria, the courts are vibrant and have developed an approach that enables them to adjudicate such cases despite criticisms.[44]

The Nigerian state is aware of the importance of human rights and has incorporated it in chapter 4 of its 1999 Constitution as amended. Under the section Fundamental Human Rights, the following are enshrined in the Constitution: (A) Article 33—Right to Life; (B) Article 34—Right to Dignity of Human Person; (C) Article 35—Right to Personal Liberty; (D) Articles 36 and 37—Right to Private and Family Life; (E) Article 38—Right to Freedom of Thought, Conscience and Religion; (F) Article 39—Right to Freedom of Expression and the Press Association; (H) Article 41—Right to Freedom of Movement; and (I) Article 42—Right to Freedom of Discrimination.[45] There are ample provisions on human rights in the 1999 Constitution and in international instruments, some of which have been domesticated in Nigeria. No doubt, upholding the tenets of human rights alongside economic growth results in sustainable economic development.

5 Law Enforcement Agencies and Human Rights Protection in Nigeria

The security services of any nation are an integral part of society that cannot be dispensed with, and their responsibilities in securing lives and properties cannot be overemphasized. Therefore, it is ironic that those who are supposed to safeguard and protect turn out to be the ones who trample upon and violate the rights of the citizenry.[46] Apart from the known internal security forces, such as the Nigeria Police Force (NPF), the Nigerian Correctional Service (NCS), the State Security Service (SSS), and the intelligence units of the armed forces, which exercise these powers, there are also para-military organizations, such as the National Drug Law Enforcement Agency (NDLEA), the Nigerian Customs Service (NCS), and the Nigerian Immigration Service (NIS), among others.[47] Some of the functions of these security agencies, as provided by law, include the preservation of law and order, the detection of any crime within Nigeria, the maintenance of internal security, and the protection and preservation of all non-military classified matters concerned with the internal security of Nigeria, among others.[48] The enforcement of laws and the maintenance of peace and order are, first and foremost, about protecting the rights of citizens, and thus the role of police personnel in protecting and respecting the rights of every individual is fundamental. However, because the police are always responding to diverse issues and problems of law enforcement, issues of rule of law and human

[44] Shankar and Mehta (1999); Kothari (2004).

[45] Ogoloma and Sampson (2015).

[46] Nzarga (2014), p. 30.

[47] Chukwuma (1997), 14.

[48] See the Agency Act 2004 51 Cap N74 LFN.

rights often arise during police interventions, including methods such as stopping people for questioning, arresting them, searching them or their property, and interrogating them after custodial arrest. Moreover, how the police take control of such circumstances, particularly in terms of the level of force they use, is also a matter concerning the rule of law and human rights.[49]

The security sector is crucial to the sustenance of emerging democracies and the protection of human rights in third-world countries. However, the readiness and ability of the security sector to play these roles, which assure citizens of the benefits of good governance, remain a question begging for deep reflection. Policemen in Nigeria are given wide powers under the Police Act of 2020 and the Administration of Criminal Justice Act 2015 in the performance of their duties.[50] These powers include arrest, search, seizure, detention, and the use of force in certain circumstances. The exercise of each of these powers affects the fundamental rights of citizens more directly than the activities of other internal security forces in the country. Personal freedom and physical and psychological integrity are often compromised by unlawful arrests, detention, and coercive interrogations.[51] Studies on the patterns of police brutality in Nigeria frequently highlight two basic situations of contact between the police and citizens: 'crime control' and 'crowd control'. These are the two areas where one can see the disproportionate use of violence and deadly force by the police in their dealings with the public. The average Nigerian policeman often approaches his duties with the assumption that his suspects are already guilty and, therefore, deserve no respect or sympathy at all.[52]

The prisons in Nigeria exist for the sole purpose of dehumanizing and degrading the offender as punishment for his crime. The sprawling prison system of Nigeria is not only infested with a myriad of human rights violations but also dependent on these violations for its very survival. The police and the government, being unable to curb or eliminate the material and non-material social pressures that encourage crime, consider the horrible conditions in the prisons as a valid and legitimate means of discouraging crime. This is despite official declarations to the contrary.[53]

A disturbing aspect of police abuse in Nigeria is the contempt that policemen have for the rule of law and the legal process. In handling cases of criminal suspects, they often assume the roles of prosecutors and adjudicators. Both the Nigerian Constitution and the Police Act permit the derogation of personal liberty for the sole purpose of arraigning a suspect before a court of law. However, these provisions have been perverted by the police, who now arrest people merely to intimidate and extort money from them. Under the Nigerian Constitution, an accused is supposed to have a trial within 3 months of arrest.[54] The suspect is also entitled to bail within

[49] Madubuike-Ekwe and Obayemi (2019).

[50] Madubuike-Ekwe and Obayemi (2019), p. 23.

[51] Soyombo (1994).

[52] Ibidapo-Obe (1994).

[53] Ehonwa (1996).

[54] Section 35 (4) of the Constitution of the Federal Republic of Nigeria 1999.

48 hours of arrest, except for certain categories of offences. It is sometimes the case that the Nigerian police detain people for several years without trial or court appearance.

Human rights violations cut across all spheres of human existence, and the Nigerian security services have been accused of being one of the greatest violators of the said rights in Nigeria. On 20 November 1999, defenceless and unarmed civilians were massacred in Odi (a village in Bayelsa State) by the Nigerian military as an offshoot of an ongoing conflict in the Niger Delta over indigenous rights to oil resources and environmental protections.[55] Meanwhile, the Human Rights Watch (HRW) in New York, in its report of 26 October 2001, condemned the massacre of over 100 civilians by Nigerian soldiers in several villages in Benue State. According to the report, the militia of the Tiv ethnic group was believed to have abducted and murdered about 19 soldiers sent to restore peace in the crisis between the Tivs and the Jukuns. The soldiers' mutilated bodies were later found in the village of Zaki Biam. Aside from police brutality and the massacre of citizens by security operatives, there is a violation of press freedom in Nigeria. Clampdowns, assaults, beatings, unfair arrests, and police raids against producers of print media have continued despite the transition from military to civilian rule in 1999.[56] A typical example is the Social Media Bill, which was recently passed by the legislature.

Given the foregoing situation, the police and other internal security forces in Nigeria no longer bother themselves about what the Constitution mandates if they are serving under a military government. The result is the entrenchment of a police state in the country, where the whims and caprices of those in power are enforced by overzealous internal security forces.[57] There is no doubt that the fundamental human rights of citizens are well provided for in the Constitution and other Nigerian statutes, which recognize that human rights are broader than the rights associated with criminal law and the criminal process. These rights encompass the individual sense of dignity, respect, and free participation in society, as well as the government's role in facilitating social exchange. Such rights need a mechanism for their protection. In democratic societies, that mechanism is the law and the judiciary, but it is often mediated by the actions of the police and the pervasive corruption that has eaten deep into the fabric of the judicial system in Nigeria.

[55] Oluwaige and Anaba (2004), pp. 21–23.

[56] ChurchHill, (2010), p. 7.

[57] Chukwuma (1997).

6 An Assessment of Governance and Human Rights in Nigeria

Nigeria's emergence as a state in 1960 legally thrust it into the web of recognized and member states of the United Nations, which, over a decade earlier, had adopted a universal framework for the observance and protection of human rights as a fundamental precept of statehood.[58] There is a nexus between governance and the protection of human rights, linked to the nature, logic, and character of the Nigerian state. This is largely due to how fragile, weak, patron-client, and dependent a state is, which goes a long way to determining the governance pattern in that state.[59] Over the decades, there has been a recurrent and sustained argument that the Nigerian state, like its counterparts in Africa and other countries of the developing world, underperforms due to a lack of state capacity to deal with the contemporary complexities of governance.[60] The nature of the state, the public institutions through which legitimate power is exercised and enforced, is germane to the study of human rights in any state.[61]

According to Onwuazombe,[62] 'dating back to the colonial era, the human rights records of the Nigerian state has been consistently poor and unimpressive and at present, the situation has not significantly improved'. In other words, the human rights records of the Nigerian state have remained consistently mediocre and unimposing even in the twenty-first century. Taking a historical perspective on the surrounding issues, Jauhari[63] compared the colonial and post-colonial human rights situations in Nigeria and found that human rights violations worsened after independence as compared to the colonial era. Jauhari[64] highlighted the long history of violations of human rights in Nigeria, which is traceable to the colonial periods.

Several years after independence, Nigerian citizens have continued to face incessant violations of their basic rights during the mixed periods of military and civilian rule as the military rule in the country became a symbol of unchecked authoritarianism. After every military coup, the country's Constitution was suspended, and the government remained unaccountable to the people; civilian regimes also became characterized by unaccountability. As Jauhari[65] surmises, in order to hold on to power, civilian leaders denied freedom of expression to the citizens, blatantly rigged elections, and engaged in unlawful and extrajudicial killings. With the end of the military rule and the emergence of a civilian regime in May 1999 in Nigeria—which

[58] Animashaun, pp. 59–64.
[59] Akintunde (2017), p. 7.
[60] Yagboyaju and Akinola (2019), p. 1.
[61] Smith (2013).
[62] Onwuazombe, pp. 116.
[63] Jauhari (2011), pp. 53–57.
[64] Jauhari (2011), pp. 53–57.
[65] Jauhari (2011), pp. 53–57.

marked the Fourth Republic—many had hoped for the establishment of good governance in the country, characterized by respect for and the promotion of the fundamental rights of the people.[66]

Fundamental rights provisions have continued to feature very prominently in the successive Constitutions of the Federal Republic of Nigeria.[67] The foundation of genuine democracy is embedded in the rule of law, a principle that demands devotion to spiritual and moral values, the common heritage of the peoples, and the true source of individual freedom and political liberty.[68] These democratic ideals are currently being assimilated into the people's consciousness in Nigeria as the nascent democratic experiment gradually solidifies. Since the adoption of the Universal Declaration of Human Rights in 1948, human rights have not only acquired global status and importance but have also grown tremendously in both conception and content.[69] While the internationalization of human rights has been energized and strengthened by several developments, the present status of human rights in Nigeria is not without any historical antecedents.

The departure of the military regimes in Nigeria in 1999 restored hope for human rights, which had been grossly abused by successive military regimes. Regrettably, however, after many years of democratic governance, human rights violations remain rife.[70] Particularly worrisome is the government security operatives' abuse of rights, resulting in casualties. Security agencies have been repeatedly accused of extensive human rights abuses and extrajudicial killings, and the number of incidents of human rights violations in Nigeria's democracy has become a major concern. More disconcerting is that the justice sector has not effectively addressed the issue, largely due to the disregard of lawful processes and orders by the Nigerian state and its machinery.

Johnson and Salau[71] studied human rights and governance in Nigeria between 2011 and 2015 and found that the human rights situation in the country remained irreconcilable with constitutionalism as there were frequent cases of encroachment of citizens' fundamental rights. They examined the human rights situation under President Jonathan's administration and assessed how human rights issues were handled. It is evident from the study that Nigeria continued to confront serious human rights challenges, including a culture of impunity where perpetrators of human rights abuses were often not held accountable for their acts of infringements and illegalities. By contemporary consensus, human rights are generally understood as the moral-political claims that all human beings are deemed to have upon their societies or governments, claims recognized 'as of right' and 'not by love, grace or

[66] Coker and Obo (2012), pp. 62–73.

[67] Nwafor (2009), 1–11.

[68] Jacobs (1975).

[69] Dada (2013), pp. 1–14.

[70] Hassan (2020).

[71] Johnson and Salau (2019), pp. 14–25.

charity'.[72] However, this is hardly the case in Nigeria, where human rights are perceived as a limited largesse, predetermined by the political elite. In this twenty-first century in Nigeria, all households which cannot afford the cost of the ubiquitous personal generating sets for electricity power supply are usually in darkness, metaphorically and in actuality. In the Nigeria current democratic process, violation, and abuse of human rights, including arbitrary arrest and detention of persons have drastically reduced as compared with the military regimes. However, a recent report from the National Human Rights Commission[73] stated that human rights violations grow worse by the day, as compared to other democratic settings in the world.

7 Conclusion

Human rights are inalienable rights that accrue to every citizen of a country and deserve the maximum and unhindered protection from infringement. This is so because human beings are said to be naturally brutish and selfish and cannot exhibit such conduct in a democratic society. Human rights are an indispensable factor when good governance is under consideration. Thus, they cannot be subject to violation at will. We also noted that human rights have been generally abused in both Nigeria and Africa as a whole. However, it is pointed out that during the military rule, particularly in Nigeria, more human rights abuses were recorded. The overarching submission of this chapter is that the governance milieu in Nigeria is dysfunctional to the extent that it is invariably unable to protect the human rights of its citizens. For decades, Nigerian leaders have spoken of the dividends of democracy and good governance but have largely been unable to effectively realize the ethos and core tenant of good governance; therefore, the problem of violation of human rights must be addressed without selective obedience to court orders.

The governance crisis that has plagued Nigeria since 1960 has had devastating consequences for the promotion of the basic rights of the people, as well as other aspects of life in society. This chapter has shown that human rights are basic liberties, freedoms, and other entitlements that accrue to a human being because of his or her human nature. But these rights would remain meaningless, unfulfilled, and mere wishes if the rulers of society do not create the conditions conducive to their realization. In protecting the rights and liberties of all Nigerians, the government must be resolute in its commitment to ensuring security, without compromising human rights. The chapter argues for strong and transparent institutions that are devoid of corrupt practices and capable of delivering essential services to the Nigerian citizenry. The key now is to look internally with a readiness to use political will in the right direction, taking significant actions to address critical human rights issues in Nigeria. The chapter concludes that human rights are an indispensable

[72] Onwuazombe (2017), p. 116.

[73] National Human Rights Commission.

factor when good governance is under consideration. It delves into the human rights discourse in Nigeria and provides workable recommendations towards strengthening the African human rights system.

References

Addaney M (2018) The African Union's agenda 2063: Education and its realization. In: Onuora-Oguno AC, Egbewole W, Kleven T (eds) Education law: strategic policy and sustainable development in Africa

Adejuwon KD (2012) The dilemma of accountability and good governance for improved public service delivery in Nigeria. Africa's Public Serv Deliv Perform Rev 1:25–25

Afegbua SI, Adejuwon KD (2012) The challenges of leadership and governance in Africa. Int J Acad Res Bus Soc Sci 2:141–157

Ajulor OV, Adejuwon KD (2010) Civil society and the challenges of democratic governance in contemporary Africa: the case of Nigeria. J Arts Contemp Soc 2:7–31

Akinola SR (2000) Balancing the equation of governance at the grassroots. In: Adedeji A, Ayo B (eds) People– centred democracy in Nigeria? The search for alternative systems of governance at the grassroots. Heinemann Educational Books (Nig.) Plc, Ibadan

Akintunde IJ (2017) Good governance and development in Nigeria: the gap between rhetoric and reality. Int J Acad Res Bus Soc Sci 7

Animashaun BO (2013) Human rights, governance and the Nigerian constitution: a historical survey. IOSR J Human Soc Sci 17:59–64

Anyanwu A (1998) Governance and African politics. In: Emezi CE, Ndoh CA (eds) African politics. Achugo Publications, Owerri

Chukwuma I (1997) The legal structure of the police and human rights in Nigeria. Third World Leg Stud 14

ChurchHill O (2010) Imprisonment of press freedom in Nigeria. This day Newspaper, Tuesday 4 May

Coker MA, Obo UB (2012) Crisis of governance and the violations of human rights: the Nigerian experience, 1999 to 2007. Afr J Polit Sci Int Relat 6:62–73

Dada JA (2013) Human rights protection in Nigeria: The past, the present and goals for role actors for the future. J Law Policy Glob 14:1–14

Ehonwa OL 1996) Behind the wall: a report on prison conditions in Nigeria and the prison system, 2nd edn. Civil Liberties Organisation, Lagos

Federal Ministry of Women Affairs and Social Development (2007) National guidelines and standards of practice on orphans and vulnerable children Abuja: Federal Ministry of Women Affairs and Social Development

Hassan I (2020) Human rights status in Nigeria since Obasanjo's second coming. In: Levan C, Ukata P (eds) The Oxford handbook of Nigerian politics. Oxford University Press, Oxford

Heyman SJ (2004) The third annual C. Edwin Baker lecture for liberty, equality, and democracy: the conservative-libertarian turn in first amendment jurisprudence. West Virginia Law Rev 117

Igwe OW (2002) Preliminary studies in human rights law. Ring and Favolit Ltd, Lagos

Jacobs FG (1975) The European convention on human rights. Clarendon Press, Oxford

Jauhari A (2011) Colonial and post-colonial human rights violations in Nigeria. Int J Humanit Soc Sci 1:53–57

Johnson I, Salau JO (2019) Human rights and governance in Nigeria, 2011-2015. Afr Res Rev 13: 14–25

Kalu O et al (2020) Nigeria: challenges in enforcement of fundamental rights in Nigeria. https://www.mondaq.com/nigeria/human-rights/986460/challenges-in-enforcement-of-fundamental-rights-in-nigeria

Kothari J (2004) Social rights and the Indian constitution. Law, Social Justice and Global Development (LGD). http://www.go.warwick.ac.uk/elj/lgd/2004_2/kothari

Lbidapo-Obe A (1994) Police brutality: dimensions and control in Nigeria. Paper presented at a workshop on Law Enforcement and Human Rights in Nieia held in Badagry, Lagos, May 30-June 1

Madubuike-Ekwe NJ, Obayemi OK (2019) Assessment of the role of the Nigerian police force in the promotion and protection of human rights in Nigeria. Annual Surv Int Comp Law 23: Article 3

National Human Rights Commission (2008) The state of human rights in Nigeria 2005–2006. A report on human rights violations monitored in Nigeria by Network of Human Rights Violations Monitors in collaboration with the National Human Rights Commission, UNDP, and NORAD

National Human Rights Commission (2018) An independent review of evidence of gross violations of the rights to participate in government, to public service, and to fair trial through the election petition process in Nigeria 2007 & 2011. Final Report

Ndehfru J (2017) Good governance and the challenges of democratic sustainability in Nigeria: policy Alert. J Pub Pol Anal 1:1

Nwafor AO (2009) Enforcing fundamental rights in Nigerian courts: processes and challenges. Afr J Legal Stud 4:1–11

Nwufor CC (2010) An overview of human rights, good governance and development. Afr Res Rev Int Multi-Discipl J 4:203–216

Nzarga FD (2014) An analysis of human rights violation by the Nigerian security services. J Law Policy Global 30:1–8

Obadan MI (1998) The state, leadership, governance and economic development. The National Centre for Economic Management and Administration

Obaseki AO (1992) The judiciary and human rights in U. Kalu and Osinbajo: perspectives on human rights. Federal Ministry of Justice, Lagos

Obidimma AE (2020) The impact of human rights on good governance and sustainable development in Nigeria. Glob J Polit Law Res 8:11–29

Ogbu ON (1999) Human rights law and practice in Nigeria: an introduction. CIDJAP Press, Enugu

Ogoloma FI, Sampson BN (2015) Boko Haram: human rights violation in Nigeria. J Law Glob Policy 1

Ojo EO (2006) Human rights and sustainable democracy in Nigeria (1999–2003). J Soc Sci 13:15–29

Oluwaige I, Anaba I (2004) Human rights situation in Nigeria. The Vanguard Newspaper Friday, 5 March

Onwuazombe II (2017) Human rights abuse and violations in Nigeria: a case study of the oil-producing communities in the Niger Delta region. Ann Surv Int Comp Law 22:115–160

Panth P (2020) 'Economic development: definition, scope and measurement' www.researchgate.net

Pegram T (2015) Governing relationships: the new architecture in global human rights governance. Millennium J Int Stud 43:618–639

Prempeh HK (2009) Africa's "constitutionalism revival": false start or new dawn? Int J Const Law 5:469–473

Sahni P (2004) Introduction. In: Sahni P, Medury U (eds) Governance for development: issues and strategies. Prentice-Hall of India Private Limited, New Delhi

Shankar S, Mehta PB (1999) Courts and socio-economic rights in India. http://www.ser.bd.com/doc/138569272/courts_and_socioeconomic_rights_in_india. 67Ibid

Smith BC (2013) Understanding third world politics: theories of political change and development. Palgrave Macmillan, New York

Soliyev II (2021) Key factors Influencing economic development. Eur J Res Dev Sustainab www.scholarzest.com

Soyombo O (1994) Traditional approaches to curbing deviant behaviour in Nigeria". unpublished paper presented at a conference on the Administration of Justice: The Challenge of Due Process, held in Baton Rouge, Louisiana, USA, February 28-March 5

Umuzurike UO (1995) Introduction to international law. Spectrum Law Publishing, Ibadan
United Nations (2007) Good governance practices for the protection of human rights. United Nations, York and Geneva
United Nations Committee of Experts on Public Administration Fifth session New York, 27-31 March 2006 (E/C.16/2006/4)
Yagboyaju DA, Akinola AO (2019) Nigerian state and the crisis of governance: a critical exposition. SAGE Open

Stanley Osezua Ehiane is a Senior Lecturer at the Department of Political & Administrative Studies, University of Botswana, Gaborone, Botswana. He is also a Researcher Fellow at the University of South Africa (UNISA), Pretoria, South Africa, and a Research Associate at the Nelson Mandela University, Port Elizabeth, South Africa.

Dr Masilo Bontle is a lecturer at the University of Botswana in the Department of Political and Administrative Studies. She holds PhD from the University of Sussex, United Kingdom.

Dr Ayoola Abuloye holds a PhD in Law and teaches Human Rights Law, and International Humanitarian Law among others at the Obafemi Awolowo University, Ile Ife. Nigeria.

International Obligation of Mineral-Resource-Rich States to Share Benefits from the Mining Sector to Local Communities

Tanzanian Perspectives

John S. Ombella

1 Introduction

Natural resources, such as minerals, have significant potential to contribute to the socio-economic development of States and local communities where they are extracted, if properly regulated.[1] Proper regulation refers to guaranteeing the effective participation of local communities in the distribution of mining benefits among the main mining stakeholders (governments and companies). Notably, the sharing of resource benefits with local communities stems from international human rights principles.[2] In essence, involvement in the disposal of natural resources includes not only being part of decision-making but also sharing the benefits accruing from their use.[3] Resources like minerals catalyse the socio-economic transformation of the economies of poor countries around the world and, in particular, Africa.[4] According to the Southern African Development Community (SADC),[5] *mining activities brings hope to most poor rural communities* in the region.

In particular, environmental degradation, limiting of resource rights such as land dispossession, and loss of economic gains from habitual socio-economic activities

[1] UN Commission on Sustainable Development (2010), p. 10; SADC (2008), para. 85.

[2] African Charter on Human and Peoples' Rights 1986. Art. 21(1).

[3] Inter-American Commission for Human Rights (2015), p. 219.

[4] UN Commission on Sustainable Development (2011), para. 47.

[5] SADC (2008), para. 85.

J. S. Ombella (✉)
Economic Law Department, Faculty of Law, Mzumbe University, Mzumbe, Morogoro, Tanzania

Private Law Department, Faculty of Law, Mzumbe University, Morogoro, Tanzania
e-mail: john.ombella@mu.ac.tz

I. Kajiru et al. (eds.), *Economic Development and Human Rights in Contemporary Sub-Saharan Africa*, Ius Gentium: Comparative Perspectives on Law and Justice 122, https://doi.org/10.1007/978-3-031-81400-6_9

prior to mining are common.[6] Although environmental impact assessments (EIAs) are required to be carried out before mining is allowed, they suffer from limitations, such as the lack of experts and impartiality.[7] EIAs aim to address all potential social and environmental impacts that may arise and suggest remedial measures if mining is to be permitted. In Tanzania, for example, mining is responsible for causing pressure on rural communities' access to land and clean water and for the continued socio-economic injustices perpetuated by mining companies.[8] Given the fact that a majority of Tanzanians are underprivileged, mining activities seem to exacerbate poverty in local communities. Parallel to that, Tanzania is reported to have lost a substantial amount of revenue from the mineral sector due to lenient laws on incentives for foreign investors.[9] Recently, it has been shown that mining companies are involved in tax evasion and money laundering and, in collaboration with locals, illicitly transfer minerals from Tanzania that are worth billions.[10] All these resonate with two key points: firstly, the resource curse, a theory explaining the paradox of poverty amidst plenty of natural resources[11] and, secondly, the concerns regarding weak legal and policy frameworks on the sharing of mining benefits with local communities in Tanzania.

According to the UN Commission on Sustainable Development (UNCSD), a weak legal framework seems to be a primary factor behind the inability of natural-resource-rich States like Tanzania to convert their resources into tangible socio-economic benefits.[12] Notably, there are international, regional and sub-regional binding and non-binding frameworks and State practices that influence the Tanzanian legal framework on the sharing of mining benefits with local communities. This chapter, therefore, examines whether Tanzania's legal framework complies with the requirements of such international, regional and sub-regional frameworks and State practices. In particular, this chapter focuses on four key points: compensation for land acquired for mining, direct benefit sharing to local communities, the legal nature of corporate social responsibility (CSR) as a mechanism for benefit sharing, and the identification of local communities.

In this chapter, the term local community refers to communities which are habitual residents and those with ancestral ties on lands in the vicinity of mines and suffer the immediate gross impacts of mining activities. This chapter is organised into six major parts, including this introduction. Part 2 presents the resource curse, exploring its relevance to the inability of States to convert their natural resources into

[6] UN Commission on Sustainable Development (2010), paras. 152–153.

[7] Environmental Management Act 2004, section 81; Bekhechi and Mercier (2002).

[8] United Republic of Tanzania, (2008); Commission for Human Rights and Good Governance (2013), para. 2.3.2; IRIN (2013), pp. 18–19; Laltaika (2017), p. 57.

[9] Policy Forum (2012).

[10] Kamati Maalumu iliyoundwa na Rais wa Jamhuri ya Muungano waa Tanzania (2017), p. 10; Kamati Maalumu iliyoundwa na Rais wa Jamhuri ya Muungano wa Tanzania (2017), p. 31.

[11] See para. 2 of this chapter for an expounded description of the resource curse theory.

[12] UN Commission on Sustainable Development (2010), para. 151.

tangible benefits for their populations, and part 3 presents the international frameworks and State practices. Part 4 discusses the Tanzanian legal framework, while part 5 presents the distilled challenges noted in part 4. Part 6 offers a conclusion and recommendations.

2 Brief Theoretical Underpinnings of Mineral Resource Benefit Sharing with Local Communities

As noted in the introduction above, many natural-resource-rich States appear to have failed to convert their resources into socio-economic gains. The Natural Resource Governance Institute (NRGI) refers to this situation as the 'paradox of plenty'.[13] A number of factors contribute to the State's inability to convert its natural resources into socio-economic gains. Among the relevant causes discussed in this chapter are government capture of benefits, the fallacy of incentivising foreign investors through a friendly fiscal regime, and social and environmental concerns. First, with regard to government capture, there is a common tendency among resource-rich States to centralise revenue collected from mining while ignoring local communities, which endure the impacts of extraction.[14]

Second, there is a fallacy commonly adopted by most resource-rich States in attracting investment from the first world.[15] The fallacy is that the adoption of a friendly fiscal regime, which lowers the tax or levy to be paid by foreign companies, will gain them more investors and thus spur employment opportunities. On the contrary, Evaristus Oshieonebo concludes that most natural-resource-rich African States do adopt a friendly fiscal regime as a means to attract more foreign investors, to their detriment.[16]

The third relevant cause of resource curse is interference with land rights and other resources like water by mining processes.[17] Land and water are prime resources that local communities rely on to support their daily livelihood. Consequently, limiting their access and use through dispossession, pollution and competing use between mines and local communities subjects local communities to mine-induced poverty.

It is also worth noting the work of Lisa Sachs,[18] which is relevant to the resource curse and the extraction of natural resources despite its focus on petroleum rather than minerals. Sachs shows that *Timor-Leste* is a poor country with inadequate

[13] Natural Resources Governance Institute (2015).

[14] Natural Resources Governance Institute (2015).

[15] Natural Resources Governance Institute (2015).

[16] Evaristus (2011), p. 235.

[17] Natural Resources Governance Institute (2015).

[18] Sachs (2013).

infrastructure in key sectors like health, education and transport.[19] She further explains that the country is rich in petroleum, which is being extracted by foreign companies. Among the factors that contribute to the situation in the country is land dispossession by multinational companies for investment in the oil sector. Consequently, local communities lose their sources of livelihood due to the loss of compensation or little compensation received from foreign companies.[20] Sachs also noted issues of environmental destruction, which negatively impacts the well-being of the local communities.[21]

In addition, the natural resource extraction sector is, by its very nature, inherently engulfed in competing interests from various groups.[22] These groups are, for example, the States, which focus on revenue generation; natural resource investors, which focus on profit maximisation; local communities, focused on safeguarding their livelihood; international financial institutions, which are looking for opportunities to finance large-scale extraction projects for profit, to name but a few. In these competing interests, the weaker, that is, the local communities, are likely to be jeopardised by the rest. Hence, there is a need to balance the interests in this sector as a means to guarantee sustainable resource extraction.

Ultimately, in order to move out of the resource curse, States need to adopt strong legal frameworks for the proper regulation of mining.[23] A strong legal regime, for example, will have to provide a balance between the competing interests of the stakeholders in the sector, local communities being one. In particular, the need for a strong legal framework resonates with the identified problems discussed above.[24]

Generally, the theory of the resource curse described above seems to be rooted in the absence of a strong regulatory framework for the proper regulation of such resources. Through a strong legal framework, the fallacy of alluring investors will be eliminated, environmental pollution and land dispossession will be abated and competing interests will be sorted out on a priority basis. In particular, the theory shows that local communities are subjected to socio-economic challenges caused by the extraction of resources, and hence they need to be considered. The next section, which presents the international frameworks and State practices, expounds on this discussion.

[19] Sachs (2013), p. 1.

[20] Sachs (2013), p. 4.

[21] Sachs (2013), p. 5.

[22] Sachs (2013), p. 5.

[23] Sachs (2013), pp. 7 and 9.

[24] See para 1 above.

3 International Regulation of Mineral Resource Revenue Sharing with Local Communities

There seems to be no comprehensive international legal instrument regulating the sharing of natural resource revenue between the central government and local communities.[25] Available international attempts to regulate the sharing of revenue from mineral resources seem to be confined to specific communities.[26] Consequently, there are more soft laws such as proclamations, declarations and plans of action. The regional and sub-regional levels, however; seem to have binding instruments that may be used to justify the sharing of revenue to local communities. This part critically discusses the non-binding international legal positions, preceded by the international binding frameworks and State practices.

3.1 Revenue Sharing with Local Communities Under Binding International Law Instruments and State Practices

This part reviews international binding frameworks relevant to sharing of benefits to local communities in the mineral sector. In particular, this part discusses the four key areas mentioned above with reference to United Nations (UN), African Union (AU) and Southern African Development Community (SADC) instruments.

Firstly, there is a need to provide compensation to local communities upon the compulsory acquisition of their land for mining. It is worth reiterating that international law principles seem silent on local communities benefiting from the mineral resources extracted from their locality as the existing legal framework is limited to Indigenous communities, as discussed below. However, at the regional level, local communities are guaranteed full compensation in case their land is used for other economic activities or is ruined due to the impacts of mining.[27] In the case of *SERAC vs Nigeria*,[28] the Nigerian government was held to have breached the provision of Article 21 of the African Charter where land in the vicinity of the extraction was polluted by crude oil. In the Niger Delta, land and water pollution grossly impacted the Ogoni peoples' means of livelihood.[29]

---

[25] UN Convention on Biological Diversity 1992, Art. 1. This article calls for benefit sharing in accessing genetic resources in a particular country/community. As may be noted, the focus is on biological-genetic resources, not mineral resources, as is the case in this study.

[26] For details, see para 3.1 below.

[27] African Charter on Human and Peoples' Rights 1986, Art. 21(2).

[28] *Social and Economic Rights Action Centre (SERAC) and Centre for Economic Social Rights (CESR) v Nigeria* [2001] ACHPR 155/96, paras. 56, 63.

[29] *Social and Economic Rights Action Centre (SERAC) and Centre for Economic Social Rights (CESR) v Nigeria* [2001] ACHPR 155/96, para. 67.

The international, African regional and sub-regional laws recognise the rights of Indigenous peoples to benefit and be compensated whenever their land is used for mineral extraction.[30] At the African regional level, for example, reference to the term 'peoples' connotes sub-national groups that enjoy the right to self-determination, such as Indigenous peoples. According to the case of *Gunme v Cameroon*,[31] some local communities may exercise autonomy within a sovereign State provided that they preserve the territorial integrity of the State. Consequently, Indigenous communities enjoy self-determination and the control of resources in their territory.[32] The use of such resources, which threatens their livelihood, should accompany a plan to compensate and benefit them accordingly.[33]

Secondly, there is a need for legal mechanisms that directly benefit local communities. As mentioned above, there is a lack of regulations obliging mineral-resource-rich States to share revenue with local communities at the international level. What exists seems to be narrowed to, firstly, resource-specific regulations, such as those under the UN Convention on Biological Diversity 1992, and, secondly, to community-specific regulations, as seen under the UN Convention on Indigenous and Tribal Peoples 1989 (UN Convention 1989). At the regional and sub-regional levels, on the other hand, the African Union (AU) requires its member States to enact laws that will guarantee peoples' effective participation in the allocation of resources in their country.[34] The main aim is to guarantee the eradication of poverty and ensure the broad-based economic empowerment of local communities through benefits accruing from mineral resources.[35]

In particular, the UN Convention 1989 regulates, among other things, the rights of the Indigenous peoples to own and manage natural resources for their development independently of the central government.[36] However, in case the government needs to extract minerals within its jurisdiction, the Indigenous peoples are entitled not only to participate fully in the process but also to derive benefits therefrom.[37] Benefit sharing is based on the extent to which their means of livelihood will be impacted by mining.[38] In the case of *Saramaka People vs Suriname*, the court was of

[30]Indigenous and Tribal Peoples Convention 1986, 1989, Art. 15(4–5); African Charter on Human and Peoples' Rights, Art. 21; Protocol on Mining 1997, Art. 2(8).

[31]*Kevin Mgwanga Gunmme et al. v Cameroon* [2003] African Commission on Human and Peoples' Rights *266*, *Communication*, para. 191.

[32]Indigenous and Tribal Peoples Convention 1989; Pereira and Gough (2013), p. 495.

[33]Barume (2010), p. 52.

[34]African Charter on Human and Peoples' Rights 1986, Art. 21(1).

[35]Treaty of the Southern African Economic Development 1992, Art. 5(i).

[36]Indigenous and Tribal Peoples Convention, 1989, Art. 15(1).

[37]See Indigenous and Tribal Peoples Convention, Art. 15(2).

[38]See Indigenous and Tribal Peoples Convention, Art. 15(2).

the view that extraction activities should not deny the Saramaka peoples of their means of survival.[39]

A similar position was reached in the case of the *Centre for Minority Development (Kenya) and Minority Rights Group (on behalf of Endorois Welfare Council) vs Kenya*,[40] where the African Commission on Human and Peoples' Rights (ACHPR) ruled that there is a need for the adoption of a specific measure to safeguard the land and survival of the Endorois through a benefit-sharing scheme in projects to be established on their land. Notably, however, although the scope of the convention covers a specialised group of communities, the fact that benefit sharing is not only their right but also a means to mend the impacts on their livelihood indicates that a similar approach may be relied upon by other communities so affected, whether or not they are Indigenous.

Thirdly, there is a need to properly identify which local communities are beneficiaries of mining. Generally, international laws provide for such identification.[41] As already noted above, the term 'peoples', as used in the African Charter, refers to both the State and the communities in the State, such as Indigenous communities.[42] At the SADC level, directives require mining companies and the respective member States to empower historically disadvantaged groups.[43] The term 'disadvantaged group' is composed of women, persons with disabilities and Indigenous peoples.[44] Unlike the Indigenous peoples shown above to identify themselves, it is unclear how other groups within the local community may be identified.[45]

In a general sense, it appears that binding international laws do not contain principles guaranteeing the right of local communities to benefit from mining activities within their vicinity. Specifically, however, it provides specialised rules to safeguard the interests of Indigenous communities. On the other hand, regional and sub-regional laws safeguard the broader rights of local communities, Indigenous communities, women and persons with disabilities. A lacuna is, however, noted regarding the mechanisms through which local communities may benefit as well as the means through which other groups, apart from Indigenous communities, are identified. The next part briefly analyses African State practices concerning local communities' enjoyment of benefits from mining.

First, consideration may be made to the grant of compensation by the government and mining companies for the land subjected to mining. In South Africa, landowners

---

[39] *Saramaka People v Suriname (Interpretation of the Judgment on Preliminary Objection, Merit, Reparation and Cost)* (Inter-American Court of Human Rights), para. 29.

[40] *Centre for Minority Rights Development (Kenya) and Minority Rights Group (on behalf of Endorois Welfare Council) v Kenya* [2009] ACHPR No. 276/03, para. 187.

[41] Indigenous and Tribal Peoples Convention 1989; African Charter on Human and Peoples' Rights 1986, Art. 21(1), which refers to all peoples in Africa, a term that includes ordinary and Indigenous peoples as well.

[42] Olaniyan (2016), pp. 282–285.

[43] Protocol on Mining, Art. 2(8).

[44] Ibid., Art. 1.

[45] *Kevin Mgwanga Gunmme et al. v Cameroon*, supra note 32, para. 175.

are compensated by virtue of an agreement between the government, mining companies and local communities.[46] Such agreement is preceded by an effective consultation of the landowners or occupiers prior to the issuance of a mining licence.[47] Notably, the landowner could be an individual or a community.[48] However, the statute seems silent on whether compensation should be a one-time lump-sum payment or whether the landowners can negotiate a contract providing for perpetual benefits. All in all, the law provides a room for local communities to negotiate agreements that determine their benefits from mining.

Second, a question may be posed as to whether the sharing of revenue with the local communities are done directly or through their established trusts. State practice, unlike international initiatives, guarantees the sharing of revenue to local communities via their trusts. A reflection on selected countries shows that mineral revenues are shared between the central government, local government and local communities based on clear statutory rates. Notably, the rates seem to differ from one country to another; for example, the rates are 3% and 10% in Uganda and Kenya, respectively.[49] In South Africa, local communities may be issued a mining licence jointly with the mining companies in case minerals from their land are to be extracted.[50] Joint ownership and participation in mining by local communities under the Mineral and Petroleum Resources Development Act (MPRDA), 2002, indicate a strong commitment to guaranteeing the broad-based economic growth of local communities in South Africa.

A third point worth discussing is the nature of the mechanism for benefit sharing with local communities. Experiences from Kenya and Sierra Leone show that local communities benefit from mining primarily through community development agreements (CDAs) rather than corporate social responsibility (CSR).[51] Moreover, CDAs are a condition for issuing and renewing mining licences.[52] This legal requirement obliges mining companies to take CDAs seriously; otherwise, their licences may be revoked. Among the key aspects to be covered under the CDA are education, health, infrastructure, economic development and the preparation of the local community for the post-mining closure era, to name but a few.[53]

The mechanism for identifying how local communities can benefit from mining makes the fourth point of this discussion. Here, experience is borrowed from South Africa, where 'local communities' are defined to include landowners and

[46] Mineral and Petroleum Resources Development Act 2002, section 50(1)–(2)(a–b).

[47] Mineral and Petroleum Resources Development Act 2002, section 10.

[48] Mineral and Petroleum Resources Development Act 2002, section 1.

[49] Mining Act 2016, section 183(5); Mining Act 2003, section 98(2), read together with the second schedule to the Act.

[50] Mineral and Petroleum Resources Development Act, 2002, sections 17(4A), 23(2A).

[51] The Mines and Minerals Act 2009, sections 138–139.

[52] Mining Act, sections 42(1)(c), 109(i), 115(c).

[53] The Mines and Minerals Act 2009, sections 139(1)–140.

historically disadvantaged communities.[54] According to the MPRDA, the term 'historically disadvantaged communities' includes individuals, communities or companies whose majority members were discriminated against before the 1996 Constitution took effect. Notably, the use of the term 'historically disadvantaged communities' under South African law resonates with the directives under the SADC Protocol on Mining, discussed above.

3.2 Regulation of Revenue Sharing Under Non-binding International Laws

As noted above, there appears to be no general internationally recognised framework regulating mining.[55] In particular this lacuna is founded on the principle of state sovereignty over natural resources, which grants states exclusive control over resources within their borders.[56] Consequently, regulation on the access, use and/or disposal of such resources and how revenue generated is to be shared remains the subject of the domestic laws of States. Notably however, some emerged initiatives seem to be capable of influencing state laws on regulation of benefit sharing in the mineral sector in particular. These initiatives range from public to private. Private initiatives are inclusive, such as the International Council on Minerals and Metals (ICMM), the Natural Resource Charter (NRC) and the Intergovernmental Forum on Minerals and Sustainable Development Policy Framework (IGF Policy Framework), to name but a few. On the other hand, public initiatives are inclusive, such as UN declarations and AU declarations, the Economic Community of West African States (ECOWAS) Directive, and the SADC implementation plan, to name but a few. This part critically presents two private initiatives, namely the IGF and the NRC. It also critically presents four public initiatives, namely UN resolutions, AU declarations, the ECOWAS Directive and the SADC implementation plan, as shown below.

3.2.1 Public International Initiatives

Firstly, local communities have the right to be compensated for the land taken from them by the government and mining companies for mining. The general idea of compensation lies in the fact that most African States entrust the ownership of all

[54] Mineral and Petroleum Resources Development Act 2002, sections 1(a–b(ii)), 12(1–2).

[55] See para. 3.1 above.

[56] UN General Assembly Resolution Permanent Sovereignty over Natural Resources 1962, Art. 1; *Democratic Republic of the Congo v Uganda* [2005] International Court of Justice 2005/5, paras. 4, 9.

natural resources to the government or the president of the country.[57] Citizens therefore do not own land but occupy the same at the pleasure of their presidents. Consequently, when land is taken for mining, its occupiers have to be consulted and compensated accordingly.[58] As noted above, the right to compensate includes the right to benefit from the mineral extraction.[59] According to a UN Resolution, there are specialised attempts aimed at safeguarding the interest of Indigenous peoples against the mainstream government's access to and use of resources located within their jurisdiction.[60] In particular, Indigenous peoples have the right not only to be consulted if the government intends to extract minerals from their area but also to benefit from the minerals extracted and to return to the land after extraction is complete.[61]

In addition, as a means to mitigate the gross impacts of mining on the environment, clean water, agricultural land and sociocultural sacred areas, ECOWAS requires every State to enact laws specifying areas where mining is prohibited.[62] Impliedly, local communities that are dependent on such environmental and sociocultural sacred areas will be immune from the severe impacts of mining activities.

Secondly, local communities need to benefit directly from mining activities in proportion to the impacts they endure. It is explained above that local communities are subjected to mine-induced poverty.[63] Consequently, the benefits have to be directed to the affected communities as a means to mitigate the impacts they have endured. Generally, international, regional and sub-regional frameworks recognise this right of direct benefit to local communities.[64] Despite the widespread underdevelopment in African countries and the SADC sub-region in particular, the SADC Plan does not specifically address the issue of benefit sharing with local communities.[65] It seems general as it calls for mainstreaming gender issues in the mining

[57] United Nations Economic Commissions for Africa, *African Governance Report v Natural Resource Governance and Domestic Revenue Mobilization for Structural Transformation* (2018), para. 2.2.2.

[58] UN Declaration on Rights of Indigenous Peoples 2007, Art. 10; Resolution on a Human Rights-Based Approach to Natural Resources Governance: The African Commission on Human and Peoples' Rights (African Commission), at its 51st Ordinary Session held from 18 April to 2 May 2012 in Banjul, The Gambia; 2012. 2; ECOWAS (2009), Art. 4(2–3).

[59] See para. I above. See also the American Declaration on the Rights of Indigenous Peoples (Adopted at the third plenary session, held on 15 June 2016). Art. XXIV(4)(5).

[60] UN (2007).

[61] UN (2007), Art. 32(2).

[62] ECOWAS (2009), Art. 4(4).

[63] See para. I above.

[64] UN (2012), para. 227; World Summit on Sustainable Development (2002), para. 7; Johannesburg Declaration on Sustainable Development 2002, para. 46 (b); UNECA (2009); Resolution on a Human Rights-Based Approach to Natural Resources Governance: The African Commission on Human and Peoples' Rights (African Commission), at its 51st Ordinary Session held from 18 April to 2 May 2012 in Banjul, The Gambia, para. 2(c); ECOWAS (2009), para. 8(5).

[65] World Summit on Sustainable Development, para. 7.

sector than local communities specific aspects.[66] In particular, the need for a direct benefit to local communities is most noticeable when the community in question is Indigenous. On a similar note, international, regional and sub-regional frameworks guarantee Indigenous communities benefits accruing from mining activities in their territory.[67] Notably, despite the fact that the ECOWAS Directive does not expressly provide for benefit sharing with Indigenous communities, it contains a general provision that may be impliedly construed. In particular, ECOWAS member States and mining stakeholders are required to establish a fund to be financed jointly by the State and such stakeholders to address the post-mining impacts of mining on local communities.[68]

Thirdly, it is worth mentioning the local communities' beneficial arrangements via CSR. Generally, most African countries' mining agreements with multinational corporations do not provide benefits to local communities.[69] This trend, however, seems to be changing, with local communities now reportedly benefitting from mining through various mechanisms, including community trust funds, joint ventures with mining companies and benefits in kind, to name but a few.[70] In other countries, benefit streams take the form of agreements such as CDAs, impact-based agreements (IBAs) and CSR initiatives.[71] While CDAs and IBAs seem to be based on contractual arrangements as they connote an agreement between the local communities and mining companies, CSR remains an amorphous term in legal parameters unless properly framed under domestic statutes. At the international and regional levels, soft laws seem silent on the approach through which local communities may derive benefits from mining. As noted above, international and regional initiatives recognise the need for mineral-resource-rich States to share their revenue with local communities but do not detail how or through what medium. Each country is at liberty to plan and enact its own approaches. Such a lacuna negatively impacts local communities' ability to benefit from mining in their area.

At the sub-regional level, ECOWAS requires State laws to include provisions for CSR as one of the approaches through which local communities can derive benefits from the extraction of natural resources, like minerals.[72] In order to guarantee the effective enforcement and implementation of CSR provisions, they are tied to the issuance and revocation of mining licences.[73] Indeed, the directive has taken

---

[66] SADC (2008), para. 88.

[67] UN Declaration on Rights of Indigenous Peoples, 2007, Art. 32 (3); Resolution on a Human Rights-Based Approach to Natural Resources Governance: The African Commission on Human and Peoples' Rights (African Commission), at its 51st Ordinary Session held from 18 April to 2 May 2012 in Banjul, The Gambia, 4.

[68] ECOWAS (2009), para. 16(7).

[69] SADC (2008), para. 86.

[70] Nyamwaya and Kenya Human Right Commission (2013), p. 28.

[71] Odumasu (2014), p. 478.

[72] ECOWAS (2009), Art. 11 (2).

[73] ECOWAS (2009), Art. 11 (3).

cognisance of the fact that CSR, unless properly articulated in statutes, may not yield its intended purpose for local communities.

Fourthly, it is worth examine the mode of identification of local communities that are to benefit from mining. The above definition of the term local community, linked it to the endurance of the gross impacts of mining in their vicinity.[74] It is imperative to properly identify local communities to not only with the view to guarantee mending of the impacts caused by the mining but also to empower them economically. Generally, international, regional and sub-regional initiatives recognize several groups such as; Indigenous and tribal peoples and historically disadvantaged groups, to name but a few.[75] These groups are generally considered to be vulnerable when mining activities commence in their vicinity, owing to the fact that mining tend to ruin the base of their livelihood.

Notably, despite such groups being recognized as vulnerable, with exception of the indigenous peoples, it is not clear how the rest can be identified fro them to participate in the benefit schemes. According to the UN Declaration on the Rights of Indigenous Peoples (UNDRIP), Indigenous peoples have the right to self-identification. Self-identification entails the right of Indigenous peoples to exist in their own identity and to determine their membership according to their traditional and customary rules.[76]

Generally, this part shows that despite the presence of a public non-binding framework for the sharing of revenue with local communities, such a framework is not immune to criticism. Notably, States are expected to be influenced by this framework so as to properly regulate mining. As such, the stronger the legal framework, the better the regulation of the mining sector, leading to improved revenue generation and more effective sharing. According to the UN,[77] one of the elements of a robust legal framework in the mining sector is how it guarantees socio-economic advantages to the State and its people and how it addresses its socio-economic and environmental impacts. It is noted above that the socio-environmental impacts of mining have a significant effect on local communities.[78] The next part discusses the private international initiatives on the sharing of benefits with local communities. The flow follows the same themes discussed in this part to facilitate logical analysis and the drawing of a conclusion.

[74] See para. I above.

[75] UN Declaration on Rights of Indigenous Peoples, Arts. 3–4; Resolution on a Human Rights-Based Approach to Natural Resources Governance: The African Commission on Human and Peoples' Rights (African Commission), at its 51st Ordinary Session held from 18 April to 2 May 2012 in Banjul, The Gambia. 4; ECOWAS (n. 59), Art. 15(3); SADC, paras 85 and 88.

[76] UN Declaration on Rights of Indigenous Peoples, Art. 33.

[77] UN, para. 227.

[78] See para. I above.

3.2.2 Private International Initiatives

Under private initiatives, there are two frameworks that are more relevant: the NRC and the IGF Policy Framework 2013. The relevance of these initiatives may be explained twofold. Firstly, Tanzania is one of the member States under the IGF.[79] Also, by its very nature, unlike other mineral-related international initiatives such as the ICMM and the Towards Sustainable Mining (TSM) initiative, the IGF Framework is composed of States, not mining companies. Bearing in mind that it is the State's duty to enact laws, regulate natural resources within its jurisdiction and guarantee the well-being of local communities, it is essential to scrutinise the IGF Framework in this chapter. Secondly, the NRC offers a neutral proposition for an ideal legal framework for the governance of natural resources. Thus, natural-resource-rich States like Tanzania may adopt their own principles accordingly. Notably, when these voluntary and non-binding frameworks are domesticated, they become binding. When a significant number of States incorporate certain practices into their domestic laws, these practices can form a basis for international customary law.

To begin with, it is essential to establish a legal framework that compensates local communities wherever they are impacted by mining. The NRC framework, under percept 5, requires model laws to address the opportunities for local communities in the extraction sector. It calls for the compensation of local communities for the impacts they endured from mining activities.[80] As mentioned above, compensation also entails benefit sharing from mining. To be noted here is that the NRC references other international frameworks, such as those addressing Indigenous peoples' rights, to be considered in the ideal framework.[81]

Next, there is a need for the direct sharing of revenue with local communities and/or their trusts. As noted above, natural resources are often controlled by the central government in most African Statesl. This, too, impacts the revenue accruing from these resources. Both the NRC and the IGF frameworks recognise the central collection of revenue when resources are exploited within a State. However, given the potential impacts of the extractive sector on local communities, both the IGF and NRC give an option for State laws to address the sharing of revenue at the sub-national levels.[82]

The call to benefit sharing to local communities' lies on the fact that, when all revenue are paid to the central government or local authorities, there is no guarantee such benefits will eradicate poverty amidist local communities. i[83] Hence need of direct beneficial connection between mining and the local communities is apparent.

---

[79] IGF (2013), p. 3.

[80] Natural Resource Governance Institute (2014), p. 20.

[81] Natural Resource Governance Institute (2014), p. 20.

[82] IGF (2013), p. 29; Natural Resource Governance Institute (2014), p. 26.

[83] Natural Resource Governance Institute (2014), p. 26.

However, while the NRC refers to communities in the vicinity of mines, the IGF instead refers generally to regional authorities.[84] Reference to regional authorities shows primacy to a political and or administratively pre-established location rather than local communities referred in this chapter.

Another point is that there is a need to clarify the legal nature of the approaches used in guaranteeing benefits to local communities (in this case CSR). In particular, private initiatives propose that governments, in collaboration with local communities, agree to assign mining rights to mining companies.[85] Hence, the agreement between the government, local communities and mining companies should form the basis for local communities' benefits. Despite the absence of clear language on the nature of the agreement, the use of the term 'agreement' presupposes the possibility of enforcing its clauses. Consequently, although CSR is not directly mentioned, such a concept may be inferred from the use of the term agreement, provided its terms are enforceable.

Furthermore, there is a need to clarify the manner in which local communities that should benefit from mining are identified. The identification of local communities is crucial due to the widespread perception that revenue from the mining sector ends up in big cities, leaving local communities impoverished.[86] According to the NRC, local communities are those within the vicinity of the mines that suffer the negative impacts caused by mining activities.[87] These include the habitual habitats in the vicinity of mining, Indigenous communities and historically underdeveloped areas.[88] As already discussed above, Indigenous peoples do identify themselves. However, there is a need to properly identify other communities so they can fit in the definition of the term 'local community' and benefit from mining. Apart from Indigenous peoples, no other potential groups within local communities are identified under both the IGF Framework and the NRC. Such a gap in these initiatives negatively influences member States' laws. As noted above and further discussed below, State laws prefer the use of the concept of politically and administratively influenced areas instead.[89]

Generally, global, regional, and sub-regional binding and non-binding initiatives offer principles that may be relied to improve domestic legal framework on mining revenue sharing to local communities. Despite the variety of mechanisms and State practices, a common thread among them is the need to guarantee local communities direct revenue from mining. It is also worth noting that non-binding initiatives seem to have yielded results in countries such as Sierra Leone, Kenya, Uganda and South Africa, where CDAs are recognised as a tool to empower local communities. The immediate section below investigates Tanzania's mechanism for the sharing of

[84] Natural Resource Governance Institute (2014), p. 26.; IGF (2013), p. 29.

[85] Natural Resource Governance Institute (2014), p. 20.

[86] IGF (2013), p. 28.

[87] Natural Resource Governance Institute (2014), p. 26.

[88] Natural Resource Governance Institute (2014), p. 20.

[89] See paras. 4–5 below for details.

mining revenue. It answers the question of whether Tanzania complies with the above-described international, regional, sub-regional and State practices.

4 Tanzania's Legal Framework on Sharing Mining Benefits with Local Communities

This section critically discusses the Tanzanian legal framework for regulating mining and the mechanism for benefit sharing with local communities. It focuses on four key aspects, as highlighted above.[90] Since, the manner in which resources are owned influences the nature of benefits arising from them, this part describes resource ownership in particular to Tanznaia.

According to the United Republic of Tanzania (URT) Constitution[91] and the Natural Wealth and Resources (Permanent Sovereignty) Act, all natural resources in Tanzania belong to Tanzanians.[92] They are entrusted to the President as the people's trustee and/or custodian on behalf of and for the benefit of all.[93] According to Elmarie, the State, as a trustee, holds natural resources in a fiduciary capacity in favour of the present and future generations.[94] Although the principle seems to be much practised in America, it was actually inherited from England.[95] English law adopted the same from Roman law.[96] Roman law is said to have recognised and distinguished resources that could be owned communally and those can be privately owned.[97] General resources were restricted from private appropriation as they are intended for public good.[98] However, the doctrine seems to have widened its scope to include not only environmental resources but also resources of value to the community that require protection, for example minerals.[99]

Under the public trust principle, governments are free to legislate on how resources may be better utilised to guarantee the broad-based socio-economic empowerment of underprivileged communities.[100] Such power is founded on the theory of custodianship or trusteeship, which holds that all natural resources belong to everyone. In addition, the States' mandates under public trust extend, for example, to the power to revoke mining permits or licences in a bid to protect the interests of

[90] See para. I above.

[91] United Republic of Tanzania Constitution 1977, Art. 27(1–2).

[92] Natural Wealth and Resources (Permanent Sovereignty) Act 2017, sections 4(1–2), 5(1).

[93] Natural Wealth and Resources (Permanent Sovereignty) Act 2017, sections 5(2).

[94] Schyff (2006), pp. 106–149; Schyff (2016), pp. 230–231.

[95] Feris (2012), p. 5.

[96] Schyff (2006), p. 81.

[97] Feris (2012), p. 5.

[98] Feris (2012), p. 5.

[99] Schyff (2013), pp. 376–378.

[100] Schyff (2008), p. 767.

the public, such as preventing environmental destruction and local community marginalisation.[101]

The extraction of minerals, due to their non-renewable nature, may impact both the current and future generations if not properly regulated. Therefore, the Tanzanian government is obliged, under the public trust principle, to guarantee that access to and use of minerals by companies benefits such generations (including local communities).

In particular, the URT Constitution requires that the harnessing of natural resources be done for public good.[102] The Constitution necessitates that natural resources, including minerals, be used equitably by all Tanzanians. A similar note is reiterated under the Natural Wealthy and Resources (Permanent Sovereignty) Act.[103] Consequently, local communities whose livelihoods are jeopardised by mining have the right, under the Constitution, to claim compensation for the adverse effects of mining on their livelihood. To examine the reflection of this constitutional position, relevant laws regulating mineral revenue and local communities (Land Act 1999, Land acquisition Act 1967, Mining Act 2018 and Local Government Finance Act 1982) are hereunder analysed.

Firstly, it has to be noted that in Tanzania, as in most African States, land is owned by the President as a trustee for all.[104] Under the Land Act 1999, all land in Tanzania is public and is entrusted to the President for the benefit of all citizens.[105] Tanzanians, therefore, do not own land but occupy it. The most common way of occupying land in Africa, and Tanzania in particular, is through the customary rights of occupancy.[106] Consequently, if the Tanzanian government intends to develop the mining sector, it has to acquire land from its occupiers. According to the Land Acquisition Act 1967, one of the criteria through which land may be compulsorily acquired by the government is when the land has potential for development in the mining sector.[107]

The Land Act 1999 requires that in every instance where land issues are concerned, the occupiers of the land must be involved in decision-making.[108] In particular, as above noted, the participation of the land occupiers also implies the right to benefit from the activities their land will be subject to. The basis for benefit sharing here lies on the compensation for the land compulsorily aquired by the government and or resettling mine-indused displaced community on an alternative land. this benefit sharing mechanism has been the fact that the government compen-

---

[101] Schyff (2008), p. 766.

[102] URT Constitution 1977, Art. 9(c).

[103] Natural Wealth and Resources (Permanent Sovereignty) Act. No. 5 of 2017, section 6(1–2).

[104] United Nations Economic Commissions for Africa, *supra note* 58, para. 2.2.2.

[105] Land Act 1999 (5), section 1(1)(a); Fimbo (2013), p. 6.

[106] United Nations Economic Commissions for Africa, para 2.2.4.

[107] Land Acquisition Act 1967, section 4(5).

[108] Land Act, section 1(1)(i).

sate the land occupiers for their resettlement or land compulsorily taken.[109] In Tanzania, however, occupiers of land are often not consulted when mining activities are set to take place on their land.[110] Notably, the Mining Commission may allocate mining rights to potential mining companies without necessarily consulting land occupiers.[111]

Experience indicates that a number of concerns arise when the issue of compensation comes into play. Among them are the small amount offered compared to the market value, delay in issuing compensation, absence of compensation (for example, the land is taken for the construction of roads leading to the mining sites) and embezzlement of compensation funds by government officials.[112] All these issues imply the impoverishment of local communities as their means of livelihood are grossly impacted.

Notably, local communities have the legal right under common law and statute to sue mining companies that either invade their land or pollute their land or waters.[113] However, local communities do not have such awareness and the necessary skills to institute legal actions against mining companies.[114] They rely on non-governmental organisations (NGOs) to aid them in court processes.[115] NGOs are, however, limited in terms of their location and independence. Firstly, they are mostly concentrated in cities and not in rural areas, where the marginalisation of local communities takes place. Secondly, they fear potential confrontation with the government when representing local communities against the State and multinational companies in courts of law.[116]

Next is the Local Government Finance Act 1982, a law that provides for the sources of funds to be used by local governments (District Councils) in Tanzania. The Act lists a number of potential sources, and levy is one of them. The District Council is allowed to charge companies a service levy not exceeding 0.3% of their annual turnover for operating within its jurisdiction.[117] Therefore, mining companies, as for other companies operating within the Councils, are duty-bound to pay for this levy. The monies so received by the District Council from the mining sector are used to further the development plans of the District Council. Notably, the composition of the District Council seems to be politicised as it is constituted by political representatives from each ward and various political parties.[118] Such a composition may not necessarily be representative of the local communities discussed in this

[109] United Republic of Tanzania Constitution, Art. 24 (2); Land Act, section 1(1)(g).

[110] Mining Act 2018, section 95(1)(b); Pocian (2019), p. 340.

[111] The Mining Act 2018.

[112] United Republic of Tanzania, 9; Kamat and others (2019), pp. 4–5.

[113] The Environmental Management Act 2004, section 5(1), (2)(a–f).

[114] Makene et al. (2012), pp. 16–17.

[115] Ibid.

[116] Ibid.

[117] The Local Government Finance Act 2019, section 7(1)(z)(aa).

[118] The Local Government (District Authorities) Act 1982, section 35.

chapter. According to Lange, mining companies have been funding local communities through a committee composed of the District Commissioner, three members of the Parliament, the Chief Councillor and the human resource officer of the mining company.[119] Notably, this committee is nowhere provided under Tanzanian laws. Such an approach to decisions on development issues is influenced by the private interests of politicians.[120] Every politician wants to see such developments implemented in their constituency as a means to guarantee their re-election. It is perceived by local communities that areas where the ruling party has control and influence are the ones that benefit from socio-economic services compared to those that are not.[121]

Furthermore, Lange noted that at the lower level, such as in villages, leaders such as village executive officers are not necessarily from the local communities. They are hired by local government authorities (LGAs) and are reported to embezzle funds allocated for local community development. Also, they often lack detailed knowledge of the local communities and are therefore unable to represent them accordingly in negotiations with mining companies.[122] For this reason, some mining companies have opted to issue their development funds to the respective communities, for example the Maasai community, which received money from AFGEM Mining in Mererani-Arusha.[123]

Generally, the sharing of revenue from the mining sector under the Local Government Finance Act 1982 and the general practice of companies appear to be an indirect approach to addressing the concerns of district authorities, councils or specially appointed committees, rather than the specific needs of mining-impacted local communities. Such a practice could contribute to resistance and unrest in local communities when natural resources, generally, are extracted and not only minerals.[124] In addition, when district authorities fail to collect levies from mining companies for a considerable period of time, local communities are denied their portion of revenue.[125]

According to research carried out by the Presidential Committee, there is a difference between the statutory requirement on the collection of a 0.3% levy and the contractual arrangements between mining companies and the government.[126] For example, under mineral development agreements (MDAs), mining companies negotiated to pay no more than 200,000 USD as levy, irrespective of their turnover per year.[127] Notably, the minister responsible for minerals has the mandate to enter into

[119] Lange (2006).
[120] Lange (2006); Reyes (2015), pp. 17 and 27.
[121] Kamat and others (2019), p. 7.
[122] Lange (2006), p. 120.
[123] Lange (2006), p. 120.
[124] Mwesiga and Kseniia (2017), p. 60; Kamat and others, p. 7.
[125] United Republic of Tanzania (2017), para. 3.1.4.
[126] United Republic of Tanzania (2017), para. 3.1.4.
[127] United Republic of Tanzania (2017), para. 2.3.7.

MDAs with such terms.[128] Such a variation undermines the efforts to empower the local communities as a means to eradicate poverty and attain sustainable development. Despite the inclusion of such clauses in previous MDAs, the current position in Tanzania prohibits lifetime stabilisation clauses.[129] Consequently, ministerial powers in this regard are limited.

It is worth noting the revenue-sharing scheme under the Mining Act 2018. Prior to the review of the Mining Act 2018, it did not provide for mechanisms through which local communities can benefit from mining. The 2018 revision, however, addressed this issue through the introduction of CSR. It required every mining right holder to submit a prepared CSR plan listing the activities to be undertaken on a yearly basis for the benefit of the local communities. It would appear that the CSR plan is a condition for issuing mining and/or exploration licences. What is not clear under the law, though, is the legal consequence of its absence.

The 2018 revision requires the CSR plan to be prepared by mining rights holders in consultation with relevant LGAs, the Minister for Finance and the Minister for Local Government Affairs.[130] It is a paradox that the beneficiaries of CSR initiatives, in this case local communities, are not involved in the preparation of the CSR plan. There also seems to be no administrative guideline on how the local communities may be involved. Recently, the minister responsible for minerals reiterated the same statutory position in her budgetary speech to the National Assembly.[131] It is questionable how local communities' interests and rights can be protected under a CSR plan in which they are not involved. Furthermore, the 2018 revision did not identify local communities as implementers or evaluators of CSR projects. As stated above, under land laws, land occupiers have to be consulted and be part of the decision on the use of their land. Such a principle is also reflected in the Environmental Management Act 2004, which derives its legitimacy from international instruments such as the Rio Declaration 1992 and Aarhus Convention 1998.[132] Under the Rio Declaration, the principle of public participation requires that those who are likely to be affected by any decision (in this case the decision to mine) should be part of the decision and evaluation processes themselves.[133]

In order to effectively ensure that mining rights holders give full effect to the CSR plan, the Mining Commission is mandated to monitor and evaluate its implementation.[134] While this approach is good because it seems to provide for enforcement

---

[128] Mining Act No. 14 of 2010, section 10(4)(a).

[129] The Written Laws (Miscellaneous Amendment) Act 7 of 2017, section 100E(1).

[130] Mining Act. section 105(1).

[131] Jamhuri ya Muungano wa Tanzania: Wizara ya Madini, Hotuba Ya Waziri Wa Madini (2019), p. 47.

[132] Convention on Access to Information, Public Participation in Decision-Making and Access to Justice in Environmental Matters 1998, Art. 6(2)(a–d).

[133] The Rio Declaration on Environment and Development 1992, 10; Environmental Management Act 2004, section 178.

[134] Mining Act, section 22(u).

mechanisms, still, there are no clear legal consequences for the non-implementation of the CSR plan by mining rights holders. This is apparent as a CSR plan is not a condition for the issuance or revocation of mining rights. As noted above, the public trust principle, which is enshrined in Tanzanian laws and the ECOWAS guideline, directs States to enact legal provisions that will safeguard the public interest in the access to and use of natural resources. The non-fulfilment of the CSR plan by mining rights holders undermines the efforts of local communities to achieve broad-based socio-economic development, which calls for a legal provision to warrant the revocation of such rights. Such an approach will deter mining companies from taking CSR as a mere social obligation with no legal status, as it currently appears under the revised Mining Act.

Furthermore, the 2018 revision defines local communities that are beneficiaries of the CSR as individuals/families/communities residing in the vicinity of mines.[135] Notably, in this definition the following aspects although relevant seem not considered; the ancestral ties the community may have to the land, gender, disabilities and nature of existing resources such as rivers and forest. In particular, based on the size of the mining operations and/or the nature of the resources involved (such as rivers, lakes and underground waters), the community may extend beyond or be limited to an area smaller than a District. In the Sierra Leon practice noted above, it is the local communities that engage with mining companies that are under the guardianship of the government and not the other way around. Such an approach makes local communities direct beneficiaries of schemes that uplift them from mine-induced poverty. Indigenous communities, for example, enjoy the right to self-identification, a fact missing in the definition of the term 'local communities' under the Act. Perhaps this is based on Tanzania's refusal to recognise the existence of Indigenous communities within its borders, as is the case for many African countries.[136]

In addition, it is noted above that only indigenous peoles group is capable of being identified under both international regional and sub-regional, binding and non-binding principles. Other groups such as disabled, historically disadvantaged needs to be identified as well in order to benefit from mining activities in their vicinity. Since prior to mining, environmental impact assessment is compulsory,[137] the report there from may scientifically provide for a guide on geographical coverage of the potential effects, nature and types of natural resources that will potentially be impacted during mining. Consequently, local communities in the particular geographical area and or those whose life is dependent on natural resources (such as rivers, forest and lakes) that are potentially to be affected by mining can easily be identified.

---

[135] Mining Act, section 105(5).

[136] Laltaika (2012), pp. 150–156, 163–164.

[137] See para. I above.

5 Noted Challenges in the Tanzanian Legal Framework

A number of challenges that may inhibit local communities from effectively benefiting from mining may be identified from the discussion above.

First is the non-participation of local communities in the process of awarding mining rights to mining companies acquiring their land. As above noted, participation in decision-making is connected to benefit sharing. Consequently, the absence of full participation undermines the potential benefits that local communities ought to have gained. It also means eviction from their land, which has intrinsic value like spiritual and ancestral linkages, and the loss of their livelihood. Impoverishment is even exacerbated by the inadequate compensation offered to them and the embezzlement of compensation funds by governmental officials.

Second, there is an indirect sharing of mining revenue with local communities. It is indirect because the revenue collected is payable to the District Council, which will later consider the socio-economic interests and priorities of the local communities. Consequently, there is a need for legal support and political will to ensure that local communities directly derive tangible benefits from mining.[138] Notably, poorly shared mining revenue between mining stakeholders paves the way for corruption, increased resistance and socio-economic inequalities.[139] It is argued that when local communities are not well involved in the benefits accruing from mining, their socio-economic well-being will suddenly deteriorate once the mining operations cease.[140] The adoption of indirect approaches also adds bureaucracy. Despite the reliance on the bottom-up approach in local government planning, local levels such as villages have a marginal influence on LGAs' plans.[141]

Third, the adoption of CSR as a mechanism for the benefit sharing of mining revenue poses a legal challenge to its enforcement. Such a status does no good to local communities, which need a clear and strong legal framework to rely on when they are negatively impacted by mining activities. In addition, the Mining Act seems silent on the possible activities that may be negotiated under a CSR plan. According to Lange, mining companies seem to have different responses towards CSR. While some argue that they are not duty-bound to build schools and hospitals, others say they are.[142] Also, local communities' perception of the social contribution of mining companies to their development differs. While companies consider the construction of roads, water infrastructure and hospitals in mining areas as CSR, local communities perceive this as necessary for the company's prosperity rather than for their benefit.[143]

[138] Makene et al. (2012), p. 17.

[139] United Nations Economic Commissions for Africa (2018), para. 2.2.2.

[140] Zarsky and Stanley (2013), p. 148.

[141] Policy Forum (2020).

[142] Lange (2006), p. 120, para. 4.4.

[143] Lange (2006), p. 120, para. 2.4.

In particular, setting parameters for activities to be covered by CSR initiatives serves three purposes. First, it maintains the uniformity of obligations to be borne by mining companies. Second, it acts as a reference point or guide for local communities in negotiating with mining companies. Third, it guides law enforcement agents in monitoring and evaluating CSR efforts. Consequently, leaving it open-ended undermines negotiation, monitoring and evaluation by law enforcement agents.

Additionally, there seems to be a contradiction in the laws regulating the amount to be paid by mining companies to local communities. It is unclear whether the already-adopted stabilisation clauses in MDAs prior to the review of the Mining Act will be affected by the non-retrospective effect of the law.

Lastly, the Mining Act seems silent on how to identify the local communities that are to be beneficiaries of CSR initiatives. The adopted definition is less specific to vulnerable groups such as geographically underdeveloped communities, Indigenous communities, women and persons with disabilities. The definition also is not liked to the environmental impact assessment which identified potential benefits and harms of large-scale projects such as mining, to community in their vicinity.[144] Moreover, the mining legal framework is silent on mandatory human rights impact assessment (HRIA) prior to mining activities. According to Nora Gotzman *et al.*, HRIA not only encompasses international human rights and standards but also assesses rights holders and duty bearers concerning specific rights that might be violated by mining companies.[145] Consequently, the combination of EIA and HRIA will offer more scientific and legal grounds for identifying local communities (including their potential groups). In particular, the proper identification of local communities would warrant direct beneficial schemes and ensure they truly benefit from mining activities.

6 Conclusion and Recommendations

Conclusively, this chapter highlights that local communities in natural-resource-rich States, Tanzania included, are subjected to mine-induced poverty due to weak legal frameworks regulating such resources. When the legal framework guarantees benefit sharing between mining companies, the central government and local communities, it does not only foster human rights but also guarantees broad-based socio-economic growth. Consequently, this chapter shows that there exists international (binding and non-binding) and State practices requiring natural-resource-rich States to share benefits with local communities in that respect.

Tanzania has attempted to ratify such international (binding and non-binding) frameworks. However, the manner in which Tanzania has ratified these framesowks does not guarantee local comunities full realization of benefits from the mining

[144] See para. I above.

[145] Gotzmann and others (2016), A.4.5.

sector. Among the evidencing factors are inadequate or lack of compensation, indirect benefit sharing with local communities, conflicting legal provisions on the extent of benefits to local communities, unclear legal status of CSR and the absence of clear scientific and legal criteria to identify local communities. Consequently, most local communities in Tanzania seem to be more victims than beneficiary of the large-scale mining projects in their vicnity owing to little or no benefits derived there from.

In order to guarantee that local communities benefit from mining in Tanzania, the mining legal framework should provide for

(i) The full participation of local communities in the sharing of mining benefits
(ii) Direct benefit sharing with local communities or their established trusts
(iii) An enforceable mechanism for benefit sharing with local communities (a condition for the issuance and revocation of mining or exploration permits and licences), and
(iv) Clear criteria to be relied on when identifying the local communities noted above

References

ACHPR Resolution on a Human Rights-Based Approach to Natural Resources Governance: The African Commission on Human and Peoples' Rights (African Commission), at its 51st Ordinary Session held from 18 April to 2 May 2012 in Banjul, The Gambia; 2012

African Charter on Human and Peoples' Rights 1986

Barume A (2010) Land rights of Indigenous Peoples in Africa. IWIGIA

Bekhechi M, Mercier J-R (2002) The legal and regulatory framework for environmental impact assessment: a study of selected countries in Sub-Saharan Africa. The World Bank

Centre for Minority Rights Development (Kenya) and Minority Rights Group (on behalf of Endorois Welfare Council) v Kenya [2009] ACHPR No. 276/03

Commission for Human Rights and Good Governance (2013) Report on Public Awareness on Land Rights. Dar es Salaam Tanzania.

Convention on Access to Information, Public Participation in Decision-Making and Access to Justice in Environmental Matters 1998

Democratic Republic of the Congo vs Uganda [2005] International Court of Justice 2005/5

ECOWAS (2009) Directive on the harmonisation of guiding principles and policies in the mining sector

Evaristus O (2011) Fiscal regime for natural resource extraction: implication for Africa's development. In: Francis Botchway F (ed) Natural resources investment and Africa' development. Edward Elgar, Cheltenham

Feris L (2012) The Public Trust Doctrine and liability for historic water pollution in South Africa. Law Environ Dev J 8

Fimbo GM (2013) Essays in land law in Tanzania law Africa. Kampala

Gotzmann N, others (2016) Human rights impacts assessment: guidance and toolbox. The Danish Institute for Human Rights, <www.menneskeret.dk/tilgaengelighed>

IGF Mining and Sustainable Development (2013) Policy Framework 2013 <http://igfmining.org>

ILO Indigenous and Tribal Peoples Convention 1986

Inter-American Commission for Human Rights (2015) Indigenous Peoples' Communities of African Decent Extractive Industries. OEA/Ser.L/V/IL Doc. 47/15

IRIN (2013) Tanzanian Famers Displaced by Mining like Refugees. <http://www.irinnews.org/report/98150>

Jamhuri ya Muungano wa Tanzania: Wizara ya Madini (2019) Hotuba Ya Waziri Wa Madini Mh. Angellah Jasmine Mbelwa Kairuki (MB); Akiwasilisha Bungenimpango Wa Makdirio Ya Mapato Na Matumizi Ya Fedha Kwa Mwaka Wa Fedha 2018/2019. Wizara ya Madini

Kamat V and others (2019) Natural gas extraction and community development in Tanzania: documenting the gaps between rhetoric and reality. Extract Ind Soc 6

Kamati Maalumu iliyoundwa na Rais wa Jamhuri ya Muungano waa Tanzania (2017) Taarifa Ya Kamati Maalum Kuchunguza Mchanga Uliokkatika Makontena Yenye Mchanga Wa Madini (Makinikia) Yaliyopo Katika Maeneo Mbalimbali Nchini Tanzania.' I

Kamati Maalumu iliyoundwa na Rais wa Jamhuri ya Muungano wa Tanzania (2017) Taarifa Ya Kamati Maalum Ya Kuchunguza Masuala Ya Kisheria Na Kiuchumi Kuhusiana Na Mchanga Wenye Madini Unaosafirishwa Nje Ya Nchi.' II

Kevin Mgwanga Gunmme et al v Cameroon [2003] African Commission on Human and Peoples' Rights 266, Communication

Laltaika E (2012) Indigenous Peoples' Rights in Tanzania and international rights law. Tuma Law Rev 1

Laltaika E (2017) Legal protection of environment from negative impacts of extractive operations in Tanzania. Afr Nazarene Univ Law J

Lange S (2006) Benefit streams from mining in Tanzania: case studies from Geita and Mererani. CMI Chr Michelsen Institute <www.cmi.no/publications>

Makene M, Emel J, Murphy J (2012) Calling for Justice in Goldfields of Tanzania. Resources

Mwesiga T, Kseniia M (2017) Mtwara gas project conflict: impacts on local communities socio-economic activities (Part 1). Soc Sci 6

Natural Resource Governance Institute (2014) Natural Resource Charter, 2nd edn. <http://www.naturalresourcecharter.org>

Natural Resources Governance Institute (2015) The Resource Curse: The Political, Economic Challenges of Natural Resource Wealth. <https://resourcegovernance.org/sites/default/files/nrgi_Resource-Curse.pdf>

Nyamwaya C and Kenya Human Right Commission (2013) Benefit sharing on extractive natural resources with society in Kenya. Friedrich Ebert Stiftung

Odumasu A (2014) Government, investors local communities: analysis of multi-actor investment contract framework. Melbourne J Int Law

Olaniyan K (2016) Corruption and human rights law in Africa. Hart Publishing, London

Pereira R, Gough O (2013) Permanent sovereignty over natural resources in the 21st century: natural resources governance and the right to self determination of Indigenous peoples under international law. Melbourne J Int Law 14

Pocian J (2019) Extractive resource ownership and sub-national resource curse: insight from Tanzania. The Extractive Industry and Society, p 6

Policy Forum (2012) Revenue losses owing to tax incentives in the mining sector: policy recommendation. Policy Forum <https://www.policyforum-tz.org/extractive-industries>

Policy Forum, Enhancing Local Government Accountability: Where Are the Opportunities <www.policyforum.or.tz>

Republic of Kenya, Mining Act 2016

Republic of Sierra Leone the Mines and Minerals Act 2009

Republic of South Africa, Mineral and Petroleum Resources Development Act 2002

Republic of Uganda, Mining Act 2003

Reyes D (2015) The rise in conflict associated with mining operations: what lies beneath? Field case study 2: Bullyanhulu, Tanzania Canadian International Resources and Development Institute

Sachs L, (2013) On solid grounds: toward effective resource based development. World Polit Rev <https://www.worldpoliticsreview.com/articles/13140/on-solid-ground-toward-effective-resource-based-development>

SADC (2008) Implementation Plan for the Harmonisation of Mining Policies, Standards and Legislative Regulatory Frameworks in Southern Africa, ECA/SA/Tpub/2008/1

SADC Protocol on Mining 1997

SADC, the Treaty of the Southern African Economic Development 1992

Saramaka People v Suriname (Interpretation of the Judgment on Preliminary Objection, Merit, Reparation and Cost) (Inter-American Court of Human Rights)
Schyff E (2006) The Constitutionality of Mineral and Petroleum Resource Development Act 28 of 2002. Unpublished PhD Thesis North West University
Schyff E (2008) Who "Owns" the country's mineral resources? The possible incorporation of the public trust doctrine through the mineral and petroleum resources development act. J South Afr Law 4
Schyff E (2013) Stewardship Doctrine of public trust: has the eagle of public trust landed on South African Soil? South Afr Law J 130
Schyff E (2016) Property in minerals and petroleum. JUTA Cape Town
Social and Economic Rights Action Centre (SERAC) and Centre for Economic Social Rights (CESR) vs Nigeria [2001] ACHPR 155/96
UN (2007) Declarations on the Rights of Indigenous Peoples
UN Commission for Sustainable Development, Johannesburg Declaration on Sustainable Development 2002
UN Commission on Sustainable Development (2010) Report on the Eighteenth Session (15th May 2009 and 3-14 May 2010). Economic and Social Council E/2010/29
UN Commission on Sustainable Development (2011) Report on the Nineteenth Session (14th May 2010 and 2-13 May 2011). Economic and Social Council E/2011/9
UN General Assembly Declaration on Rights of Indigenous Peoples 2007
UN General Assembly Resolution Permanent Sovereignty over natural resources 1962
UN General Resolution No. 66/288, The Future We Want (2012)
UN Rio Declaration on Environment and Development 1992
UNECA (2009) Africa Mining Vision. <http://www.africaminingvision.org/reports.html>
United Nations Economic Commissions for Africa (2018) African Governance Report V: Natural Resource Governance and Domestic Revenue Mobilization for Structural Transformation
United Republic of Tanzania (2008) Report of the Presidential Mining Review Committee to Advise the Government on Oversight of the Mining Sector. <http://www.policyforum-tz.org/sites/default/files/BomaniReport-English_0.pdf>
United Republic of Tanzania Constitution 1977
United Republic of Tanzania Mining Act 2018
United Republic of Tanzania the Environmental Management Act 2004
United Republic of Tanzania the Land Acquisition Act 1967
United Republic of Tanzania the Land Act 1999 (5)
United Republic of Tanzania the Local Government (District Authorities) Act 1982
United Republic of Tanzania the Local Government Finance Act 2019
United Republic of Tanzania the Natural Wealth and Resources (Permanent Sovereignty) Act 2017
World Summit on Sustainable Development (2002) Plan of Implementation of the World Summit on Sustainable Development
Zarsky L, Stanley L (2013) Can extractive industries promote sustainable development? A net profit framework and case study of the Merlin Mine in Guatemala. J Environ Dev 22

John S. Ombella LL.B (Mzumbe University 2005) LL.M (University of Western Cape 2007), LL.D (OUT 2023), Certificate on Sustainable Development and Human Rights Law (SUSTLAW) (Antwerp University-Belgium 2017), Certificate on Climate Change International Legal Regime (UNITAR/UNEP 2024), Lecturer, Private Law Department, Faculty of Law, Mzumbe University, Founder and Director of Mine-host Communities Initiative (MHCI 2022), An Advocate of the High Court and Subordinate Courts – Tanzania. Contacts: majaliwaj.sinato@gmail.com

Three Decades in the Constitution

Analysing the Contribution of the Bill of Rights to Economic Development in Mainland Tanzania

Leonard Chimanda Joseph and Sekela Kalangson Mlungu

1 Introduction

The Bill of Rights was incorporated into the Constitution of the United Republic of Tanzania (CURT) in 1984 through the Fifth Amendment to the Constitution.[1] The enforcement of the Bill of Rights began in 1987 before the formulation of the formal procedural rules. The court began to handle human rights cases while there were no formal procedures in place. The case of *Chumchua Marwa v. Officer of Musoma Prisons and the Attorney General* marked the first case on the enforcement of the Bill of Rights (violations of human rights) heard by the High Court of Tanzania, as empowered by article 30(4) of the Constitution.[2] Several reasons drove the government to embark on the business of incorporating the Bill of Rights into the Constitution. These include, among others, pressure from international organizations like the International Monetary Fund (IMF) through its structural adjustment policies (SAPs) as lending requirements from international financial institutions, pressure from human rights activists within Tanzania and the unilateral inclusion of the Bill of Rights in the Constitution of Zanzibar.

The Bill of Rights of the Constitution of the United Republic of Tanzania encompasses both enforceable and non-enforceable rights. The rights found in articles 12 to 29 are enforceable before courts of law, while the rights depicted in articles 6 to 11 of the Constitution are not enforceable. The Bill of Rights forms a

[1]Lubuva (1988), pp. 853–854, available at https://www.tandfonline.com/doi/abs/10.1080/03050718..9985970. See also Peter (1992), p. 1.

[2]Wambali (2009), p. 35.

L. Chimanda Joseph · S. Kalangson Mlungu (✉)
School of Law, University of Dodoma, Dodoma, Tanzania
e-mail: sekela.mlungu@udom.ac.tz

I. Kajiru et al. (eds.), *Economic Development and Human Rights in Contemporary Sub-Saharan Africa*, Ius Gentium: Comparative Perspectives on Law and Justice 122, https://doi.org/10.1007/978-3-031-81400-6_10

basic part of the Constitution of the United Republic of Tanzania, where basic rights and duties of individuals are provided and expressed. It identifies various fundamental rights, including but not limited to right to life, right to freedom of movement, right to personal freedom, equality before the law, right to just remuneration, right to work, right to own property and right to freedom of conscience. It also provides and expresses duties, including the duty to participate in work, the duty to safeguard public property and the duty to abide by the laws of the land.[3]

At the time of the conception of this chapter, thirty-nine (39) years (almost four decades) had passed since the landmark adoption of human rights jurisprudence in Tanzania. There are various pieces of literature on the interpretation, applicability and features of the Bill of Rights of the Constitution of the United Republic of Tanzania. However, there is a noticeable dearth of academic writings as far as the discussion on the contribution of the Bill of Rights to economic development in Tanzania is concerned. The linkage between human rights and economic development traces its roots to the African Charter on Human and Peoples' Rights, which stresses the need to pay particular attention to the right to development.[4]

This chapter aims to discuss the role that the Bill of Rights has played in promoting economic development in Tanzania since its incorporation into the Constitution. It also discusses its positive contribution to economic development in the country. The chapter argues that the manner in which the Bill of Rights is incorporated and the political will towards its implementation do not support its contribution to Tanzania's economic development. The chapter comprises six parts: the first is the introductory part, the second part discusses the background of the Bill of Rights and economic development in Tanzania, the third part deals with the role of the Bill of Rights and its contribution to economic development in Tanzania, the fourth part of the chapter presents the reality on implementation of the Bill of Rights towards economic development in Tanzania and the fifth part discusses the hurdles facing the enforcement of the Bill of Rights in manifesting economic development in the country. The last part deals with the conclusion and recommendations of the chapter.

2 Background of the Bill of Rights and Economic Development

The historical background of the Bill of Rights in the Constitution of the United Republic of Tanzania appears in different phases related to the debates on whether it should be incorporated in the Constitution, the era of its incorporation, its existence in the Constitution and its enforcement before the courts of law currently. It is undeniable that although there were various arguments as to whether the Bill of

[3]Part III of the Constitution of the United Republic of Tanzania (1977).

[4]Preamble of the African Charter on Human and Peoples' Rights (1983).

Rights should be incorporated into the Constitution, this did not occur before independence. This means that for decades, there was no Bill of Rights in the Constitution during the colonial economy in Tanganyika, currently mainland Tanzania. The German and British governments ruled the country with no legal recognition and without the enforcement of a Bill of Rights. However, there were various opinions and influences on the significance of including the Bill of Rights in the Constitution especially during the British colonial rule which turned futile.[5] Occasionally, though not consistently, the judiciary, during British colonialism, ruled in favour of human rights protection. This can be recalled from the judgments in the cases of *Fatuma d/o Kazi v DC Bukoba*[6] and *The Iron & Steelwares Limited v C.W. Martyr & Company*[7] on the right to equality and non-discrimination, respectively.

During independence, Tanganyika, currently mainland Tanzania, adopted both the political and economic systems of the British colonial government. The adoption of British political and economic systems during independence was influenced by the colonial economy that existed at that time. The British government suggested the inclusion of the Bill of Rights in the Independence Constitution to protect its interests in Tanganyika. However, this willingness was not realized by Tanganyika since the independent government considered human rights as a threat to the economic development of the country. Therefore, the new independent state (Tanganyika) established the Constitution without the Bill of Rights. Nevertheless, debates on the need for a Bill of Rights, prevalent during the colonial period, continued after independence.[8]

Since the period of independence, Tanganyika has, over time, experienced various constitutional changes. The current Constitution (1977 Constitution) was preceded by three other constitutions: the 1961, 1962 and 1964 Constitutions.

The first constitution of Tanganyika was the Independence Constitution, titled the Tanganyika (Constitution) Order in Council of 1961. The Independence Constitution was adopted in 1961 during independence when the United Kingdom granted independence to Tanganyika which was formally achieved from the United Nations trusteeship under the British administration.[9] The Independence Constitution was based on the Westminster model, and it lasted for one 1 year, from 1961 to 1962.[10] This Constitution empowered the Governor General to represent the Queen as the official head of state. Apart from that, the Prime Minister was considered the head of the executive branch.[11] Although the colonialists wanted to incorporate the Bill of

[5] Peter (2000), p. 1

[6] *Fatuma d/o Kazi v. DC Bukoba* (1957) Dig 94.

[7] *The Iron & Steelwares Limited v. C.W. Martyr & Company* (1956) 23 E.A.C.A 175.

[8] Wambali (2009), p. 35.

[9] Shivji et al. (2004), p. 47.

[10] Pfeiffer (1978), p. 39.

[11] Madenge (2021), available at https://unitedrepublicoftanzania.com/government-of-tanzania-and-the-society/education-in-tanzania.

Rights in the Independence Constitution to protect their interests, it was not possible with the government of the Tanganyika African National Union (TANU).[12] Among the reasons for the refusal to incorporate the Bill of Rights was that the new government had its priorities, and the Bill of Rights was not among them.[13] At that time, the government's priority was economic development, and it was considered that the Bill of Rights would hinder this goal.[14]

The second constitution was the Republican Constitution, adopted in 1962.[15] The Parliament was transformed into a Constituent Assembly and revised the Independence Constitution of 1961. The Republican Constitution led to the formation of a republican form of government.[16] Under this Constitution, a strong presidential system was built, empowering the President as the head of state and government and the commander in chief.[17] But like its predecessor, the Republican Constitution was short-lived, lasting for 2 years only, from 1962 to 1964. Also, this Constitution excluded the Bill of Rights among its provisions. However, for the first time, the government formally considered, but then rejected, the incorporation of the Bill of Rights in the Constitution.[18]

The third constitution was the Interim Constitution of Tanganyika and Zanzibar of 1964. The Interim Constitution succeeded the Republican and Independent Constitutions of 1961 and 1962, respectively. This Constitution was scheduled to last for 1 year following the union under the Articles of the Union of Tanganyika and Zanzibar of 1964.[19] However, this timeline was practically endlessly extended, and the Interim Constitution lasted for 12 years until the adoption of a permanent constitution in 1977.[20]

This Constitution of the United Republic of Tanzania of 1977 was the product of the modification made to the Republican Constitution of 1962 through the agreements between the two political parties such as the Tanganyika African National Union (TANU) and the Afro-Shirazi Party (ASP) merged to form *Chama cha Mapinduzi* (CCM).[21] Through Acts of the Union, these agreements were ratified as the Articles of Union, which became part and parcel of the Constitution of the United Republic of Tanzania. Therefore, it was this Constitution that established the

[12]Peter (1995), p. 46.

[13]Ibid., 47.

[14]Ibid., 47.

[15]Edward (2016), p. 77.

[16]Constitutionnet (2014), Constitutional History of Tanzania, available at https://constitutionnet.org/country/tanzania.

[17]Shivji et al. (2004), p. 48.

[18]Amankwah (1988), p. 207, and Wambali (2009), p. 35.

[19]Katundu and Kumburu (2015), p. 107.

[20]Edward (2016), p. 77.

[21]Constitutionnet (2014), Constitutional History of Tanzania, available at https://constitutionnet.org/country/tanzania.

state called the United Republic of Tanganyika and Zanzibar. The nature of the government established under this Constitution was a dual government, that is, a government for the Union and an independent government for Zanzibar.[22] The President of Zanzibar served as the Vice President of the Union.[23]

The Parliament, in its capacity as a Constituent Assembly, adopted the Articles of Union by virtue of its power to amend.[24] This Constitution took note of the adjustments made by the Union and adopted the majority of the recommendations made by the One Party Commission, including the decision not to include the Bill of Rights in the Constitution and the placement of the fundamental rights and freedoms in the Preamble. This means that the Bill of Rights had no impact because it could not be enforced, given that the Preamble is not part of the constitutional provisions that can be enforced.[25] Additionally, the ruling party constitution of 1977 was added to the schedule of the current Constitution of the United Republic of Tanzania of 1977.[26]

The fourth constitution is the Permanent Constitution of 1977, in effect to this day. The Constitution of the United Republic of Tanzania of 1977 underwent various amendments to suit the economic environment of the country, which was at its early stage after independence. It was enacted 16 years after the independence of mainland Tanzania. The Constitution of the United Republic of Tanzania, 1977, was followed by various constitutional amendments to cover different important matters not included during the time of its enactment. The Fifth Amendment to the Constitution, made in 1984, is its most remarkable constitutional amendment as it introduced the Bill of Rights in the Constitution of the United Republic of Tanzania. This amendment changed the course of the country's history, which was previously ruled without the enforcement of a Bill of Rights.

It is observed that for 3 years, the Bill of Rights was not enforceable in the courts of law as the government was undergoing internal reform. Its enforcement began in 1987, when an application for unlawful detention was lodged before the court.[27] This marked the beginning of a new era and practice in the country. However, it is noted that at the time, there were no procedures and rules for the courts to follow in handling human rights cases in Tanzania. It was not until the government enacted the Basic Rights and Duties Enforcement Act in 1994, for the implementation of the Bill

[22] Katundu and Kumburu (2015), p. 108.

[23] Constitutionnet (2014), Constitutional History of Tanzania, available at https://constitutionnet.org/country/tanzania.

[24] Shivji (1990), p. 44.

[25] Peter (1995), p. 47.

[26] Constitutionnet (2014), Constitutional History of Tanzania, available at https://constitutionnet.org/country/tanzania.

[27] Wambali (2009), pp. 36–37.

of Rights, that procedural rules were set up. This law provides for the procedures to follow when there is a violation of the rights enshrined in the Bill of Rights.[28]

Along the same lines, the Constitution was modified in 2020 with the amendment of section 4 of the Basic Rights and Duties Enforcement Act.[29] The amendment added sub-section 2 to section 4 of the Basic Rights and Duties Enforcement Act and introduced the requirements for filing a petition for human rights violations.[30]

The amended provision requires the High Court of Tanzania (HCT), as a court of competent jurisdiction, to admit a human rights application or petition only if accompanied by an affidavit detailing the extent to which the violation of rights under the Constitution has personally affected the applicant or petitioner.[31] It is argued that the implication of the requirement of a "personally affected affidavit" is that it potentially limits organizations or individuals from filing a petition on behalf of a group of people affected by violations of fundamental rights and freedoms.

3 The Bill of Rights and Its Contribution to Economic Development

The Bill of Rights has played a tremendous role in the economic development of Tanzania. The incorporation of the Bill of Rights led to a shift in the economic paradigm—from a state-owned to a privately owned economy. During independence, the economy was under private ownership, which means that the economic sector was controlled by individuals.[32] However, 7 years after independence, the government embarked on the establishment of state-owned economy and state operated enterprises through a nationalization programme, which altered the existing private economy ownership structure.[33] The reason behind this approach was to consolidate the newly attained independence and replace the private sector with the public sector.[34] Through the nationalization programme after independence, the state became the main player in the economy, which previously was privately controlled.

The introduction of the Bill of Rights influenced and enhanced individual rights and freedoms recognized by the Constitution. The Bill of Rights ensures that citizens

[28] The Basic Rights and Duties Enforcement Act (1994) Cap. 3 [R.E 2019].

[29] Part III of the Written Laws (Miscellaneous Amendments) Act (2020) GN No. 6 (2020 amends the Basic Rights and Duties Enforcement Act (1994).

[30] Section 4(2) of the Basic Rights and Duties Enforcement Act (1994) and Rule 4 of the Basic Right and Duties Enforcement (Practice and Procedure) Rules, GN No. 304 of 2014.

[31] This provision requires an affidavit on how one is personally affected; see Rule 4 of the Basic Right and Duties Enforcement (Practice and Procedure) Rules (2014).

[32] Nellis (2005), available at https://papers.ssrn.com/sol3/papers.cfm?abstract_id=828764.

[33] Constitutionnet (2014), Constitutional History of Tanzania, available at https://constitutionnet.org/country/tanzania.

[34] Musoke (2008), pp. 10 and 51.

are entitled to various fundamental liberties and rights,[35] including the right to education,[36] the right to equality before the law,[37] the right to life,[38] the right to freedom of expression,[39] the right to freedom of association,[40] the right to freedom of religion,[41] the right to work[42] and the right to own property, among others.[43] The Bill of Rights incorporated in the Constitution demonstrates the nation's dedication to promoting individual rights and freedoms. It establishes a legal framework for the protection of individual rights and liberties and makes sure that the government is held accountable in case of violations.[44]

The link between the Bill of Rights and economic development can be derived from these individual rights and freedoms guaranteed by the Constitution.[45] However, many variables can influence the relationship between the Bill of Rights and economic development, including the general government structure, institutional capability, and sociocultural context.[46] A strong and effective enforcement of the Bill of Rights can foster stability, inclusion and personal liberties, which assist in economic development.[47] Below is a discussion of specific individual rights and freedoms under the Bill of Rights and their role in economic development.

The constitutional protection of the right to own property under the Bill of Rights contributes to the economic development of the country.[48] Also, the protection of the right to own property upholds the ownership of property and protects the owner of the property against unjustified deprivation.[49] It is said that the constitutional guarantee of the right to own property provides assurance to the owner that there

---

[35] Ruhangisa (1998), p. 136.

[36] Right to education; see Art. 11 of the Constitution of the United Republic of Tanzania (1977).

[37] Right to equality before the law; see Art. 13 of the Constitution of the United Republic of Tanzania (1977).

[38] Right to life; see Art. 14 of the Constitution of the United Republic of Tanzania (1977).

[39] It provides for the right to freedom of expression under Art. 18 of the Constitution of the United Republic of Tanzania (1977).

[40] The right to freedom of association is provided under Art. 20 of the Constitution of the United Republic of Tanzania (1977).

[41] It provides for the right to freedom of religion; see Art. 19 of the Constitution of the United Republic of Tanzania (1977).

[42] The right to work is enshrined under Art. 22 of the Constitution of the United Republic of Tanzania (1977).

[43] It provides for the right to own property as per Art. 24 of the Constitution of the United Republic of Tanzania (1977).

[44] United Nations (2018), pp. 4–9.

[45] Icelandic Human Rights Centre, Human Rights and Development, available at https://www.humanrights.is/en/human-rights-education-project/human-rights-concepts-ideas-and-fora/human-rights-in-relation-to-other-topics/human-rights-and-development#.

[46] Uutela et al. (2021), p. 2.

[47] United Nations (2007), pp. 7, 75.

[48] Howard-Hassmann, (2013), available at https://www.tandfonline.com/doi/full/10.1080/14754835.2013.784667.

[49] Article 17 of the Universal Declaration of Human Rights, 1948.

will be no interference with their property. Because of this, businesses and investors will have confidence and security in their business and investments, which will lead to economic development in the long run.[50]

Furthermore, it is said that the Bill of Rights leads to a stable and dependable legal system that ensures the free execution of contracts, the ownership of property and protection from arbitrary government actions.[51] The fundamental right to own property encourages people and firms to take risks and engage in economic activities that can enhance investment and entrepreneurship.[52] Therefore, the Bill of Rights encourages economic growth as it increases investors' confidence and creates trust in the legal system.

There is also a right to equality before the law among the fundamental rights provided under the Bill of Rights in the Constitution.[53] Equality before the law ensures that everyone has equal access to economic opportunities, resources and services.[54] The Bill of Rights, which ensures equality and non-discrimination, is important to ensure equal opportunities. Furthermore, the right to equality before the law enhances the circumstances in which everyone has an equal chance to succeed in building a productive society.[55] Therefore, the Bill of Rights encourages inclusive growth as it lowers barriers that hinder marginalized people from fully engaging in the economy by reducing social and economic inequities.

Another role of the Bill of Rights in economic growth can be realized through the freedom of expression.[56] The right to freedom of expression is essential because it allows people to express their opinions and share information.[57] Also, it enables people to participate in the public dialogue on policies, laws and regulations related to economy and development strategies. Additionally, freedom of thought is vital for creativity and economic growth since people are more likely to come up with new ideas, advance technology and enhance economic growth when they are free to voice their thoughts, share their knowledge and challenge the current state of the economy.[58] Therefore, the Bill of Rights is important for the country's economic development through the freedom of expression, which is the foundation of democracy.

---

[50] Besley (1995), p. 903.

[51] Kalley and Graglia (2017), available at https://www.newamerica.org/future-land-housing/blog/why-property-rights-matter/.

[52] Sullivan et al. (2007), p. 33.

[53] Article 13 of the Constitution of the United Republic of Tanzania (1977).

[54] Atuguba (2014), available at https://www.ohchr.org/sites/default/files/Documents/Issues/Development/RTDBook/PartIIChapter7.pdf.

[55] Icelandic Human Rights Centre (2015), available at https://www.humanrights.is/en/human-rights-education-project/human-rights-concepts-ideas-and-fora/substantive-human-rights/the-right-to-equality-and-non-discrimination.

[56] See Art. 18 of the Constitution of the United Republic of Tanzania (1977).

[57] See Art. 19(2) of the International Covenant on Civil and Political Rights, 1966. See also Art. 19 of the Universal Declaration of Human Rights, 1948.

[58] Gurkaynak (2019), available at https://papers.ssrn.com/sol3/papers.cfm?abstract_id=3543433.

Furthermore, the promotion of social and economic rights, like the right to work, the right to education and the right to good health, can lead to economic development. The provision of access to these essential services encourages the development of human capital, reduces poverty and establishes the framework for sustainable economic development in the country.[59] Also, the Bill of Rights leads to a more productive and engaged workforce since it protects labour rights, including the freedom of association, collective bargaining rights and the right to equitable working conditions. The fair treatment of employees and their freedom to organize and bargain can result in better working conditions, greater job satisfaction and higher production.[60] Therefore, the Bill of Rights can spur innovation and efficiency, which in turn can have a good effect on economic development.[61]

Generally, the Bill of Rights plays an important role in the economy of the country because the protection of these rights guarantees the people's freedom to engage in economic activities without unjustified interference or prejudice. People's well-being is also enhanced when they have the chance to work productively and earn a living wage, which in turn helps the economy as a whole by boosting output and consumption.

4 The Bill of Rights and Economic Development in Tanzania

This section seeks to explore the extent to which the Bill of Rights has contributed to various aspects of economic development in Tanzania. The economic development that is the subject of this discussion is at two levels: individual and national. The authors selected only a few key areas, albeit not exhaustive. The contributions of the Bill of Rights can be traced from its incorporation into the Constitution in 1984 to the present day. These contributions are discussed below.

4.1 Enhancing Land Ownership

Specific to the Constitution of the United Republic of Tanzania, the protection of land rights can be reflected in five provisions: articles 12, 13, 14, 22 and 24.

Article 12 provides for the equality of human beings, human dignity and non-discrimination. From its conception, the provision has aimed to protect all persons against unequal treatment in various spheres of life. This includes treatments

---

[59] Besley (1995), p. 904.

[60] International Labour Organization, available at https://www.ilo.org/global/topics/dw4sd/themes/freedom-of-association/lang%2D%2Den/index.htm.

[61] Adams (2011), pp. 231–235.

and entitlements concerning ownership and control of land. The provision essentially opposes all practices and laws that treat human beings differently with regard to ownership of land due to their stations in life, such as sex, gender, race, political opinion, and ethnicity.

Article 13 provides for equality before the law. The provision, inter alia, ensures that all persons have equal access to the law, including its enforcement bodies, such as courts, the police and quasi-judicial bodies. This provision enables individuals in Tanzania to approach courts and other dispute settlement bodies whenever their land rights are encroached upon. In enshrining this right, the Constitution is embodied with the spirit of non-discrimination and the inclusion of all people.

Article 14 provides for the right to life. Under this provision, every person in Tanzania has a right to life in accordance with the law. Land being a major means of production, people make a life out of it. In other words, the deprivation of one's land can be equated to the deprivation of one's life. Article 14 can therefore be used in conjunction with other provisions to accord protection to diverse land-related rights in Tanzania.

Article 22 provides for the right to work. In the Tanzanian context, especially in rural areas, land is the major asset through which people work. The working avenue for people in rural areas is highly limited to cultivating land. Thus, the protection of their access to land also safeguards their right to work. Conversely, the encroachment of their right to land leads to the deprivation of their right to work.

Article 24 provides for the right to own property. The Constitution states that "every person is entitled to own property and has a right to the protection of his property held in accordance with the law". Land is not only property but is also often considered the most significant property because it is the foundation of agricultural production.[62] Therefore, article 24 is the leading provision in the Constitution of Tanzania for the protection of land rights.

In mainland Tanzania, human rights constitutional protection have enhanced land ownership in two major areas; equality of women over land ownership and equality of customary land rights over granted right of occupancy as herein below elucidated.

4.1.1 The Bill of Rights and Women's Rights in Tanzania

Prior to the inclusion of the Bill of Rights in the Constitution of the United Republic of Tanzania, women's entitlement to land ownership was uncertain; as a result, women were deprived of the right to own land in most cases. While deprivation of women's right to own land was more pertinent under customary laws the status led to the deferral of application of statutory laws which was nonetheless weak at that particular moment being majory regulated by the Land Ordinance whose content was not comprehensive. The situation was made even worse due to the fact that in 120 ethnic groups in Tanzania, the majority are not only Bantu originated but also

[62] See Garance and Maria (2022), p. 153.

patrilineal, in which property inheritance is through the male lineage, where the primogeniture distribution rule gives priority to the eldest son.

Before 1984, the customary practices in Tanzania undermined the entitlements of women under that of men. As a result, society and the community at large presumed a congruence of interest between family members to the extent that, men's access to land was believed to also guarantee women's access to land.[63] Such subjugation of women's land rights made women vulnerable bearing in mind that, in the context of Tanzania especially in rural areas, land is an important property for women with unique advantages over employment and other non-land income forms.

With the incorporation of the Bill of Rights in 1984, especially the provisions of articles 12, 13, 22 and 24 of the Constitution, the protection of women's land rights was enhanced. This was evident in both the judiciary and the legislature. In the judiciary, courts boldly declared null and void all laws and practices that undermine women's entitlement over land. A good example is the case of *Bernado Ephraim v. Holaria Patory and Gervazi Kaizilege*, where the court ruled that customary laws that restrict women's land rights are null and are in violation of international human rights instruments to which Tanzania is a party.[64]

The legislature (Parliament), on its side, enacted two laws in 1999 in response to the enhancement of land rights for all persons in the country: the Land Act, Cap. 113, and the Village Land Act, Cap. 114. These Acts were preceded by the National Land Policy of 1995, which that to a large extent grounded their content. The Land Act regulates various aspects related to general land and reserved land. While general land covers "all land that is not reserved and it included unoccupied or unused village land",[65] reserved land includes "all land set aside for special purposes, including forest reserves, game parks, game reserves, land reserved for public utilities and highways, hazardous land and land designated under the Town and Country Planning Ordinance".[66] The Village Land Act regulates all used and occupied land in villages primarily through customary laws and practices.

The two Acts are liberative when it comes to women's rights. This is because these laws have provisions that ensure the equality of all people over land rights, preventing gender discrimination. The Land Act, for instance, unequivocally enshrines the principle that "the right of every woman to acquire, hold, use, and deal with, land shall to the same extent and subject to the same restrictions be treated as a right of any man".[67] The same principles are embodied in the Village Land Act.[68] Besides women's ownership of land, the Village Land Act contains

[63] See Ambreena (1996), pp. 11–38.

[64] *Bernado Ephraim v Holaria Patory and Gervazi Kaizilege*, Civil Appeal No. 70 of 1989, High Court of Tanzania at Mwanza, Mwalusanya, J (Unreported).

[65] Section 2 of the Land Act (1999) Cap. 113 [R.E 2019].

[66] Section 2 of the Land Act (1999) Cap.114 [R.E 2019].

[67] Section 3 (2) of the Land Act (1999) Cap. 114 [R.E 2019].

[68] Section 3(2) of the Village Land Act (1999).

provisions on women's participation in decision-making over all matters affecting land rights, which are found in sections 23(2)(c), 30(4)(b), 35(2), 36(2) and 60(9).

Despite these gender-neutral provisions and the declarations made by the Tanzanian legislature and judiciary with regard to land rights, problems on the discrimination of women over land rights persists to a significant extent.[69] The literature shows that in Tanzania at present, married women, especially those in rural areas, still own less land compared to their husbands and have limited rights over jointly owned land. It is further reported that although members of institutions responsible for dispute resolution over village land hold pro-women opinions on land rights, they do not always make gender-neutral recommendations in cases of land disputes.[70] Admittedly, however, despite the current gender equality challenges with regard to land ownership in Tanzania, the situation has improved compared to the time before the incorporation of the Bill of Rights.

4.1.2 The Bill of Rights and Customary Land Tenure

It is a fact that customary land tenure is the leading system in agrarian communities and, generally, in Africa.[71] The tenure has evolved from a communal to an individual framework in response to socio-economic developments. Simply put, customary land tenure is a central system of land ownership in developing countries, especially in rural areas.

The right to own property and its collateral rights, enshrined in the Bill of Rights, has had an impact on guaranteeing customary land rights. Proceeding from the discussion above, it should be cemented that, the Land Acts of 1999 did not only impact women's land rights but also rights of persons holding land under customary laws. This is because prior to 1984 and, more particularly, 1999, persons who held land under customary law were considered inferior to persons who held land under the Granted Right of Occupancy. As a result, persons holding land were, in most cases, forcefully evicted from their lands, oftentimes without any compensation. Authorities with the mandate to regulate land in villages often gave away land used by villagers to commercial farmers and public corporations without the villagers' consent.[72] Simply put, prior to the implementation of the Bill of Rights in Tanzania, clans and tribes were deprived of their entitlement to and ultimate control over land. This was undoubtedly a violation of the right to own property.

The deprivation of customary land tenure can be traced back to 1967 and 1974, during the Arusha Declaration and the villagization programme, respectively. During these times, millions of people were evicted from their ancestral lands and were resettled in communes. The Arusha Declaration and its resultant villagization

[69] See Helen (2012).

[70] See Garance and Maria (2022), p. 153.

[71] See also Jenesta (2022), p. 22.

[72] See Ben (2010).

programme have been considered in the literature as illegal and criminal in both their conception and implementation.[73]

Since the incorporation of the Bill of Rights into the Constitution of the United Republic of Tanzania in 1984, courts and Parliament have been in favour of protecting customary land rights, as shown in their pursuit of equality between customary land tenure and granted rights of occupancy. Courts, on various occasions, have been uniformly ruling that customary land tenure is equal to granted rights of occupancy and that no person should be deprived of such tenure without following due process of law.[74] The Village Land Act states that "a customary right of occupancy is in every respect of equal status and effect to a granted right of occupancy".[75] Similarly, the Land Act defines the right of occupancy as a "title to the use and occupation of land and includes the title of a Tanzanian citizen of African descent or a community of Tanzanian citizens of African descent using or occupying land in accordance with customary law".[76] These definitions demonstrate that land laws in Tanzania no longer consider customary land tenure as inferior to granted rights of occupancy.

4.2 Enhancing Investment Environment

Investment, especially foreign private investment, is a key source of foreign exchange flows and capital, which can highly contribute to a country's economic growth. Prior to 1984, the United Republic of Tanzania practised a strict socialism policy, which was unfriendly to foreign investments and trade liberalization. With the guarantee of human rights that came with the incorporation of the Bill of Rights into the Constitution of the United Republic of Tanzania in 1984, the environment for investment was given a green light. With the privatization and trade liberalization policy that began in around 1985 during the second phase of government, investments, particularly foreign direct investments (FDIs), began to accelerate.

Normally, FDIs are closely associated with the democratic maturity of the host country. Foreign investors are always attracted to countries with a mature level of democracy and where human rights adherence is at its peak. This is true since foreign investors will always want their property rights to be protected when investing in the host state. It is therefore important to state that the Bill of Rights was incorporated in

[73] See Ben (2010).

[74] See *Tito Saturo and 7 Others v Matiya Seneya and Others*, Civil Case No. 27 of 1985; *National Agricultural and Food Corporation (NAFCO) v Mulbadaw Village Council and 66 Villagers*, 1985 TLR 88; *Attorney General v Lohay Akonaay and Another*, Civil Appeal No. 31 of 1994; *Alameni Kambini and 14 Others v Orkesumet Village Council and 2 Others*, Civil Case No. 39 of 1994; and *Lekengere Faru Parutu Kamunyu and 52 Others v Minister of Tourism, Natural Resources and Environment and 3 Others*, Civil Appeal No. 53 of 1998.

[75] Section 18(1) of the Village Land Act, 1999, Cap. 114 (R.E 2019).

[76] Section 2 of the Land Act, 1999, Cap. 113 (R.E 2019).

1984 and its resultant effects such as introduction of multiparty democracy in 1992, made Tanzania a potential attraction for Foreign Direct Investment.

By year 2000, the United Republic of Tanzania was considered a fast becoming Foreign Direct Investment (FDI) front runner country in the African Union. This is because as of 2000, market reforms reached critical mass and the country received a billion dollars of investment inflows in 1995-2000 compared with only USD 90 million in the preceding six years.[77] The stock of foreign direct investment increased to USD 15,392.9 million in 2017 distinct from USD 14,634.3 million in 2016.[78] Again, despite the global deterioration, FDI inflows to Tanzania were 24.2 per cent higher in 2017 compared with the inflows registered in 2016.

In addition to that, at the beginning of the year 2000, the most attracting sector for foreign investment in Tanzania was mining. By 2023 the sectors prone to foreign direct investment have multiplied. Currently, sectors that attract foreign direct investment albeit with varying rates are mining, agriculture, manufacturing, health, education, aquaculture development, livestock, economic infrastructure, tourism and ICT.[79]

4.3 Women Empowerment

In addition to the empowerment of women regarding land ownership, the Bill of Rights has also empowered women in various aspects, including political participation, early marriage, employment and educational rights. Empowering women is key to fostering inclusive economic development in any country.[80] Women's empowerment in the identified areas stems from the recognition and protection of various rights under the Bill of Rights, such as the right to equality and non-discrimination, the right to education, the right to work and receive just remuneration, the right to participate in government affairs, the right to freedom of movement and the right to freedom of expression. All of these rights are recognized and protected under the Constitution of the United Republic of Tanzania.

Prior to 1984, due to discriminatory cultural practices, women were dependent on men. Where a man was employed, a woman was also considered to be employed on that basis. Women were not considered independent. As a result, the number of salaried women workers was negligible. By 1980, out of 100 salaried workers in Tanzania, one was a woman, despite the fact that, population wise, the number of women was bigger than men.[81]

Currently, the rate of employed women has increased in pursuit of the Bill of Rights of 1984 in Tanzania. The women's labour force rose in 2019 to 80%,

[77] United Nations (2002), p. 1.

[78] See National Bureau of Statistics (2018).

[79] See Tanzania Investment Centre (2023).

[80] See Esther (2012), pp. 1051–1079.

[81] See Ruth (1996), pp. 39–90.

compared to 67% in 2000. This percentage is above the reported 63% average of the female labour force in sub-Saharan Africa. Also, the number of women participating in unpaid agricultural work fell from 78% in 2004–2005 to 64% in the years 2015–2016.[82]

With regard to participation in government affairs, although the representation of women leaders has remained at 34% at the local level over the last three general elections, Tanzania is nonetheless ranked number 34 in the globe for women in national assemblies. Also, notably, Tanzania in 2000, was the first partner state in the East African Community to introduce a 20% constitutional quota to increase the political participation of women.[83] This was through a formal constitutional amendment.[84]

Further, towards women empowerment, in 2019 the Court of Appeal of Tanzania made an order the result of which was to fight early marriage for a girl-child in Tanzania. The court declared sections 13 and 17 of the Law of Marriage Act, 1971, Cap. 29, to be unconstitutional and hence null and void. The provisions were held to be against the constitutional rights of dignity and equality.[85] These provisions allowed a girl-child below 18 years of age but above 14 years to be married at the consent of a parent (or guardian) and/or a court of law. The court held these provisions to be discriminatory since laws in Tanzania ban any boy below 18 years from entering into marriage. The court also observed that the provisions were likely to infringe on the girl's right to education and dignity, in violation of the many international human rights instruments to which Tanzania is a party. This decision of the Court of Appeal is considered significant for the economic development of women and in alleviating their risk for poverty. Early marriage denies a girl-child opportunities for self-development and access to education, making them victims of extreme poverty.

4.4 *Development in ICT*

Information and communication technology (ICT) plays a significant role in the economic development of any country. More often, ICT offers an environment for fundamentally changing the lives of many people in the world.[86] ICT plays a key part in creating and operating employment, contributes to the provision of health services, transport services, educational services, energy services, agricultural as well as manufacturing industry. Undoubtedly, there is a very close nexus between

---

[82] See World Bank (2022).

[83] See Alistair (2021), available at https://storymaps.arcgis.com/stories/6077c18b29c2461688c4ea83c28b8527.

[84] The 2000 Thirteenth Constitutional Amendment.

[85] *Attorney General v. Rebecca Gyumi*, Civil Appeal No. 24 of 2017.

[86] See UNCTAD (2012).

ICT and national development at large. Literature indicates that developed countries have achieved positive economic development from high internet penetration in their territories. It is also noted that developing countries are starting to benefit from ICT.[87]

Essentially, the development of ICT is fundamentally grounded in the right to access information, which is considered an engine for democracy, openness, good governance and accountability. The right is based on the fact that the government is always supposed to serve its people.[88]

In the United Republic of Tanzania, the right to access information is provided under article 18, broadly within the right to freedom of expression.[89] The Constitution, under article 18, entitles every person to the right to seek, receive and disseminate information regardless of national boundaries. In addition to the constitutional guarantee of the right to information, the Tanzanian Parliament has enacted various laws to protect and regulate the realization of this right. These include the Access to Information Act No. 6 of 2016; the Newspapers Act, 1976; the National Security Act, 1970; the Cybercrimes Act, 2015; the Media Services Act, 2015; the Statistics Act, Cap. 351 (R.E 2019); and the Electronic and Postal Communications Act (EPOCA), 2010. These laws are also coupled with implementing regulations, which are adopted by the relevant parent ministries. Among others, they regulate the manner of access to information to be exercised by individuals. They also provide limitations on access to information. Additionally, some institutions have been vested with various powers in relation to the regulation of access to information. The four institutions responsible for regulating access to information are the Ministry for Information, Communication and Technology; the Tanzania Communications Regulatory Authority; Tanzania Telecommunications Company Limited; and the Tanzania Commission for Science and Technology.

As said earlier, one of the means to protect the right to information is laws. While this is true, nonetheless, ICT is one of the ways the improvement of which may lead to realization of the right to access information. The use of ICT through forums such as email and social media (Twitter, Facebook etc.) vehemently implements the right to access to information.

In Tanzania, the use and utilization of ICT have developed significantly. According to the Tanzania Communications Regulatory Authority (TCRA), by 2013, there were 1.4 million Internet subscribers in Tanzania.[90] By April 2023, there were 33.1 million Internet users in the country. This is about a 97% increase within a span of 10 years. In April 2023, the Parliament approved the budget of 212.4 billion for the transformation of the information sector in the United Republic of Tanzania. This demonstrates the extent to which the right to information, as

[87] See Meta (2022), pp. 2–18.

[88] See Ashnah et al. (2015).

[89] The right to freedom of expression; see Art. 18 of the Constitution of the United Republic of Tanzania (1977).

[90] See Steve and Lishan (2013).

enshrined in the Bill of Rights, has highly influenced developments in ICT in Tanzania.

5 Concluding Remarks and Way Forward

On 1 July 2020, the World Bank acknowledged that the economy of the United Republic of Tanzania has moved from a low-income to a lower-middle income status.[91] While this chapter has maintained that the Bill of Rights has contributed significantly to such development through the realization of some rights in the Bill of Rights, thus it is important to state that, the implementation of the Bill of Rights in Tanzania was not only factored by economic development. There are other key factors that shaped the timing and mode of implementing the Bill of Rights. These factors are the political will of the government of the United Republic of Tanzania and pressure from external actors such as the United Nations in general, the European Union, the International Monetary Fund and the World Bank.

Despite the significant pace in implementing the Bill of Rights in Tanzania, there are still some challenges which hinder its implementation. Below are those challenges with respective recommendations or way forward:

First, the arbitrary partitioning of the Bill of Rights to enforceable rights and non-enforceable rights. Rights provided under articles 6 to 11 are not enforceable before courts of law.[92]As a result, some rights, such as the right to education, which is provided under article 11, has become obsolete. It is recommended that an amendment of the Constitution of the United Republic of Tanzania should be effected to remove such partitioning which goes against the principle of equality and indivisibility of human rights.

Second, under the Constitution of the United Republic of Tanzania, some rights are arbitrarily dedicated to citizens and denied to non-citizens. For instance, the right to freedom of movement under article 17 is accorded to citizens only and excludes non-citizens. Under international human rights instruments, this right should be accorded to all persons, except for justifiable reasons.[93] It is therefore observed that, since the Bill of Rights of Tanzania is subject to some limitation clauses, designating some rights on citizens alone is unscientific. The Constitution should be amended to eliminate such a flaw.

Third, the Constitution of the United Republic of Tanzania contains a general limitation clause, which states that "the human rights and freedoms, the principles of

---

[91]See World Bank (2020), available at https://www.worldbank.org/en/news/press-release/2021/03/03/. See also William (2020), World Bank Blog.

[92]See Art. 7 (2) of the Constitution of the United Republic of Tanzania (1977).

[93]See Art. 13 of the Universal Declaration of Human Rights, 1948; Art. 12 of the International Covenant on Civil and Political Rights, 1966; and Art. 12(1) of the African Charter on Human and Peoples' Rights, 1981.

which are set out in this Constitution, shall not be exercised by a person in a manner that causes interference with or curtailment of the rights and freedoms of other persons or of public interest".[94] Based on this provision, public interest may be invoked to curtail individual rights. Unfortunately, the Constitution does not define the term 'public interest'. This makes the limitation clause essentially unlimited as it may be invoked discretionarily to violate human rights. It is recommended that the Constitution specifically the general limitation clause be amended to clearly specify its limits. A lesson can be drawn from the SIRACUSA Principles on the Limitation and Derogation Provisions in the International Covenant on Civil and Political Rights, 1985.

Fourth, on 14 November 2019, the United Republic of Tanzania withdrew its declaration that accepted the jurisdiction of the African Court on Human and Peoples' Rights (AFCtHPR) to receive and determine human rights applications from aggrieved individuals and non-governmental organizations (NGOs). This has exempted Tanzania from the jurisdiction of any binding human rights international court at the regional level on matters brought by individuals and NGOs. This is because the AFCtHPR is the only binding regional human rights court in Africa. The situation is even more appalling due to the fact that the human rights jurisdiction of the East African Court of Justice is still uncertain. It is therefore recommended that Tanzania should consider reinstating the withdrawn declaration.[95]

Fifth, article 26(2) of the Constitution of the United Republic of Tanzania entitles any person, including legal persons, to bring an action to the courts of law for the protection of the Constitution. The provision was used as an enabling provision for NGOs and Civil Society, in general, to approach courts in Tanzania on behalf of vulnerable groups whose rights were being violated or likely to be violated. This avenue is commonly known as public interest litigation. This avenue was largely affected by the Written Laws (Miscellaneous Amendments Act) No. 3 of 2020 which under section 4(2) requires that any person who petitions before the court any human rights case must accompany an affidavit stating the extent to which the claimed violation has affected such person personally. This indirectly amended article 26(2) of the Constitution of the United Republic of Tanzania and consequently affects the prospect of public interest litigation. It is recommended that the Parliament of Tanzania should repeal section 4(2) of the Act No. 3 to avoid its encroachment of the doctrine of public interest litigation which is an eminent doctrine across many democratic countries across the globe.

Sixth, the content of the Bill of Rights is inadequate for want of other essential rights. Some rights commonly found in international human rights instruments are not included in Tanzania's Bill of Rights. This puts those rights at risk of violation due to the lack of constitutional guarantees. Entitlements such as the right to nationality, the right to a clean and healthy environment and the right to development

94 Art. 30 (1) of the Constitution of the United Republic of Tanzania (1977).

95 On the legal possibility of Tanzania of reinstating the withdrawn declaration, see Leonard (2021), pp. 29–45.

are not found in the Bill of Rights of Constitution of the United Republic of Tanzania. It is therefore recommended that the Constitution add the omitted rights.

Last but not least, seventh, the political will with regard to respect, promotion and fulfilling human rights in Tanzania has been highly unpredictable. In most cases it has never been at the auspices of constitutional recognition rather the will of the government in power. As a result, during the fifth government from 2015 to 2021 in the reign of His Excellence the late John Pombe Magufuli Tanzania experienced human rights crisis while the Bill of Rights was the same as that existed during the preceding regimes. It is recommended that sensitization and capacity building should be embarked to top leaders in the country on the sanctity of human rights.

References

Adams S (2011) Intellectual property rights, innovation and economic growth in Sub-Saharan Africa. J Third World Stud 28:231–243

Alistair T (2021) Women's Political Participation in Tanzania. HAKIZETU, Available at https://storymaps.arcgis.com/stories/6077c18b29c2461688c4ea83c28b8527

Amankwah AH (1988) Constitutions and Bill of Rights in third World Nations: issues of form and content. Comp Int Law J Southern Africa 21:190–201

Ambreena SM (1996) The case for Women's rights to land in Tanzania: some observations in the context of AIDS. UTAFITI (New Series) 3:11–38

Ashnah K et al (2015) Citizens perceptions of using ICT to make right to information requests in Uganda. CIPESA ICT Policy Research Series, No. 02/15

Atuguba RA (2014) Equality, non-discrimination and fair distribution of the benefits of development. Available at https://www.ohchr.org/sites/default/files/Documents/Issues/Development/RTDBook/PartIIChapter7.pdf

Ben L (2010) Dispossession and land tenure in Tanzania: what hope from the courts.? Cultural Rights and Survival Series, 5

Besley T (1995) Property rights and investment incentives: theory and evidence from Ghana. J Polit Econ 103:903–937

Edward B (2016) New constitutional making in Tanzania: an examination of actors roles and influence. Afr J Polit Sci Int Relat:74–88

Esther D (2012) Women empowerment and economic development. J Econ Liter 50:1051–1079

Garance G, Maria H (2022) Women's land rights and village institutions in Tanzania. World development. Elsevier

Gurkaynak G (2019) Maximising welfare through freedom of expression: the interface between human rights and innovation. Human Rights Law Committee of the Public and Professional Interest Division of the International Bar Association, Available at https://papers.ssrn.com/sol3/papers.cfm?abstract_id=3543433

Helen ED (2012) *Shamba ni Langu* (The *Shamba* is Mine): a social-legal study of women's claims to land in Arusha, Tanzania. DPhil (Law Studies) Thesis, University of Sussex

Howard-Hassmann RE (2013) Reconsidering the right to own property. J Human Rights, 12 Available at https://www.tandfonline.com/doi/full/10.1080/14754835.2013.784667

Icelandic Human Rights Centre (2015) The Right to Equality and Non-Discrimination. Available at https://www.humanrights.is/en/human-rights-education-project/human-rights-concepts-ideas-and-fora/substantive-human-rights/the-right-to-equality-and-non-discrimination

Jenesta AEU (2022) Changing customary land tenure regimes in Tanzania: the case of Women's land rights in matrilineal and patrilineal communities. Doctoral Thesis in Real Estate and Construction Management, Ardhi University Tanzania

Kalley P, Graglia M (2017) Why Property Rights Matters. Available at https://www.newamerica.org/future-land-housing/blog/why-property-rights-matter/
Katundu MA, Kumburu NP (2015) Tanzania's constitutional reform predicament and the survival of the Tanganyika and Zanzibar Union. J Pan Afr Stud 8:104–118
Leonard C (2021) From a host country to no access: Tanzania's "Withdrawal" from the African Court. Zanzibar YearBook Law 9:29–45
Lubuva DZ (1988) Reflections on Tanzania's Bill of Rights. Common Wealth Bull 14:853–854. Available at https://www.tandfonline.com/doi/abs/10.1080/03050718..9985970
Madenge P (2021) Constitution of Tanzania-overview and history. Available at https://unitedrepublicoftanzania.com/government-of-tanzania-and-the-society/education-in-tanzania
Meta AK (2022) Analysis of the impact of ICT on economic growth: empirical, evidence from Asian countries. J Asian Bus Econ Stud 29:2–18
Musoke JK (2008) The impact of privatization on state-owned enterprises: a case study of Uganda Commercial Bank, now Stanbic Bank of Uganda. Masters Thesis, University of Oslo
National Bureau of Statistics (2018) Bank of Tanzania and Tanzania Investment Centre, Tanzania Investment Report: Foreign Private Investments
Nellis J (2005) The evolution of enterprise reform in Africa: from state owned enterprises to private participation in infrastructure-and back.? September, 4-5 Available at https://papers.ssrn.com/sol3/papers.cfm?abstract_id=828764
Peter CM (1992) Five years of the rights in Tanzania: drawing a balance sheet. Afr J Int Comp Law
Peter CM (1995) Civil and political rights in Tanzania: the Bill of Rights of 1985. The African Review. J Afri Polit Dev Int Aff 22:45–72, p. 46
Peter CM (2000) Constitution-making in Tanzania: the role of the people in the process. University of Dar es Salaam, Dar es Salaam
Pfeiffer SB (1978) Notes on the role of the judiciary in the constitutional systems of East Africa since independence. Case Western Reserv J Int Law 10:11–53
Ruhangisa JE (1998) Human rights in Tanzania: the role of the judiciary. PhD Thesis, University of London
Ruth M (1996) Situational analysis of education of Girls/ Women in Tanzania. UTAFITI (New Series) 3:39–90
Shivji IG (1990) Tanzania: the legal foundations of the union. Dar es Salaam University Press
Shivji IG et al (2004) Constitutional and legal system of Tanzania: a civics sourcebook. Mkuki na Nyota Publisher Ltd: Dar es Salaam
Steve E, Lishan A (2013) What is happening in ICT in Tanzania: a supply and demand, side analysis of the ICT sector. Evidence for ICT Policy Action, 11
Sullivan JD, Rogers J, Bettcher KE (2007) The importance of property rights to development. SAIS Rev Int Aff 27:31–43
Tanzania Investment Centre (2023) An overview of investment climate, opportunities, trends and services provided by Tanzania Investment Centre
UNCTAD (2012) Measuring the impacts of information and communication technology for development UNCTAD current studies on science, technology and innovation
United Nations (2002) Investment policy review: Tanzania" UN Conference on Trade and Development. United Nations
United Nations (2007) Good governance practices for the protection of human rights. United Nations
United Nations (2018) Human rights and constitution making. United Nations
Uutela AL et al (2021) Legal rights of private property owners vs. sustainable transitions.? J Clean Prod:1–11
Wambali MKB (2009) The enforcement of basic rights and freedoms and the state of judicial activism in Tanzania. J Afr Law 53:34–58

William B (2020) What does Tanzania's move to lower-middle income status mean.? World Bank Blog
World Bank (2020) Maintaining Tanzania's lower-middle income status post-COVID-19 will depend on strengthening resilience. World Bank
World Bank (2022) Tanzania has much to gain by expanding women's access to opportunities. World Bank

Leonard Chimanda Joseph LL.B, LL.M (University of Dar es Salaam), Advocate, Contributor to the Local Engagement Refugee Research Network, Member to the University of Dar es Salaam Research Chair on Forced Displacement, PhD in Law Candidate at University of Sussex (United Kingdom).

Sekela Kalangson Mlungu, a Lecturer (the University of Dar es Salaam-School of Law) LL.B, LL.M (Ruaha Catholic University), Ms. CLEF (International University College of Turin (Italy), PhD in Law (the University of Dar es Salaam-School of Law. She may be contacted through sekela2009@gmail.com/sekela.mlungu@udom.ac.tz and +255716858 849/+255685634729.

Power Sharing Following Violation-Marred Elections and Its Implication on the Protection of Human Rights in Africa

Amiri Sharifu

1 Introduction

Power-sharing arrangements address competition over power, resources, and democratic deadlock. These arrangements, which often lead to the formation of coalition governments or governments of national unity, are typically established by political parties with conflicting interests following violence-marred elections.[1] The impacts of these arrangements have been studied from many perspectives. Most studies have examined their effects on socio-economic development, democracy, security, and peace.[2] The impact of these arrangements on the protection of human rights has been addressed in only a few studies. This underscores the relevance of a study examining the implications of power-sharing arrangements in the context of the protection of human rights in Africa. Among the three countries under consideration, only Tanzania Zanzibar currently has an active government resulting from power-sharing schemes. In Kenya and Zimbabwe, governments that resulted from power-sharing arrangements were transitional. This chapter explores the implications these arrangements had in Kenya and Zimbabwe and continue to have in Tanzania Zanzibar, particularly regarding the protection of human rights.

[1] See Havard and Gates (2008), p. 1.

[2] See Minde et al. (2018), p. 163.

A. Sharifu (✉)
Dar es Salaam CPA Review Center, Dar es Salaam, Tanzania

Anjarwalla & Khanna Tanzania, Dar es Salaam, Tanzania

I. Kajiru et al. (eds.), *Economic Development and Human Rights in Contemporary Sub-Saharan Africa*, Ius Gentium: Comparative Perspectives on Law and Justice 122, https://doi.org/10.1007/978-3-031-81400-6_11

2 Nature of Power Sharing

Power-sharing agreements are deployed to promote better governance and resolve protracted conflicts. There is no uniform method for crafting and implementing power-sharing arrangements, which provides the necessary flexibility to political actors. Power-sharing arrangements that seek to achieve a durable peace would have a sunset clause, while those focused on the governance aspect would be permanent.[3] The involvement of political actors would result in either an exclusive or inclusive government. An inclusive government works towards integrating as many voices as possible into the decision-making body, while an exclusive government creates autonomous political spheres. Inclusive institutions assume that exclusion is the key to violent conflicts and are non-exclusive. This type of arrangement allows certain political parties that participated in the election to be part of the government.[4] All three countries under consideration have experience with inclusive governments, as described below.

2.1 Tanzania Zanzibar

The Government of National Unity established under the Constitution of Zanzibar is neither transitional nor temporal. It was established with a view to ensure that the electoral violence experienced in 1995, 2000, and 2005 is avoided by allocating certain number of political seats to the first runner-up with the highest number of votes.

The Constitution of Zanzibar has created positions for the first runner-up with the highest number of votes, regardless of the state of election. It does not matter whether the election has resulted in violence or not. This government is formed in the event any political party garners at least 10 percent of the total votes or holds the second-largest number of seats in the House of Representatives. On basis of this constitutional arrangement, the first Government of National Unity came into power between 2010 and 2015. The Government of National Unity resurfaced in 2020 and will remain valid until the new government is sworn in after the 2025 general election.

Between 2015 and 2020, the country was not under the Government of National Unity because the ruling party emerged victorious after securing 91.4% of all the votes cast, and the minimum threshold for the formation of the Government of National Unity was not met.[5] This unprecedented victory occurred after the 2015 elections were nullified, and the Civic United Front (CUF), which claimed victory, boycotted the run-off -election.[6]

---

[3] See Havard and Gates (2008) p. 1.

[4] See Havard and Gates (2008) p. 1.

[5] Art. 39(3)(i) of the Constitution of the Revolutionary Government of Zanzibar.

[6] See Minde et al. (2018), p. 162.

In case one political party manages to secure a huge win and the runner-up does not meet any of the above requirements, as occurred in 2015, the Government of National Unity cannot be formed. The electoral results of the 2015 elections halted the formation of the Government of National Unity for five years, until 2020. In 2020, the main opposition party, ACT-Wazalendo, came second in the presidential election after securing 19.87% of the votes, thereby becoming eligible to share power with CCM, which garnered 76% of all the votes cast.

2.2 *Kenya*

The December 2007 elections led to widespread intercommunal violence, which erupted after the Electoral Commission declared President Mwai Kibaki as the winner of the presidential race. This was despite significant irregularities in the vote-counting process. Following the deaths of over 1000 people and the displacement of at least 300,000 others, a power-sharing agreement or accord between Kenya's two main political parties— the Party of National Unity (PNU) and Orange Democratic Movement (ODM)—was executed on 28 February 2008.[7] The accord provided for the creation of a grand coalition government in which both political parties would share power on an equal basis. The coalition government established through the power-sharing agreement led to the dissolution of the tenth parliament, in accordance with section 6(a) of the National Accord and Reconciliation Act.

2.3 *Zimbabwe*

The power-sharing agreement, namely the Global Political Agreement, led to the creation of the Government of National Unity in 2009.[8] This agreement was negotiated and executed by the Zimbabwe African National Union-Patriotic Front (ZANU-PF) and the Movement for Democratic Change (MDC) as a solution to end electoral violence and civil unrest resulted from the contentious 2008 general election. Accordingly, both the MDC and ZANU-PF constituted the government from 2009 to 2013. Executive positions were created and allocated to individuals from the two political parties.[9] This government was also transitional and temporary in nature, as it was formed solely to ensure the introduction of the new constitution and the enactment of other relevant laws to uphold human rights and enshrine democratic principles.[10]

---

[7] See Agreement on the Principles of Partnership of the Coalition Government.

[8] Art. XX of the Global Political Agreement of 2008.

[9] Art. 20(1)(6) of the Global Political Agreement of 2008.

[10] Art. VI of the Global Political Agreement of 2008.

3 Power-Sharing Leading Factors

An arrangement to share power is the result of several factors, including competition over resources, ethnicity, self-determination, and democratic deadlock. For the purposes of this chapter, only democratic deadlock, as one of the factors leading to a power-sharing agreement, is discussed. Democratic deadlock occurs when incumbent parties refuse to surrender power to other political parties by violating electoral laws in their favor. The incumbent political parties manipulate elections by leveraging their control over power and coercive institutions, using these to disadvantage opposition parties.[11]

Political unrest often arises when these tactics are deployed, and opposition parties question and challenge the legality of the election outcomes. In most cases, the opposition parties declare themselves the winners of the elections.[12] These actions breed deep-seated and long-standing divisions, chaos, violence, and humanitarian crises, with the most widely accepted solution in Africa being the distribution of power among the participating political parties.

The following section covers the democratic deadlock that led political parties in Tanzania, Zanzibar, Kenya, and Zimbabwe to resolve to share power among themselves.

3.1 *Democratic Deadlock*

3.1.1 Tanzania Zanzibar

The bill to amend the Constitution of Zanzibar to introduce the Government of National Unity was prompted by a series of violent events occurred during the elections in 1995, 2000, and 2005. These events occurred as an expression of disagreement over the election results between CUF and CCM. For CCM, through President Karume, and Seif Hamad of CUF, power-sharing was seen as a solution to end the widespread violence. To better understand what led to the constitutionalization of the power-sharing arrangement in Zanzibar, it is necessary to review some political and democratic events in Tanzania Zanzibar as detailed below.

The first multiparty election after independence took place on 22 October 1995. This was one week prior to the general election for the Union Government. The period leading up to the elections in Zanzibar was characterized by widespread human rights abuse and biased news coverage favoring the ruling party. Many people were denied the opportunity to register in the official voters' roll and the right to make an independent and informed voting choice.[13]

---

[11] See Fjelde and Hoglund (2014), p. 298.

[12] See Minde et al. (2018), pp. 176–177.

[13] See Kildal (2016), p. 21.

Furthermore, the vote-counting process was delayed for 2 days, and CUF argued that this gave CCM sufficient time to manipulate the election results in their favor.[14]

This sparked protests as a result of CUF's non-acceptance of the election results. CUF's reaction to the election results led to widespread clashes between CUF supporters and state machinery, which CUF claimed was deployed and operated in favor of CCM. The clashes claimed the lives of 30 people and left several hundred injured. Pemba, CUF's stronghold, was the most affected, with allegations that more than 2,000 people fled to Kenya. To end the tension and political crisis in the Isles, the Muafaka I agreement was brokered on 9 June 1999 between CUF and CCM. "Muafaka" is a Swahili word that unofficially translates to "settlement" in English.[15]

The second multiparty election was held in 2000. Similar to the 1995 general election, the 2000 election was also characterized by widespread tension and violence. The increased tension during the 2000 election led to a new round of negotiations that resulted in Muafaka II.[16] According to Muafaka II, the opposition party reserved the right to appoint two members to the Zanzibar Electoral Commission. This represented a limited penetration of the opposition party into state power and demonstrated the possibility of forming a shared government in the event of a contested election.

The 2005 election did not result in violence on the same scale as the previous elections. Despite this, CUF refused to recognize the government, alleging abuses of electoral laws and practices. This triggered another round of settlements, known as Muafaka III. Negotiations for Muafaka III took place between January 2007 and March 2008, chaired by Hon. Jakaya Kikwete. It was the Muafaka III that paved the way for political power-sharing in Tanzanian Zanzibar, which is the subject of this chapter.[17]

There were some serious concerns following the signing of Muafaka III, one of which was a lack of trust. CUF lacked trust in CCM regarding the implementation of Muafaka III. This led to further discussions between President Amani Karume and the General Secretary of CUF, the late Maalim Seif Sharif Hamad. The two leaders met for the first time on 5 November 2009.

The post-Muafaka III discussions were secretive and were not converted into writing. However, those discussions were impactful.[18] They resulted in the tabling of a bill proposing amendments to the Constitution of Zanzibar to provide for the establishment of the Government of National Unity. A referendum was prepared, and the people of Zanzibar were to vote for or against the establishment of the Government of National Unity prior to the 2010 general election. On 31 July 2010, the people of Zanzibar voted in favor of the establishment of the Government of National Unity. Subsequently, the House of Representatives passed the

---

[14] See Kildal (2016), p. 21.

[15] See Kildal (2016), p. 23.

[16] See Kildal (2016), p. 24.

[17] See Kildal (2016), p. 25.

[18] See Kildal (2016), p. 27.

amendments, allowing for the formation of the Government of National Unity anytime any of the previously mentioned thresholds is met.[19]

The 2020 elections did not spare the incumbent government from credible accusations of human rights abuses and calculated malpractices by opposition parties and observers. This time, ACT-Wazalendo, whose presidential candidate had run for the presidential seat with CUF in 2010 and was the first runner-up, held the ceremonial office of the First Vice-President from 2010 to 2015, was at the forefront as the main opposition party. The party claimed, among other things, that nine people were killed a day before the election, on 28 October 2020.[20]

The Isles held their latest general election in 2020, in which CCM was declared victorious. On 30 November 2020, ACT-Wazalendo alleged that the right of its own presidential candidate to participate in the polls were flagrantly violated by security forces, which frustrated his cause.[21] The party claimed that its supporters were also assaulted and some molested in full view of the police force. They further alleged that the police force refused to investigate the incidents. Human Rights Watch and the United Nations High Commissioner for Human Rights corroborated the claim, reporting that the police force killed at least three people and injured scores of others the night before the 2020 elections. At least ten other people were killed in the two days leading up to the elections. However, only two deaths were confirmed by the Inspector General on 11 November 2020, who attributed them to sporadic violence.[22]

Prior to joining the Government of National Unity, ACT-Wazalendo strongly claimed that the 2020 elections were flawed. ACT-Wazalendo implicated CCM in electoral malpractice and vote stuffing. As expected, CCM did not accept what ACT-Wazalendo contended. This created a fear of continued violence in the Isles. However, the tension ended when ACT-Wazalendo joined the Government of National Unity, as per the provisions of the Constitution of Zanzibar.

3.1.2 Kenya

The violence of 2007/2008 was nothing but an outcome of the highly disputed elections.[23] Post-election violence alarmed both Kenyans and the international community. After initial failures to settle the critical issues underlying the political uprising, the former UN Secretary-General, Mr. Kofi Annan, and the fourth President of the United Republic of Tanzania, who was also the Chairman of the African Union, witnessed the adoption of a power-sharing agreement.

---

[19] See Kildal (2016), p. 27.

[20] See Zanzibar, "Opposition Claims 9 Killed, Leader held Ahead of Polls," www.aljazeera.com.

[21] See Makoye (2021).

[22] See Human Rights Watch, "Tanzania: Repression Mars National Elections," www.hrw.org.

[23] See Preamble to the Agreement on the Principles of Partnership of the Coalition Government.

3.1.3 Zimbabwe

Since independence, ZANU-PF won all elections that were perceived to be flawed. After withholding the results for over a month, on 2 May 2008, the electoral commission announced that the late President Robert Mugabe and Tsvangirai, MDC's presidential candidate, had garnered 47.9% and 43.2% of the votes, respectively. Following these election outcomes, the electoral commission announced a runoff.[24] Zimbabwe's presidential runoff election was held on 27 June 2018. This time, the late President Robert Mugabe garnered 90% of all votes.

Following the declaration of these election outcomes, the MDC accused the Zimbabwe Electoral Commission of colluding with ZANU-PF, the incumbent party, to rig the elections. In response to the economic crisis and the deterioration of human rights and humanitarian conditions, the Southern African Development Community (SADC) initiated efforts to resolve the escalating tension, resulting in the signing of a Global Political Agreement between ZANU-PF and the MDC on 15 September 2008.

On account of the above, it is evident that democratic deadlock is the main driver behind the power-sharing arrangement in all three countries of reference: Tanzania Zanzibar, Kenya, and Zimbabwe.

4 Objective of Power Sharing

Power-sharing is one of the measures employed to manage post-election violence. The overall objective of power-sharing arrangements is to establish a more equitable balance of power, making negotiation an alternative to violence in order to promote stability and restore peace to a society. This arrangement fosters cooperation through a shared cabinet (a grand coalition cabinet) and parliament, bringing together the majority and opposition parties. In Tanzania Zanzibar, power-sharing arrangements aim to address tense situations that arise during contested general elections. The purpose is to prevent electoral violence, which often leaves many innocent people intimidated or killed, thereby endangering their fundamental human rights. From Kenya, we learn that power-sharing arrangements can have the objective of moving the country forward and initiating the healing and reconciliation process. It is not simply an approach designed to create positions that reward individuals. Rather, it seeks to enable national political leaders to look beyond partisan interests and promote the greater good of the nation.

Power-sharing arrangements also provide a framework to implement a coherent and far-reaching reform agenda, addressing the root causes of recurrent conflicts and creating a more secure and prosperous nation for all.[25] Such arrangements may also

[24] See Kirkengen (2013), p. 26.

[25] See Preamble to the Acting Together for Kenya Agreement on the Principles of Partnership of the Coalition Government, p. 1.

be invoked to end violence and improve humanitarian conditions. For example, in Zimbabwe, the power-sharing arrangement following the contested 2008 general elections aimed to permanently resolve the multiple threats to the well-being of Zimbabweans. According to the preamble of the Global Political Agreement of Zimbabwe, its objectives included ending polarization, divisions, conflict, and intolerance that had long characterized politics and society. Power-sharing arrangements may also aim to build a society free from violence, fear, intimidation, hatred, patronage, and corruption, instead fostering one founded on justice, fairness, openness, transparency, dignity, and equality. Additionally, they seek to enhance democratic values such as justice, fairness, openness, tolerance, equality, and respect for all persons and their human rights.

5 Common Shared Area

5.1 Tanzania Zanzibar

Between 2010 and 2015, the Government of Zanzibar was led by Ali Mohammed Shein of CCM as President, with Seif Shariff Hamad (CUF) serving as the largely ceremonial First Vice President. Hon. Seif Ali Iddi (CCM) served as the Second Vice President and leader of government affairs in the House of Representatives. The President subsequently appointed a cabinet comprising sixteen (16) line ministers and three (3) ministers without portfolio, ensuring a fair balance between CCM and CUF in key ministries. However, CCM retained the most powerful and significant positions within the government.[26] The Government of National Unity, which came into power in late 2020 and will remain until 2025, is constitutionally shared by CCM and ACT-Wazalendo. While the President and Second Vice President are from CCM, the First Vice President is from ACT-Wazalendo. Ministerial positions are held by two (2) nominees from ACT-Wazalendo and thirteen (13) nominees from CCM. There are no deputies, as the President is on record that there is no need to have them. The two ministries held by ACT-Wazalendo are the Ministry of Trade and Industrial Development and the Ministry of Health, Social Welfare, Elderly, Gender, and Children. Similar to the first Government of National Unity, the most powerful and important ministries related to human rights and good governance in the current Government of National Unity are held by CCM. With these vital ministries controlled by those alleged to be perpetrators of human rights violations during elections, the Government of National Unity in Zanzibar is not expected to provide a durable solution to such abuses.

[26] See Minde et al. (2018), p. 166.

5.2 *Kenya*

In Kenya, the agreement to form a grand coalition government allowed PNU to retain the presidency, while the ODM filled the position of Prime Minister. The arrangement saw ministerial positions distributed according to the number of seats each party had in the parliament, considering the principle of portfolio balance.[27] Consequently, ODM, PNU, ODM-K, NARC-K, and others secured twenty (20), fourteen (14), three (3), one (1), and two (2) ministerial positions, respectively. Positions for deputy ministers were twenty-two (22), eleven (11), three (3), two (2), and twelve (12) for ODM, PNU, ODM-K, NARC-K, and others, respectively.[28]

5.3 *Zimbabwe*

The Global Political Agreement signed between ZANU-PF and MDC incorporated provisions for power-sharing, in which the late President Mugabe remained the head of state, while MDC's Tsvangirai, Arthur Mutambara, and Thokhozani Khupe held the positions of Prime Minister and deputy prime ministers, respectively.[29] Additionally, thirty-one (31) ministries were established, shared among ZANU-PF, MDC-Tsvangirai (MDC-T), and MDC-Mutambara (MDC-M). In that order, fifteen (15) were nominated by ZANU-PF, thirteen (13) by MDC-T, and three by MDC-M.[30] The number of deputy ministers was fifteen (15): eight (8) were nominated by ZANU-PF, six (6) by MDC-T, and one (1) by MDC-M.[31]

6 Power-Sharing and Protection of Human Rights

Power-sharing arrangements are commonly regarded as instruments for resolving violence and paving way for lasting peace. Opposition parties often use victims of human rights violations as the basis for negotiating and securing positions in government. However, once in power, they often fail to influence or hold perpetrators of human rights violations accountable. Considerable energy and effort are typically expended by the opposition to associate the incumbent government with human rights abuses during elections, before the commencement of power-sharing negotiations. However, once they assume power through negotiations with the ruling political parties, those who were previously advocating for justice for victims of

[27] Sect. 4(3) of the National Accord and Reconciliation Act No. 4 of 2008 [R.E 2012].

[28] See Horowitz., "Power-Sharing in Kenya," http://www.prio.no/CSCW/Research-and-Publications/Project/?=65122.

[29] See Mutisi (2011), p. 3.

[30] Art. 20(1)(6)(5) of the Global Political Agreement of 2008.

[31] Art. 20(1)(6)(6) of the Global Political Agreement of 2008.

electoral irregularities often fail to pursue these causes. The section below describes how human rights violations were a concern for opposition parties in Tanzania Zanzibar, Kenya and Zimbabwe before, during, and after negotiations to share power.

6.1 Pre-Power-Sharing Period

6.1.1 Tanzania Zanzibar

The pre-power-sharing period in Tanzania Zanzibar is divided into two phases. The first phase covers the period before the Muafaka negotiations following the 2005 elections, and the second phase covers the period before ACT-Wazalendo agreed to join the Government of National Unity following the 2020 elections. In the 2005 election, Hon. Amani Abeid Karume was declared the winner. According to CUF, the 2005 election was marred by electoral irregularities, and they resolved to outrightly reject the results and not recognize the government led by President Amani Abeid Karume. CUF reported several incidents of human rights violations, which were alleged to have been sponsored and executed in favor of CCM. CUF amplified these incidents before both the domestic and international press. The party reported a number of deaths, unjustifiable arrests, long custodial incarcerations, assaults, and attacks targeting its supporters.[32] Multiple calls were made to halt the situation in the country.

The second phase is marked by several unique features, with the most significant being that the strongest opposition party is ACT-Wazalendo, rather than CUF, as was the case in the first phase. This shift allows us to explore how human rights abuses remain a concern, even with the change in the leading opposition party. The objective is to examine whether ACT-Wazalendo's rise as the leading opposition party in the 2020 general elections altered the approach to using human rights abuses to advocate for power-sharing, as CUF did following the 2005 elections. ACT-Wazalendo was not expected to focus heavily on publishing and reporting the magnitude of human rights violations in order to have the opportunity to form the Government of National Unity, since they had an automatic right to join the Government of National Unity under the provisions of the Zanzibar Constitution. However, they did release a series of reports highlighting how state apparatuses were deployed by the incumbent government, led by CCM.

ACT-Wazalendo claimed that the 2020 election was coupled with gross violation of basic human rights, vote rigging, and systematic tampering with the voting process. The party reported incidents of violence and torture, unlawful and arbitrary intimidation, threats, arrest, and detention. Furthermore, the party resolved to lodge an application before the African Court on Human and Peoples' Rights against the government of the United Republic of Tanzania in relation to such incidents. The

[32] See Hamad (2017), p. 88.

application was filed by its presidential candidate, the late Seif Sharif Hamad, and 6 others[33] on 20 November 2020. Following the death of Seif Sharif Hamad, the applicant was replaced by Ado Shaibu.

Pursuant to the decision of the African Court on Human and Peoples' Rights, released on 4 May 2021, the order to strike out the name of Seif Sharif Hamad, the first applicant, due to his death, did not affect the general consideration of the application. The applicants alleged that, before, during, and immediately after the 2020 elections, the ZEC, the Tanzania Police Force, the Tanzania Intelligence and Security Services, the Tanzania Defence Force, and the Special Forces engaged in multiple violations of citizens' rights to participate in the elections.

In the context of protection of human rights, this approach is progressive, moving beyond merely reporting incidents of human rights abuses as was previously the case. However, the application filed—mainly by individual leaders of ACT-Wazalendo—was not without discrepancies in terms of ensuring justice for the victims. To begin with, the application was not filed by ACT-Wazalendo itself. The late Mr. Seif Sharif Hamad, a presidential candidate for ACT-Wazalendo in Zanzibar, and Mr. Ado Shaibu, the Secretary-General of ACT-Wazalendo, along with other applicants, acted in their individual capacities.

Given the nature of the applicants, it can be inferred that the decision to bring the case before the African Court on Human and Peoples' Rights was not a collective one by ACT-Wazalendo. The application submitted to the African Court on Human and Peoples' Rights seemed beneficial to certain individuals rather than the people of Zanzibar.

These two phases present mixed approaches to addressing human rights violations committed by opposition parties. Although, as of the time of writing this chapter, the application submitted to the African Court on Human and Peoples' Rights has yet to be considered, its filing by leaders of ACT-Wazalendo demonstrates that human rights violations are indeed a concern. However, such efforts appear to benefit only a few individuals driven by a thirst for power. Notably, in all instances where opposition parties in Zanzibar agreed to share power with the ruling party (CCM), they showed little commitment to bringing justice or protecting human rights.

Opposition parties have consistently pushed for the nomination of their leaders to ministerial or top executive positions without strongly advocating for discussions on how victims of electoral abuses or violations would be redressed. They have rarely, if ever, urged the government to hold all perpetrators of human rights abuses accountable for their actions before, during, and after elections. Instead, opposition parties have set various conditions that would lead to the creation of more high-ranking executive positions within the government, but with no concern for those affected by electoral violence.

Considering the approach taken by opposition parties in negotiations for power-sharing, the link between human rights abuses and the actions of the incumbent

[33] Appl. No.046/2020.

government is used by opposition party candidates not as a means to ensure justice for the victims of these abuses, but rather as a tool to influence the incumbent government to accept their power-sharing proposals. In most cases, the ruling party tends to agree to offer more seats for opposition leaders to appease them. If the ruling party does not agree to create additional positions for opposition leaders or refuses to allocate the highest positions in government to them, such leaders often threaten to withdraw from discussions and incite widespread protests against the government.

6.1.2 Kenya

Prior to agreeing to share power with PNU, ODM rejected election results in 2007. ODM, did not just reject such election results. It went further to accuse the incumbent government of perpetrating abuses against supporters of the opposition parties.[34] This period was marked by widespread condemnation of the ruling party by opposition parties. ODM called for the involvement of regional and international actors in the post-election situation, documenting the number of injured individuals, listing those arrested by law enforcement agencies, and recording instances of targeted attacks, threats, intimidation, and deaths.

During this time, every media report focused on the accusations made by opposition parties. This gave ordinary people confidence that their grievances were being heard through the officials of these parties. Along with other political groups, ODM called for all perpetrators of human rights violations to be held accountable, regardless of their status, race, political affiliation, or ethnic background. It also urged the heads of law enforcement agencies to ensure an end to indiscriminate arrests, custodial incarceration, and kidnapping.

New cases were reported daily, and it was almost impossible to miss news of alleged abuses committed by PNU. Testimonies from victims were broadcast live and used by ODM to support their claim of government involvement in electoral and general human rights violations. These strategic actions, however, were more beneficial to the political parties (seeking power) than to the victims of abuse or the general protection of human rights. The negotiations to end violence following the 2007 elections hinged on the distribution of political power through a power-sharing agreement between PNU and ODM, ultimately leading to the enactment of the National Accord and Reconciliation Act.

[34] See the Report of the United Nations Office of the High Commissioner for Human Rights Fact-Finding Mission to Kenya, 6–28 February 2008.

6.1.3 Zimbabwe

Zimbabwe held the runoff election on 27 June 2008. The Norwegian Resource Bank for Democracy and Human Rights reported sharp contrasts between the 29 March 2008 elections and the runoff election and by-elections held on 27 June 2008. While the first election, despite its faults and shortcomings, was viewed as a legitimate expression of the people's will, the second was marred by pre-election violence, restrictions on campaigning, lack of transparency, and total control of the media by the ruling party.[35]

The MDC alleged widespread violence, intimidation, election bans, arrests, and media abuse orchestrated by ZANU-PF. These claims heightened tensions and led to negotiations facilitated by South Africa under the auspices of SADC. These negotiations culminated in the signing of a Memorandum of Understanding (MoU) between ZANU-PF, the MDC factions, and SADC on 21 July 2008. ZANU-PF and the MDC committed to engaging in dialogue aimed at creating a genuine, viable, permanent, and sustainable solution to the Zimbabwean crisis.

During this period, the MDC focused on exposing actions taken by the incumbent government against opposition supporters and on increasing regional and international pressure regarding the Zimbabwean situation. In this context, the actions of the MDC in Zimbabwe resembled those of opposition parties in Kenya and Tanzania Zanzibar during the periods leading up to the establishment of power-sharing arrangements.

6.2 Power-Sharing Negotiation Period

In this section, we examine whether addressing human rights abuses during power-sharing negotiations has ever been a priority for the political parties involved in elections that resulted in episodes of electoral violence in Tanzania Zanzibar, Kenya, and Zimbabwe—the three countries of reference. This analysis aims to determine the extent to which the protection of human rights is prioritized when opposition parties resort to power-sharing arrangements as a solution to end widespread post-election violence. Additionally, it seeks to assess whether opposition parties genuinely prioritize delivering justice to victims of electoral violence—often alleged to be sponsored by the ruling party—or if their primary focus is on securing positions in the government, with human rights concerns either relegated to secondary importance or ignored altogether.

[35] See Kirkengen (2013), p. 26.

6.2.1 Tanzania Zanzibar

The discussion on whether the protection of human rights was a concern raised or considered during power-sharing negotiations dates back to the period following the 2005 elections. The period following the 2020 elections is irrelevant, as there were no negotiations between CCM and ACT-Wazalendo leading to the formation of the Government of National Unity. Discussions on whether CCM and ACT-Wazalendo should form or allocate seats in the Government of National Unity were internal matters for ACT-Wazalendo, as the Constitution of Zanzibar already stipulated that ACT-Wazalendo was entitled to join CCM in forming the Government of National Unity.

Following the 2005 elections, CCM and CUF entered into negotiations to share power. These negotiations paved the way for the establishment of the Government of National Unity. However, the points discussed between the two political parties were never disclosed or made public. As a result, there is no information about any terms agreed upon by both parties that contributed to the creation of the Government of National Unity. Consequently, it is extremely difficult to state with certainty whether human rights violations during the 2005 general elections were a concern during the Muafaka talks or whether any points related to the protection of human rights were discussed.

To assess whether human rights issues were truly a concern, a review of the constitutional provisions related to the establishment of the Government of National Unity is imperative. The review of the provisions of the Constitution of Zanzibar has revealed that the Constitution of Zanzibar is silent on any matters pertaining to human rights. Instead, it focuses on the distribution of power between the winning political party and the first runner-up. Specifically, the provisions address the allocation of ministerial and higher executive positions among political parties eligible to form the Government of National Unity.

The fact that there are no constitutional provisions addressing the protection of human rights, especially following the violence-marred elections, suggests that the protection of human rights and people's economic rights—rights that could be achieved through effective constitutional provisions—did not receive sufficient consideration during the negotiations between CUF and CCM. Had it not been for the way this chapter concludes, we might have had constitutional provisions addressing how to deal with human rights issues before, during, and after elections, or representatives might have rejected the bill to introduce the Government of National Unity until relevant human rights clauses were introduced into the Constitution of Zanzibar

6.2.2 Kenya

It is likely that in Kenya, ODM and PNU discussed key terms regarding the protection of human rights during their power-sharing negotiations. This can be inferred from the provisions of the National Accord and Reconciliation Act, which reflect the key areas of negotiation between PNU and ODM. The Act contains human-rights-related provisions, suggesting that the two political parties addressed issues related to human rights. The second clause of the agreement negotiated between PNU and ODM states that the power-sharing arrangement was necessary to begin the healing process. Impliedly, the healing process includes the establishment of a system where victims of human rights abuses could seek redress. This indicates that the negotiations between the two political parties considered some aspects of human rights, particularly for victims of electoral violence, some of whom lost loved ones, property, and employment, among other things. ODM was also firm in its position that the power-sharing agreement was not about creating positions to reward certain individuals. Accordingly, the agreement concluded between ODM and PNU addressed issues beyond the division of power among the competing political parties. ODM took a strategic approach to ensuring that victims of abuse were redressed and accorded the justice they deserved.

6.2.3 Zimbabwe

It was necessary to review the Global Political Agreement negotiated between ZANU-PF and MDC to determine whether redress for the violation of human rights was addressed during the power-sharing negotiations. The objectives of the Global Political Agreement are outlined in its preamble. They include the enhancement of human rights protection and respect for human rights. The two parties agreed that the Government of National Unity would fully and impartially apply the laws of the country to bring all perpetrators of politically motivated violence to justice. This is provided for under Article 18(5)(c) of the Global Political Agreement. Under Article 7(1)(c) of the Global Political Agreement, the Government of National Unity would establish a mechanism to advise on what measures were necessary and practicable to achieve national healing, cohesion, and unity for victims of pre- and post-independence political conflicts. From the provisions of the Global Political Agreement, it appears that MDC not only focused on the distribution of power but also sought justice for victims of the misuse of state apparatus, including the police force. MDC did not forget the importance of protecting human rights during the power negotiations and successfully pushed for the inclusion of human rights-related provisions in the Global Political Agreement.

6.3 Post-Power-Sharing Arrangement Period

6.3.1 Tanzania Zanzibar

The examination of the post-power-sharing period is divided into two parts. The first part covers the period following the amendments to the Constitution of Zanzibar that introduced the Government of National Unity. During this period, CUF did not advocate for any action addressing the abuse of human rights following the 2005 elections. No action was taken against those whom CUF had publicly accused of perpetrating abuses. No special inquiry was conducted to bring the perpetrators to justice, as CUF had desired before agreeing to share power with CCM. This inaction was largely due to the fact that the amendments to the Constitution of Zanzibar introducing the Government of National Unity did not include human rights-related provisions. The amendments to the Constitution of Zanzibar did not address how human rights should be protected before, during, and after the post-power-sharing negotiation period. Until the Constitution of Zanzibar undergoes further amendments, it is unlikely that provisions ensuring human rights considerations during power-sharing negotiations will be introduced.

The amendments to the Constitution of Zanzibar did not address how human rights should be protected before, during, and after the post-power-sharing negotiation period. Until the Constitution of Zanzibar undergoes further amendments, there will likely be no provisions ensuring human rights considerations during power-sharing negotiations.

The second part covers the period from when ACT-Wazalendo decided to join forces with CCM to form the Government of National Unity on December 20, 2020, through to 2025. Since joining CCM in forming the Government of National Unity, ACT-Wazalendo has not been observed advocating for justice for the victims of the 2020 electoral violence. Given the history of the United Republic of Tanzania in complying with decisions made by human rights bodies, ACT-Wazalendo could have adopted alternative approaches to promote the protection of human rights and foster development by prioritizing human considerations in its agenda before agreeing to collaborate with CCM. As the main opposition party, whose goal was to advocate for justice for the victims of the 2020 electoral violence, ACT-Wazalendo was expected to ensure that the perpetrators of these violations were held accountable. The failure to urge the government to deliver justice for the victims reflects a broader disregard by political parties for human rights violations once they attain power.

6.3.2 Kenya

To break the cycle of impunity at the core of the post-election violence, the Waki Report recommended establishing a special tribunal with the mandate to prosecute human rights-related crimes committed during this period.[36] The purpose of this recommendation was to provide remedies for victims of human rights violations and to hold perpetrators accountable for their actions. However, the Kenyan Parliament failed to approve the creation of such a tribunal, as recommended by the Waki

[36] See Republic of Kenya, Report of the Commission of Inquiry into Post-Election Violence of 2008.

Committee of Inquiry. This denied victims the opportunity for justice and allowed perpetrators of post-election violence to evade accountability.[37]

Failure of the Kenyan Parliament to approve the establishment and operations of a special tribunal to address electoral violence stands in stark contrast to the principles that ODM leaders had ardently championed prior to agreeing to share power with PNU. This decision to reject the creation of a tribunal to provide redress for victims of violence suggests a broader issue: once opposition parties secure political positions in a power-sharing arrangement, they often overlook or even abandon the human rights issues they previously used as a platform to gain political leverage. This failure to act on the recommendation of the Waki Committee of Inquiry, which called for a comprehensive and progressive approach to addressing electoral violence and human rights abuses, demonstrates the challenges in holding political leaders accountable for their pledges. It highlights a troubling pattern where, despite the initial commitments to justice and accountability, the political calculus of those in power shifts, leaving victims of violence without redress. The inability to establish the tribunal thus not only undermines the principles of justice but also weakens the credibility of the power-sharing government, revealing how political expediency can overshadow the pursuit of long-term human rights reforms.

6.3.3 Zimbabwe

The Office of the Attorney General and the Police Force either failed or were unwilling to implement the provisions of the Global Political Agreement, which called for the full and impartial application of the law to bring all perpetrators of politically motivated violence to justice. As a result, perpetrators of human rights violations continued to roam free, despite being clearly identified by their victims.[38] The operating environment remained highly restrictive, as evidenced by the infringement on free political activities, including the disruption of rallies, peaceful marches, and meetings organized by political parties and civil society organizations. The crisis in Zimbabwe, for example, saw several disruptions of civil society events and MDC rallies by the police and ZANU PF supporters.

From the above highlights, it is clear that, once in power, political leaders from opposition parties often stop defending the common good and instead align themselves with those they once accused of human rights abuses, thereby failing to advocate for justice for the victims. These opposition leaders typically convince the public to overlook past electoral abuses and instead focus on national development, without ensuring that victims of human rights violations receive the protection and justice they deserve. This drastic shift in focus from opposition leaders is a

[37] See Mburu (2020), pp. 170–171.

[38] See "Zimbabwe's Global Political Agreement Implementation: 4 Years on at Best Faltering at Worst Failing," http://archive.kubatana.net.

profound disappointment to the electorate, who, having participated in elections, are subjected to intimidation, threats, wrongful imprisonment, insults, attacks, forced displacement, and even death, particularly in cases of intense violations.

It is common for opposition leaders to remain silent about human rights abuses once they are in power. This silence persists until the next general election, when they once again denounce electoral misconduct and exploit the human rights violations of the incumbent government to further their own ambitions. Greed for power often transforms many African opposition leaders into human rights defenders only when it suits their efforts to join the government and share power. However, this approach does little to resolve the ongoing impunity for human rights violations during elections.

7 Protection of Human Rights Terms in Power-Sharing Agreements

In Kenya, the two-page power-sharing agreement, signed by His Excellency Mwai Kibaki of the Party of National Unity (PNU) and Hon. Raila Odinga of the Orange Democratic Movement (ODM), and witnessed by the Fourth President of Tanzania and Chairman of the African Union, Jakaya Kikwete, as well as Kofi A. Annan, notably failed to include any provisions addressing the human rights abuses and the economic stagnation experienced by the victims of political violence. The omission of such provisions in the power-sharing agreement is particularly concerning given the magnitude of the human rights violations that occurred during the election crisis. Victims of violence, displacement, and various forms of abuse were left without access to justice or support for their economic recovery. This oversight in the agreement left unaddressed the critical issues of accountability and the restoration of livelihoods for those impacted by the violence. By failing to incorporate mechanisms for addressing these abuses, the power-sharing agreement not only neglected to acknowledge the suffering of the victims but also undermined the broader objectives of reconciliation and national healing. Consequently, the human rights violations remained unresolved, and the economic challenges faced by the victims endured, further complicating efforts to foster a stable and inclusive society.[39] In Zimbabwe, the Global Political Agreement featured no substantial provisions for addressing and ending human rights violations. While approximately four pages of the agreement outlined how various government positions were to be shared between ZANU-PF and MDC political leaders, the phrase "human rights" appeared only twice in the entire 14-page document. This reflects a significant disregard for the protection of human rights during the negotiations between political parties aimed at establishing a power-sharing arrangement following electoral violence.

[39] See Schedule of the Accord and Reconciliation Act.

The minimal mention of human rights in such a critical document highlights the stark imbalance in priorities during the negotiations. Instead of focusing on the urgent need for justice for the victims of political violence, the discussions appeared primarily driven by political expediency. The key concern was the distribution of power, while the profound human rights violations and the suffering of countless victims were largely sidelined. By neglecting to adequately address these human rights concerns, the Global Political Agreement risked perpetuating a culture of impunity. The failure to integrate justice and accountability mechanisms for the victims undermined efforts to build a foundation for lasting peace and reconciliation in the country. Without concrete provisions to hold perpetrators accountable and provide redress for the victims, the agreement ultimately weakened the prospects for meaningful national healing and stability.

Through the lens of the constitutional provisions in the Constitution of Zanzibar, which outlines the establishment of the Government of National Unity, it becomes evident that the Muafaka talks were initially driven by the need to address widespread human rights violations. However, despite the emphasis on national unity and reconciliation, the redress for these violations was never adequately addressed, as highlighted in the Constitution of Zanzibar itself. While the Muafaka talks aimed to resolve political differences and foster a more inclusive governance structure, they failed to incorporate comprehensive mechanisms for holding perpetrators of human rights violations accountable. This oversight in the agreement reflects a broader tendency to prioritize political stability and power-sharing over justice for victims. The Constitution of Zanzibar, which envisions a more just and equitable society, arguably falls short of fulfilling its potential by not sufficiently addressing the crucial issue of human rights redress. As a result, the absence of effective measures to address past abuses continues to impede efforts towards genuine reconciliation and healing, leaving the victims of human rights violations without the justice and compensation they deserve. This gap underscores the challenge of achieving lasting peace when the human rights of affected populations are not fully acknowledged and addressed within the framework of national governance.

8 Effect of Deferring Human Rights in Power-Sharing Agreements

The purpose of limiting the scope of negotiations and producing a concise accord may explain why many critical issues are left unaddressed. However, it is both inhumane and unjust to defer the resolution of human rights violations that occur during elections, while focusing solely on the distribution of political power within the government. There are several compelling reasons why the issue of how victims of human rights abuses are to be redressed should be prioritized. First and foremost, human rights are fundamental, and any violation of these rights must be remedied in a timely and effective manner. Delaying justice not only prolongs the suffering of the victims but also undermines the principles of equality and fairness that underpin democratic societies. Second, in Tanzania Zanzibar, Kenya, and Zimbabwe, opposition political parties have strategically used the plight of victims of human rights abuses to garner support from national, regional, and international communities for the idea of power-sharing with the ruling parties. They presented power-sharing as a means to resolve political tensions and deadlocks, positioning it as a necessary step towards national unity and peace. However, by deferring discussions on human rights, these agreements leave victims without any recourse for justice or meaningful support. Many victims are left helpless, without any legal or social mechanisms to address their grievances. In many cases, they are forced to take matters into their own hands, attempting to repair or rebuild their properties, including homes, that were damaged during electoral violence. This lack of redress only exacerbates the trauma they have experienced, leaving them to struggle in isolation without state support. The failure to prioritize human rights redress not only perpetuates the suffering of these victims but also undermines the broader goals of justice, reconciliation, and long-term peace. When human rights abuses are neglected in the pursuit of political power-sharing, the potential for healing and unity is diminished, and the foundation for a stable and inclusive society is weakened. A lasting peace cannot be achieved without addressing the injustices that have occurred and ensuring that victims receive the justice and support they deserve.

9 The Impact of Power-Sharing Arrangements on the Right to Development

Development as a right is a broad and multifaceted discipline that encompasses areas such as infrastructure and urban planning, economics, the sustainable exploitation of natural resources, health, and education. In the context of Tanzania Zanzibar, power-sharing has served as a long-awaited beacon of hope, fostering development across both Pemba and Unguja. Following the implementation of the power-sharing agreement, significant progress was made in terms of infrastructure development. The construction of roads, ports, and other essential infrastructure projects increased on both sides of the Isles. In addition to physical infrastructure, there were notable investments in social services, including health and education, which contributed to the overall improvement in the quality of life for many Zanzibar residents. Despite the sharp political divisions and competing interests between the parties involved, the power-sharing arrangement provided a framework that allowed for cooperation and resource allocation to areas of vital need. The agreement facilitated a balance between political rivalry and the practical necessities of governance, allowing for development to take place even in a politically charged environment. This demonstrates the potential for power-sharing arrangements to serve as platforms for advancing development, even in the face of significant political challenges and crisis.

In Kenya, the power-sharing arrangement has played a crucial role in mitigating the violence that erupted after the disputed elections, which left the country in a state of turmoil. By bringing together key political players from opposing parties, the power-sharing agreement helped stabilize the political landscape and created a platform for dialogue, cooperation, and national healing. This cooperation between the parties was essential in reducing tensions and preventing further escalation of the violence that had previously gripped the nation. In addition to the political stabilization, the Kenyan Parliament has taken significant steps to promote peace by passing several pieces of legislation aimed at addressing the root causes of the post-election violence and ensuring long-term stability. These legislative measures include reforms in areas such as electoral processes, governance, and the protection of human rights, all of which contribute to the broader goal of national reconciliation and peacebuilding. As a direct result of these efforts, economic activities have flourished across various sectors of the economy, including agriculture, trade, and infrastructure development. The restoration of peace and the establishment of a stable environment for investment have empowered businesses to operate freely and efficiently. This economic growth has, in turn, enabled citizens to more effectively exercise their right to development, as they can engage in productive activities without the fear of violence or instability impeding their progress. Access to education, healthcare, and other vital services has also improved, further contributing to the overall well-being of the Kenyan population.

Not much information is available on how the power-sharing agreement impacted the right to development of the people of Zimbabwe. However, it is undeniable that as a result of the Global Political Agreement, the country stabilized, allowing people to resume their economic activities. To simply put, while power-sharing arrangements may appear to have certain positive impacts on the right to development, in Tanzania (Zanzibar), Kenya, and Zimbabwe, these agreements were primarily brokered to accommodate a few individuals in executive positions within the shared governments. As a result, they did not have significant positive impacts on the broader economic development of the people.

10 Analysis

It is an undeniable fact that power-sharing arrangements can offer a beneficial alternative by granting access to power, fostering broad participation, and bestowing legitimacy upon the government and its actions. However, in the contexts of Tanzania Zanzibar, Kenya, and Zimbabwe, power-sharing arrangements have, arguably, been narrowly defined to mean simply the sharing of top executive positions within the government. As a result, these arrangements have not been effective in protecting human rights or ensuring that those who have suffered the most from electoral violations are properly considered and adequately remedied.

11 Recommendations

There are multiple ways in which human rights violations during elections can be effectively addressed through power-sharing arrangements. One key approach is to include explicit provisions within the power-sharing agreements that outline clear measures for redressing these violations. Such provisions should not only acknowledge the harm done but also provide specific mechanisms for reparations, including compensation, rehabilitation, and guarantees of non-repetition. This approach ensures that the victims of electoral violence are not overlooked and that their rights are respected within the political settlement. To ensure accountability and measurable progress, political parties involved in the power-sharing arrangement could establish defined timeframes for implementing the agreed-upon human rights terms. These timeframes would create a sense of urgency and accountability, preventing delays that might undermine the victims' trust in the process. Regular progress reports and independent oversight bodies could further reinforce transparency and ensure that commitments are fulfilled. The establishment of a commission to investigate and address human rights violations during elections could also serve as a viable mechanism for delivering justice and fostering reconciliation. Such a commission should be independent, impartial, and empowered to thoroughly investigate violations, hold perpetrators accountable, and provide recommendations for systemic reforms. By addressing grievances and ensuring justice, this mechanism would contribute to restoring public confidence in the political system and fostering national healing. Electoral human rights tribunals could be another effective tool for addressing violations. These tribunals could be constitutionalized and empowered to handle cases of electoral violence, ensuring justice for victims while deterring future violations. Operating on an ad hoc basis, these tribunals could follow the model of the Special Constitutional Court established under Article 125 of the Constitution of the United Republic of Tanzania, which provides a legal framework for addressing disputes with a constitutional dimension. Additionally, establishing a robust domestic institutional framework to address human rights violations following elections is essential. Such a framework could include dedicated institutions tasked with protecting human rights, such as national human rights commissions, ombudspersons, or specialized judicial bodies. These institutions should be accessible to victims, adequately funded, and equipped to handle cases of electoral violence efficiently and effectively. Lastly, power-sharing arrangements must also prioritize preventive measures to address the root causes of electoral violence and human rights violations. This could involve strengthening electoral systems, promoting civic education, and ensuring that security forces act impartially during the electoral process. By addressing these underlying issues, power-sharing agreements can lay the foundation for more peaceful, just, and inclusive societies.

12 Conclusion

With reference to Tanzania Zanzibar, Kenya, and Zimbabwe, this chapter critically examines the role of human rights in power-sharing arrangements across Africa. A desktop review highlights that human rights violations are often treated as significant concerns only in the absence of negotiations or agreements to share power among contesting political parties. During periods of political stalemate, opposition parties frequently leverage the plight of victims of electoral violence to garner national, regional, and international support for their demands. However, once power-sharing arrangements are reached and positions are created for the opposition parties, their leaders often abandon the pursuit of justice for victims of electoral violence and their advocacy for the protection of broader human rights. This pattern leaves victims of electoral abuses unremedied and marginalized. Survivors of violence—many of whom have suffered physical, emotional, and economic harm—find themselves without meaningful recourse or acknowledgment of their suffering. The failure to prioritize accountability for these violations perpetuates a culture of impunity, where perpetrators are rarely held responsible for their actions, leaving victims to bear the consequences alone. Furthermore, the neglect of human rights considerations within power-sharing arrangements undermines efforts to establish sustainable peace and reconciliation. Without addressing the root causes of electoral violence and ensuring justice for victims, the cycle of violence is likely to repeat in subsequent elections, further destabilizing societies. This inaction also erodes public confidence in political institutions and the rule of law, fostering the perception that power-sharing agreements serve the interests of political elites rather than the needs of the broader population. Breaking this cycle requires power-sharing arrangements to go beyond political expediency by incorporating robust mechanisms for addressing human rights violations. These mechanisms could include provisions for truth and reconciliation commissions, reparations for victims, and commitments to institutional reforms designed to prevent future abuses. Such measures would not only restore the dignity of victims but also lay the foundation for a more inclusive and just political landscape.

References

Fjelde H, Hoglund K (2014) Electoral institutions and electoral violence in Sub-Saharan Africa. Br J Polit Sci 46:297–320

Hamad HO (2017) Government power sharing in Zanzibar: a solution to political conflicts? J Law Policy Global 59:86–95

Havard S, Gates S (2008) Lessons learned from power-sharing in Africa. Centre Study Civil War Policy Brief 8:1–4

Kildal ABO (2016) Come together: the effects of power-sharing on peace and democracy in Zanzibar. University of Oslo

Kirkengen KL (2013) The constitutional history and the 2013 referendum in Zimbabwe: a Nordem special report. The Norwegian Centre for Human Rights, Oslo

Mburu DM (2020) The lost Kenyan Duel: the role of politics in the collapse of the International Criminal Court cases against Ruto and Kenyatta. In: Cullen H et al (eds) The politics of international criminal law. Brill

Minde N et al (2018) The rise and fall of the government of national unity in Zanzibar: a critical analysis of the 2015 elections. J Afr Elect 17:162–184

Mutisi M (2011) Beyond the signature: appraisal of the Zimbabwe global political agreement (gpa) and implications for intervention. Policy Pract Brief 1:1–7

Republic of Kenya (2008) Report of the commission of inquiry into post-election violence. Government Printer, Nairobi

Amiri Sharifu LL.B (Mzumbe University), Advocate of the High Court, Associate at Anjarwalla & Khanna Tanzania, and a Law Tutor at Dar es Salaam CPA Review Center. Email: amiri.sharifu@alnafrica.co.tz.

MIX
Papier aus verantwortungsvollen Quellen
Paper from responsible sources
FSC® C105338

If you have any concerns about our products,
you can contact us on
ProductSafety@springernature.com

In case Publisher is established outside the EU,
the EU authorized representative is:
Springer Nature Customer Service Center GmbH
Europaplatz 3, 69115 Heidelberg, Germany

Printed by Libri Plureos GmbH
in Hamburg, Germany